7·6

Theater Wagon

Plays of Place
and Any Place

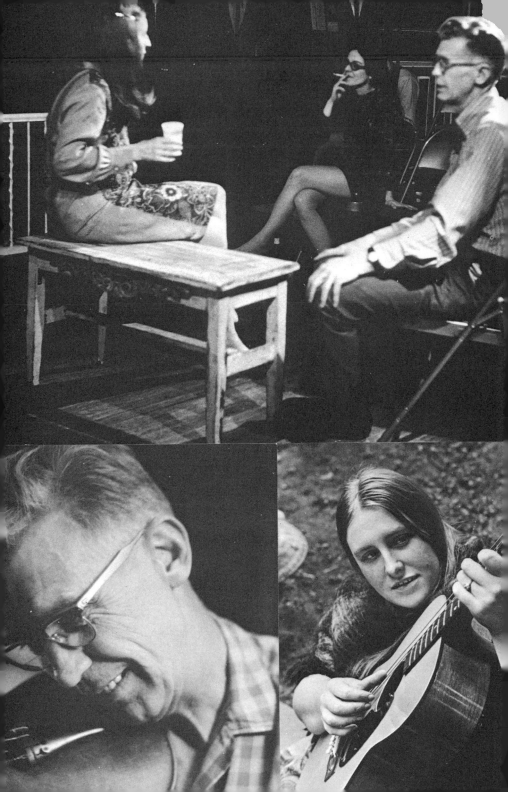

THEATER WAGON
Plays of Place and Any Place

Love Is A Daisy
Birdwatchers
A Merry Death
On the Corner Of Cherry And Elsewhere
Sandcastle
3 Filosofers In A Firetower
Styopik And Manya

Edited by
Margaret and Fletcher Collins, Jr.

University Press of Virginia
Charlottesville

The University Press of Virginia

First published 1973

The publication of
Theater Wagon Plays Of Place And Any Place
was sponsored by Mary Baldwin College.

ISBN: 0-8139-0535-4
Library of Congress Catalog Number: 73-84160
Printed in the United States of America

CONTENTS

ACKNOWLEDGMENTS

Theater Wagon gratefully acknowledges deep and specific in-debtedness to three neighboring institutions:

THE OAK GROVE THEATER, a grant from which made possible the first new-play tour to Chapel Hill and Annapolis in 1960, and which thus encouraged the formation of its new-play branch, Theater Wagon. Four Theater-Wagon plays have had their premieres during the regular subscription season of the Oak Grove. In addition, three other Wagon plays have played there as part of subscription seasons.

MARY BALDWIN COLLEGE, which has been truly an alma mater, first to Oak Grove and later to Theater Wagon. Many of our most profici-ent members are Mary Baldwin students and graduates, some of them in on the founding of Oak Grove in 1954, others joining the Grove and Theater Wagon over the years since then. 3 Filosofers In A Firetower was originally presented at the first Mary Baldwin Arts Festival, and toured to the Greenwich Mews Theatre in New York through the generosity of Jeanne Taylor Block, Mary Baldwin Class of 1954. Theater Wagon has played four of its repertory for the benefit of Mary Baldwin scholarship aid and for the entertainment of its trus-tees. As further testimony to our filial relationship to the College, it graciously accepted the role of sponsor of the present publica-tion.

VIRGINIA COMMISSION OF THE ARTS AND HUMANITIES, which has made repeated grants to Theater Wagon for the encouragement of its new-play program.

FOREWORD

These prefatory remarks are written by an Englishman, a stranger, who has experienced the unique capacity of the Shenandoah Valley to absorb strangers.

I was partly assimilated by my teaching at Mary Baldwin College; I was even more assimilated by my marriage to a Valley girl. This, though fundamental, is also "normal" and might reasonably have been anticipated. But there was also the delight of being assimilated by a group under whose auspicies could be found not only recreation but also an outlet for whatever creative energies one might have. Theater Wagon, together with the Oak Grove Theater, provided just such opportunities.

The plays in this volume offer a glimpse of those opportunities, though it will remain a very meager glimpse if the plays are simply read; these are plays to be acted. There are two broad groups: original plays by members of the Theater-Wagon troupe and plays of a Russian master translated by another gifted member. The illustrations show something of the performances, though they cannot hope to convey the excitement of the playing nor the diverse characters and professions of the performers.

However, that diversity is the clue to Theater Wagon's success, and to its attraction. Where else can a newcomer from any background find the opportunity not only to act but to act plays written by himself or his friends? Where else can the enthusiast for foreign plays find the encouragement to test his own powers of translation and put these plays on the stage where they properly belong?

The original plays and the translations in the volume show the same urgent desire: they ask to be spoken. Christopher Collins'

translations are not chiefly concerned with the play as a "literary"
product: a play is a play, and no amount of preoccupation with fine
language or subtle ideology will save it if it cannot be performed
onstage. Ultimately even its "literary" value must stand or fall by
its performance. This does not mean, of course, that drama should be
written in what Wordsworth ambiguously called "the real language of
men"; only that it has to sound as if it were. The original playwrights in this volume have worked on the same assumptions, even
those that have created worlds that never were; and Theater Wagon
gave them the opportunity to prove that they can do it successfully,
as their audiences have enthusiastically testified.

I suppose this is a warning against a rapid reading of these plays:
some of them do not read easily. They were not designed for that. Theater Wagon, while very far from being anti-intellectual, is more concerned
with the living experience as the basis for the intellectual process. I
can speak from the heart: not so long ago I offered my students a semi-
nar in the plays of Ibsen and Strindberg, and I think it went well. It
was, nonetheless, a "literature" course; we spent so much time enjoying
a useful and genuinely enlightening discussion of the origins and ideas
of the plays that we rarely considered them as documents for the stage
rather than the study. I hope we can be forgiven. If not, let the
playwright throw the first stone, but let Theater Wagon throw the second.
It's here, after all; and it's open to new ideas, or, even, the explora-
tion of old ones by those who have never had the chance to explore.

I have enjoyed exploring with Theater Wagon.

I'm not a stranger any more.

                                                    F. R. Southerington

The question for playwrights is whether, in the age of McLuhan, theater will survive. Who needs it? More people respond to the image. The key word is more. Television makes it, theater is in search of an audience. Television is global, theater a provincial handcraft in a machine society. Who wants it? It can't compete.

As Theater Wagon's provincial producers, we think this is cultural lag--like architects who build houses without fireplaces, like people who think candlelight doesn't compete with electricity or sailboats with jets. We admit to being a handcraft; we admit that more people prefer machine reproductions. But the more machines there are, the more some of us need to work with our hands. The more we are enveloped by numbers, the more essential is the intimacy of person to person. The greater the crowds, the more necessary our humanity. In a dehumanized society, if art isn't on the side of humanity, we are lost.

Theater Wagon is a company of players and playwrights who perform their own plays in gardens, homes, churches, in college theaters, community theaters, dinner-theaters, and for guests at resorts, historic homes, national parks. Our plays are upbeat comedies, a natural form for writers who have a prevailing faith in the worth of each human being. To the comic vision all things are possible. In comedy opposites can be reconciled, misery transcended. The price of salvation is the pratfall for all of us. Comedy never gives up on the human condition. It celebrates hope.

For decades, optimism has not been fashionable with trendy
directors who play comedies as "period," tragedies as "relevant,"
and pillage the classics to yield Furies for Now. Split personali-
ties use millions of dollars of light and sound to express disgust
at technology. Compulsive outsiders try to relate by clobbering
people. Serious artists take themselves seriously. If they laugh,
it's at the audience. Alienation is blamed on the times. But the
times have nothing to do with it. In a century oppressed by the
destruction of wars and the crisis in institutions, Petrarch wrote
his great love poems, and Chaucer wrote The Canterbury Tales.

Chaucer's relation to his audience was personal, as was his
art. "The measure of all arts' greatness can be but in their intimacy," said Yeats. "A deep of the mind can only be approached
through what is most human." He thought we should distrust "bodily
distance, mechanisms, and loud noise." And even Brecht, no stranger
to distance, asked "What is art without friendliness?"

Theater is a social art, whether it's for the masses at Epidau-
rus or the few at the court of the Sun King. Today between the
mass and the few there are the Many with new skills and fresh ideas
who emerge from all backgrounds and classes. In modern societies
their ranks increase each day. They work in city planning and architecture, are biochemists and engineers, make jewelry or build
harpsichords; people of all backgrounds serve on school boards,
work in clinics, run hospitals, teach retarded children, are college
trustees. This is their idea of direct experience.

These people are the new audience. But playwrights seem slow
to realize that this audience is not only bright, they are involved.

Alienation is not their thing. They believe everyone deserves a
fair chance to develop to full potential. They respond to the quality of experience, not just its labels. They radiate energy. Prag-
matic, ongoing, they move easily from technology to handcraft and
back to technology, and can readily tell the difference between
good amateurs and mediocre professionals. Eclectic, knowledgeable,
they think ideas are fun, language is exciting, and art challenging.
They are fascinated with images, symbols, and words.

Broadway underestimates this audience, Off-Broadway downgrades
it, but dance companies and music ensembles, being less verbal,
have also been less doctrinaire, more creative. Each creates its
own repertory and more crucially its own audience of individuals
from many backgrounds, drawn together by a common enthusiasm and
often a common skill. Marlboro buffs perform chamber music. Pro
Musica fans have recorder consorts. An audience of practitioners
gives art its best base, whether it's electric guitar or a flute
concerto dedicated by Haydn to a prince who could play it.

Much nonsense has been talked about the pit and the galleries
at Elizabethan public theaters. The pit relished the poetry, the
spectacle, and seeing the "rude mechanicals" have their day, but
the poetry was created for the practitioners in the gallery who
expected a playwright to out-Caesar Caesar and Mark Anthony, toss
in King Henry, and round out a Falstaff.

Today the pit has a hundred diversions, and kings aren't what
they used to be, but a playwright can learn from an earlier day,
for the very good reason that he knows he must not imitate it.
The playwright's job is the theatrical idiom. Central to that idiom

is language--half folksy, half genius, active with gesture, image,
and the rhythms of living speech.

There is a current superstition that Americans speak only Basic
English. The truth is that people of all ages and backgrounds talk
in a rich flow of language, garrulous, elliptical, rampant with
metaphor. Brilliant talk, both polished and Rabelaisian, is tossed
off daily by the wits in a small town. Farmers talk in splendid
rhythms that are half barnyard and half theology. Mechanics talk
their love of machines and frustrations with people. Through it
all runs laughter. Not just at the other guy. At themselves.

A playwright needs to listen until he tunes into the wealth
of variants in his native tongue. These rhythms can't be borrowed.
If there is a theater audience, it is an audience for living speech.

Of course Broadway can no longer afford language. Producers
explain that straight plays don't pay production costs. Off-Broadway prefers the primal scream or the higher frequencies heard only
by dogs. The missing wave lengths are words. If theater is human,
we need them.

Theater Wagon has its own solution for playwrights. No script
is a play until it is acted. Wagon playwrights are members of the
company. As actors and directors they discover the difference between dialogue that lives on stage or dies on the page. They feel
the pull of mime toward language, the attraction of language to
action. With audiences they know when a play works and where it
bogs.

Few theaters are able to offer playwrights this opportunity.

"Audiences are what we need. My own illusion was that I was talking to all the people when I began. At least I had a wider theater than I do now." (Miller) "What theater artists lack most is
a sense of being involved beyond our own personal needs and ambitions, of being part of a larger theater community." (Schneider) "New York isn't it any more. But no one knows what is."
(Dunnock)

Yesterday's playwrights had a national audience. Now theater
is described as splintered, fragmented, threatened, in search.
Perhaps all that is splintered is the artist's pride of place in
the cosmos. He's being cut down to size. He's being told to go
back and sit down. Play on the team or drop out.

The source of his distress lies deep in the paradox of American folkways. Americans may believe in the worth of the individual,
but they also believe from the womb that value is created by number. The unique is of value only if everyone thinks so. Do your
thing, but that thing is more important when more people do it--
which goes for iconoclasts as well as those they deride. What else
is relevance but how many and how much? Artists who scorn to count
dollars, count people. Foundations count people. Universities
count people.

The whole thrust of democracy is number. Number is our mys-
tique, and television is the result of our individualism, the perfect popular art. Popular art is simply what most people like.
It doesn't have to be sold. It appeals. From Russian ballet to
Spanish bullfights and Italian opera, popular art has always been
visual rather than verbal, packed with action and spectacle more

than idea, vulgar as often as beautiful. Its professionals are
craftsmen, its artists are talents. Its forms are habits. Its
genius is anonymous, even though its stars may be legendary. Imitation is how it communicates. Skill is its recognition. Popular
art reproduces prolific variations and seldom creates. It isn't
geared to the individual. The highly original is displaced.

But the highly original is the job of the artist. His problem
is always orthodoxy. Today it's eclectic creeds and fashionable
tyrannies. The Big Ideas no less than Big Money. Broadway, competing for Big Money, locks into television--the Now model of an
old theatrical custom, a technical marvel with many voices and a
one-track mind. You can preset the whole thing for direct experience. And Off-Broadway, competing for power over people, locks
into tortured obsessions with Big Ideas, like blowing your mind
is no longer enough, we've got to blow your ass off and get a
broader base.

In the struggle for money and power the artist is usually sac-
rificed. But no artist is willing to be immolated. At least he
struggles. Playwrights are caught in an identity crisis, which,
like other identity crises, is less due to confusion without than
to the confusion within them.

If theater is decaying, it's because it is busting out all
over. Broadway still has its island, Off-Broadway its beachhead,
but today all theater--as opposed to film and tape--is regional.
Regional theater is less a place than a state of mind. In regional
theater audiences are choices.

Dinner-theaters and music tents, devoted to commerce, spring
up cheek by jowl with street theater dedicated to radical politics.
Shakespeare plays in the park. Culture is In. Arts councils and
foundations, handing out subsidies, talk enthusiastically of theater
as an "enriching part of the daily life of the American people"
and a "celebration of the American experience."

But somehow the plays being subsidized are eighty percent
European. Is this the new internationalism or the old colonialism?
Civic centers start off zoom and threaten to go bust until someone
brings in the schoolchildren on the premise that if Americans don't
want culture, they want their children to have it. Managing directors, competing with theme parks and coliseums, import more television stars, while artistic directors, competing for prestige,
cut loose with assault and orgy until the audience opts out, the
director resigns, a new director comes in with the same ambitions,
and everyone starts over again.

A lively scene but more compulsive than creative. Offered new
options in the provinces, regional theater repeats the urban di-
chotomy. If, as Brecht concluded, didacticism is finally destruc-
tive of art, contamination is at a rather high level. As for the
art that refreshes, when it tries to compete with Coca-Cola, it's
a drag. We still function either too privately or too publicly,
as many writers have suggested. Theater continues to be commerce
or cult, not communion.

Communion begins with the playwright and goes on from there,
through fashions in acting to the price of real estate. Genius is
never enough. Communion is a whole environment which includes

audience and artist in what Brecht called their "high naive desire
for the transformation of the world."

Playwrights cannot go it alone. The experience of live theater is clear on this point. From the Globe to the feudal courts
of Japan and back to O'Neill at the Provincetown, a playwright needs
a company with its own audience.

Regional theaters build audiences with Broadway's "good junk"
and the "classic workhorses," but they can't risk unknowns. To
be produced, a playwright has to be certified as a Genius, or at
least Important, which takes time and often death. Regional theaters can't originate because they are mere dependencies of empire.
At best they succeed as provincial capitals, not city-states.

The mark of a city-state, whatever its wealth or lack of it,
is supreme self-confidence. Numbers don't matter. To citizens
of all classes, Florence was the world, and in Romeo's eyes there
was "no life without Verona's walls." Free cities supported their
own painters, architects, sculptors; duchies and principalities had
their own composers; universities fostered the language arts. We
think of these patterns as aristocratic, but they were also the
patterns of free republics.

In our democratic society, people everywhere, in reaction to
standardization, are in search of community. In flight from con-
formity, they hunt meanings in the past that are important now.
They learn to weave. They buy dulcimers. They flock to aristocratic old houses and backcountry festivals in search of new life
styles. Local distinctions are newly valued. There are even lo-
calities with the independence--part historical, part geographical,

part commercial--to act like city-states.

Few artists, however, are willing to become citizens. Community may be a **good** word, but they **can't** commit themselves. Who wants to be buried alive? Their eyes are still on New York and Hollywood, or London. Other places are way stations. So the playwrights flock to New York and its satellites when they'd do better to head for the boondocks and dig in. Where community is real, there is communion. Good things can happen. People talk to each other. Artists, patrons, audiences get together. Some dreams can be realized. Community comes alive when it creates new forms. Reality is touched with magic. There is zest. There is laughter. There is even compassion. The rest is imagination.

The plays in this collection were created by Theater Wagon in Virginia for audiences from everywhere. Plays of Place and Any Place, they are comedies made of the fantasy of facts, the reality of character, the foolery of human situations danced by all of us.

Margaret Collins

SOURCES OF QUOTATIONS

Ezra Pound and Ernest Fenollosa, with introduction by W. B. Yeats, Certain Noble Plays of Japan, 1916.
Richard L. Coe, "In Search of an Audience," Washington Post, Oct. 29, 1972.
Alan Schneider, Theatre Quarterly, III (1973).
Manfred Wekworth, Brecht Today, in Drama Review, XII (1967).

LOVE IS A DAISY

By Margaret Collins

CHARACTERS

Ann
Susan
Hugo
Kelly Shepherd
Garland, her youngest son, home from the University
Robert J. Spivey, a rural sociologist
Jess, Kelly's oldest son, an artist
Scott Martin

SCENE

A mountain cove not far from Skyland Drive.   A parachute.
And later at the Shepherds' farmhouse.

Act One: April 30
Act Two: May 1

ACT ONE

(As the house-lights dim, we hear bluegrass and country music.
Ad lib until a recorded voice interrupts:)

VOICE   We interrupt this program for a late news bulletin....
One of America's brightest young stars is missing.   Barbara Logan
is overdue at a Long Island airport.   Miss Logan left St. Louis
this afternoon by private plane.   Severe thunderstorms have been
reported in the Appalachians and it is feared the plane may have
crashed.

(The music comes up again, then fades as lights go up on a strip
of upland pasture.   Shrubs.   A stump.   A parachute spread out.
At the end of the sweeping line of the shrouds, and apparently out
cold, is SUSAN.)

ANN (offstage)   Su ... san...!   (Entering, seeing the parachute.)
Susan...?   (Following the shrouds at a run.)   Susan!   (Kneeling.)

SUSAN (opening her eyes)   I dreamed of falling!   (Goofy look.)
Do you think it's a sign of insecurity?

ANN (worried)   Susan, are you all right?

SUSAN (getting up)   I think so ...   (On her knees.)   Somewhere I
heard a dog bark as I ... (Weaving) floated down ...   (Stands.)
Where's the plane?

ANN   It crashed in the mountains!

SUSAN (walking, chute and all)   The twentieth century's very confusing!   One minute you're racing the sun!...   The next you're no
better than an old Indian in a buffalo tent!   (Tangled and trying
to unbuckle the chute.)   Where are we?

ANN   Virginia, I think ...   (Helping unbuckle the harness.)   Susan,
are you really all right?   How do you feel?

SUSAN (stepping free)   Like Zeus on a cloud!   (Up on the stump
at a leap.)   Isn't the world beautiful!...   I could hug those round
hills down there, covered with orchards!   And kiss each cow in those
green sloping fields!...   Do you think anyone will look for us?

ANN   In these mountains?   Not for hours.

SUSAN   There's a farm down there by the river!   Can you walk?
The sun's in the top of the tallest trees.   It soon will be dark.
(Jumping down.)   Come on....   How would you like to sleep in a
chickenhouse?

ANN   Why not in the woods?   Think of Lewis and Clark.

SUSAN   Think of Dan Boone and come on!

ANN   Do you think we'll get lost?

SUSAN (on her way)   We have eyes, haven't we?   (Suddenly backing
up.)   Ugh!   (Wiping her face.)   I didn't see it!   Ugh!   A cobweb!
(Laughing and brushing it off.   Suddenly she freezes.)   What was
that!

ANN   What?

SUSAN (tense)   Listen...!

ANN   Maybe someone...?   (A few steps forward.)   Hello...?   Some
animal maybe...?   (Sudden flight.)   Cows!

SUSAN (confident)   Cows are harmless.   (She moves ahead.   Quick
retreat.)   These look wild!

ANN   Huge!

(They bolt center.)

I thought you wanted to kiss them!

1

SUSAN   Kiss them...? (Remembering and laughing.) Don't you know
we worship the cow? She's more respected than Queen Victoria was!

(They move cautiously ahead again.)

Do you see any bulls?

ANN   There probably aren't any.

SUSAN (firmly)   There have to be.

ANN   Oh no. They can breed in absentia!... Father thinks it's
obscene!

SUSAN   I suppose any man would. Oh ... here they come!

(They bolt again up center, hide behind the shrubs, peer out and
see emerging not wild bulls but HUGO, a country man in a loud shirt,
and carrying a battered suitcase.)

HUGO   Never pass by, I say, never pass by. You can sell a man right
off his mule, make schoolgirls late to school, daffy with new ribbons
and combs in their hair, and their books lost by the side of the road.
(Setting his suitcase on the stump and opening it.) Never pass
by, I say, till the old woman sets down her bucket of slops and
off for her purse and the pigs not fed! (Showing a plush pillow
in livid colors.) Pretty, ain't it? Why, I've got poems here about
babies, and gardens, and mothers. Pictures of sunsets and rainbows,
houses with hollyhocks ... and look at this now, an original oil
paintin'! (Holding it up.) I seen the artist myself--there in
the store window--and in no more'n ten minutes, she painted that
lake and them Indian tents, right out of her head! Beautiful, ain't it?

SUSAN   It's incredible!

HUGO (pleased)   That's what it is, ma'am. Though I mightn't have
called that particular word to mind. I don't know much myself,
but I know what appeals to people that's educated. Why, I've sold
schoolteachers and minister's wives!

ANN   Where is the nearest road?

HUGO   Nearest road, reckon, is Skyline Drive. But it's closed.

SUSAN   Closed...?

HUGO   From the storm! Trees down and all.... My folks lives down
aways on the other side. Over towards Luray.

SUSAN   Is there some place we could telephone?

HUGO   Lady, that Drive's one of them fancy highways in the sky!
Loneliest damn uninhabited road! Scenery by the mile--and not a

a nickel in none of it! Why, when they began puttin' that road
through, my pappy planned on buildin' a roadhouse up there, but
the Park Service won't give no permission. Says they want scenery!

ANN   Is there a path?

HUGO   Scenery! City folks is crazy for scenery! We'd have had a
dance hall up there, juke box, place all lit up, and the cars thick
as flies on a puddin'! Like at them caverns!

SUSAN   Did you say there's a path?

HUGO (pulling a bunch of plastic roses from the suitcase) Yonder aways.
Bit overgrowed. (Gesturing with the flowers.) Mind that house down
there?

SUSAN   Near the river?

HUGO   That's where it comes out. (Waving the roses in her face.)
Clever ain't they? Like I said to the last lady, "They're clean,"
I says. "Them flowers won't fade nor drop on your table." (Taking
out another object.) This bowl and candlestick set (Demonstrating.)
goes with them.

SUSAN   No thank you, we don't -

HUGO   One dollar for this little house with the hollyhocks, but
this head here (Garish object.) I'd say was a bit finer and well
worth the extry dollar.

ANN   We haven't any money. You see our plane crashed and we -

HUGO   Sorry, ma'am, it don't pay to give credit.

(Tossing things in the suitcase, he is now facing downstage, with a
girl on each side.)

Yes'm, first house you'll come to is Kelly Shepherd's. I tell you,
Kelly Shepherd's a workhorse, but she can't do it all.

(Bluegrass music comes on low. Shrubs upstage are removed to reveal
KELLY SHEPHERD sitting on a simple cot with afghan spread. She is
holding an earthenware pitcher and a bunch of lilacs. Her dress
is a cotton print. She wears an apron and a man's old brown felt hat.)

Got her two sons ... don't amount to nothin'.

(JESS and GARLAND remove more shrubs, revealing a beat-up old pie-safe,
right, and a fine old washstand with bowl and pitcher, left. KELLY
moves to the pie-safe, puts pitcher and lilacs on top of it, opens
the safe and takes out props which she places on the oilcloth-covered
kitchen table the boys have carried into place.)

Jess, he's the one that took off for Pittsburgh ... says he's an
artist. I tell you there's some folks too mean to better theirselves,
or too ignorant, one. Some that'll lay a corpse someday ...

(JESS and GARLAND carry the cot into position below the washstand.)

in a house no mcre fittin' than wnat their grandaddies had, that's
a fact. Nothin' **but** old-timey stuff ...

(The boys are placing splint-bottomed chairs at the kitchen table.)

few sticks of furniture they made for theirselves ... Like I say,
Kelly Shepherd can't do it all. Sprayin' her orchards, killin'
her hogs. Old man dead, Garland home from the University, doin'
nothin' but set there all day gawkin' at the television.

(GARLAND has wheeled in small TV in rack and placed it left of the
cot.)

Not for me, no ma'am.

(HUGO closes the suitcase. Music fades. KELLY, JESS, and GARLAND
disappear behind flats upstage indicating the rest of the house.)

I'm a-goin' to Florida. Get me a boat that sleeps six or eight, and
take people fishin'! Ten dollars a hour with me at the wheel, and
a client now and again givin' me a nip of his bottle! (Picking up
suitcase and starting left.) Well ... pleased to meet you. Mind
you ladies don't get lost. Good luck! (He goes left.)

ANN   The Good Samaritan!

SUSAN   Don't you know what appeals to people that's educated?
It's tne Common Man! (Picking up tne chute narness and dragging
the shrouds after her.) Come on. "Never pass by, I say ..."

ANN   "Never pass by!"

(Struggling with folds of the chute, they move right.)

HUGO (appearing left)   If you ladies ever get down to West Palm
Beach, come round and I'll take you fishin'! (He picks up the stump,
and leaves left.)

ANN   "Never pass by!"

(Laughing, they go out right, carrying the chute. Upstage KELLY
enters, carrying a small chair, and places it downstage right.)

KELLY (singing)
If you kill a chicken,
Save me the wing.

You think I'm workin'
I ain't doin' a thing.
'Cause it's nobody's business,
Nobody's business,
Nobody's business if I do!

(GARLAND has entered upstage, carrying in one hand two stools, and
in the other a third stool with a checkerboard. He places the stools
down left, checkerboard in the center, takes a newspaper which is
under the checkerboard, and begins to read.)

Three more hens is a-cluckin', old Betty's farrowed, six in the litter,
and the Jersey's dropped her calf! We're overrun with propagatin'
and procreatin', and two more days yet till full of the moon. Did
y' get the mail? Anything from Jess?

GARLAND   No. Except for what's in the paper.

KELLY   If you ain't a catbird, settin' there and sayin' nothin', and
Jess wrote up in the paper!

GARLAND   It's no credit to him.

KELLY   Well, what is it? What's he done?

GARLAND   Last night at the William Penn Hotel a young man from
the hills mowed down the band, knocked ten gentlemen flat, and was
takin' the ladies two at a time when -

KELLY   If you ain't a mess! Now you read me the truth.

GARLAND   If you want the truth, you shouldn't look for it in the
paper.

KELLY   Well, read what it says then. Hear?

GARLAND (reading) "J. Douglas Stuart, Pittsburgh businessman, awards
annual art fellowship to Hall Shepherd, Virginia farm boy."

KELLY   That ain't all, is it? They've got Jess down as no more'n
a cocklebur in the cow's tail of it! I reckon Mr. Stuart's proud
to help Jess.

GARLAND   Proud of a cheap way to buy advertising.

KELLY   Is that what they learned you over to the University? It's
a wonder you ain't too smart to stay on the farm!

GARLAND   I'm a philosopher.

KELLY   Go on now! Is there anything else?

GARLAND (reading) "'One sentimental requirement I shall make of each holder of the fellowship,' Mr. Stuart continued, 'that he paint my daughter's portrait.'"

KELLY His daughter? Lord!

GARLAND (reading) "'I venture to think this will not prove an unpleasant task.'"

KELLY "Unpleasant," says! To Jess?

(GARLAND puts down the paper, and is on his way to the TV.)

Now what're you doin'?

GARLAND It's Saturday night.

KELLY (following) It's not time yet. Anyhow, you'd ought to be off over the hills after some girl 'stead of settin' there at the television. Jess, now, likes a girl where he can catch hold of her!

GARLAND This is love, not biology.

KELLY "Biology," says! Settin' there moonin' over a fool girl on TV.

GARLAND Have you heard of dryads locked in a tree, singing?

KELLY You'd ought to be courtin'.

TV One of America's brightest young stars is missing this evening. Barbara Logan is long overdue at a Long Island airport ...

(GARLAND freezes, listens anxiously.)

TV Miss Logan left St. Louis this afternoon by private plane. Severe thunderstorms have been reported in the Appalachians and it is feared the plane may have crashed.

KELLY Lord, the poor thing may be killed!

TV At the UN today Israeli ambassador -

(GARLAND switches channels.)

SPIVEY (offstage) Good evening!

KELLY Now who's that? (Calling.) Come in the house!

(SPIVEY steps nervously inside. He is a finicky academic and is carrying a briefcase.)

SPIVEY   I regret to intrude on strangers, but indeed we are all
interdependent, are we not?

KELLY   Law, Garland, here's a man from the gov'ment.

SPIVEY   Indeed I -

KELLY (to SPIVEY)   You can write down I'm a Democrat without plumbin'.
Five sons, three cows, a good pair of mules, my daddy livin', my
husband dead, three hundred acres, Episcopalian, mumps, measles,
eighth-grade schoolin' -

SPIVEY   It's my automobile!

KELLY   What?

SPIVEY   My automobile!

KELLY   What about it?

SPIVEY   I grease it regularly. Change the oil. Is there anyone
here who could repair it?

KELLY   Lord help my time, his car's broke down! Here I was goin'
on like the devil whippin' his wife! Five sons, I says! Three
cows! And him standin' there with his car broke down! (Calling.)
Come in here, Garland!

SPIVEY   The name is Spivey. Robert J. Spivey.

(GARLAND turns off the TV, crosses to the kitchen.)

KELLY   I'm Miz Shepherd, and this here's my son Garland.

SPIVEY   I grease it regularly. Change the oil. And now -

KELLY   Have a chair, Mr. Spivey.

SPIVEY   Thank you, but my car -

KELLY   Pour Mr. Spivey some liquor, Garland.

SPIVEY (alarmed)   No, no, I couldn't! Not really ...

(GARLAND is pouring a glass from the jug.)

Well ... thank you. My car -

GARLAND (handing him the glass)   Pure corn. Hate to see a man die
of rotten liquor.

SPIVEY   Good heavens! (Looks at the glass. Cautious sip.) I was
late leaving Charlottesville. A colleague failed to keep an appointment.

Very well, he is a clever man. But should he be chairman of the
department? Here I am. I work under great pressure. Indeed sometimes
I feel I shall break!... I expected a modicum of encouragement.
I had planned this field trip for a month. You see I am a busy
man. I waited until six o'clock. I was infuriated! My head was
seething! Somehow--I cannot imagine--I am a man of regular habits.
Perhaps duress explains it. I drove off--without my briefcase!

GARLAND (baiting him)   Not your briefcase?

SPIVEY (soberly)   Yes. I had to return to town. And now my car -

GARLAND   Is it missing?

SPIVEY   No, no, it's all there so far as I know.

GARLAND   Kick over at all?

SPIVEY   Kick? Well, no.

KELLY   Garland thinks you're drivin' a mule.

SPIVEY (sober)   As a matter of fact, I have never driven a mule.
The Spiveys have never been farmers.

GARLAND   And what is your diagnosis?

(SPIVEY looks baffled.)

About the car.

SPIVEY   Well, I should say--that is, I know nothing of a car's
anatomy--but I estimate that the ... uh ... the motor ... (Hesitating
and then coming through triumphantly.) has failed.

GARLAND   A modern man, born to machines! A denizen of elevators!
Habitue of bathtubs!

SPIVEY (desperate)   If you don't mind...? I am rather anxious about
the car...? That is, could we...? (Gesturing helplessly with his
glass.)

GARLAND (taking the glass)   Here, Spivey, let me fill 'er up!

SPIVEY (drawing back in alarm)   No, no really I -

(But GARLAND is already pouring from the jug.)

KELLY (ominous)   Nothin' wrong with the liquor?

SPIVEY (taking the glass)   No, no, nothing ... but if you don't
mind, I am rather anxious about -

GARLAND   Be with you in a minute.

(He goes back to the cot, turns on the TV. SPIVEY stands glumly
looking at his glass.)

SPIVEY (to KELLY)   I beg your pardon, but do you know the time?

KELLY (sociable)   My dad always kept his jug in a hole in the
ceiling. Right over the kitchen table it was, and every meal he
passed it around to us kids. Said a woman wasn't no woman that
didn't chew nor take snuff. Oh, he was a daddy all right! He had
twelve of us. There was eight boys and four girls and -

SPIVEY   What time...?

(KELLY picks up an alarm clock which is face down on the table.)

KELLY (looking at the clock)   It don't go standin' up. Law, Mr.
Spivey, it's no more'n five till nine.

SPIVEY (upset)   8:55? I should be now--precisely now -

(Behind them, JESS has entered, carrying a guitar. JESS is older
than GARLAND, lusty as his mother. He grabs KELLY from behind.
She squeals.)

KELLY (turning)   Jess!... I declare, Jess Shepherd, you'd best
get your hair cut or pay taxes, one.

JESS   I can't waste money on haircuts. Get out your horseclippers.

KELLY   If he hasn't come home from Pittsburgh to save the price
of a haircut! (Turning to SPIVEY.) This is my boy Jess ... Mr.
Spivey. (To Jess.) Have you had your supper?

JESS   Don't you bother. Portraits! I'd sooner paint frog's eggs.
I simply got on the bus. Telephoned Stuart from the bus station.

KELLY   Lord help!

JESS   I told him his filly was bred for show and no other purpose
and I was a farm boy who had my prejudices. He got his tail in an
uproar, cancelled the fellowship -

KELLY   Lord!... What's wrong with the girl?

JESS   What girl?

KELLY (to JESS)   "What girl," says! (Turning to SPIVEY who waits
glumly.) I reckon she's downright plain!

JESS   I don't know.

KELLY (to SPIVEY)   Listen to him! (She whoops.)

JESS   I didn't see her. I don't want to.

(KELLY stares at him open-mouthed.)

She's one of those social dolls with a face like a lacquered clam-
shell. You can't paint them. The thickness of a brushstroke over-
weights them. Hell with them. (Conversational.) Wealth's a sin.

KELLY   Cash money for paintin'?... No hog killin'? No plowin',
no sprayin', no plantin'?

JESS   He can keep his cash. Where's Garland?

KELLY   In there at the television worryin' hisself to death over
that Barbara Logan.

JESS   Drag him out.

KELLY   Hush!... The poor thing may be killed!

JESS   Killed?

KELLY   Haven't you heard, they's lookin' for her plane everywhere
Don't nobody know what become of her! Lord, the pretty young thing
never knowed fear nor hunger and never had her hair uncurled!

SCOTT (offstage)   Oh, Kelly!

KELLY   Now who's that?

(SPIVEY is in a sweat about more delays as SCOTT MARTIN enters.
He is about Kelly's age, wears a shapeless brown sweater, old pair
of pants, old grey felt hat.)

Evenin', Scott.

SCOTT   Evenin'. Well, Jess, I see you got here all right. Just
like you say in your telegram. (Taking a Western Union envelope
from his pocket.) I figured there wasn't no hurry. No matter of life
and death. (Handing telegram to KELLY.)

KELLY   Sure enough it's from Jess!

JESS (to SCOTT)   Why didn't you mail it?

SCOTT   Accordin' to the telegram you was to arrive at nine, so I
come on out with it to welcome you home.... Come by train, you
could a been here this mornin'.

KELLY (sniffing)   You know why he come on the bus.

2

SCOTT   Looks to me like the train is worth a extry dollar.

KELLY   Scott, this is Mr. Spivey. Mr. Spivey meet Scott Martin.
Scott's our agent over to the railroad.

SCOTT   Evenin'. (Eyes fixed on SPIVEY's glass.)

KELLY   Help yourself to some liquor, Scott.

SCOTT   Don't mind if I do. (Picking up the jug.) Understand I
don't mean to talk none against a competitor, but them buses is
slow.

KELLY   Meanin' no criticism, trains is dirty.

SCOTT (indignant)   Woman! They've got fine commodes where you've
got a privy! On buses -

SPIVEY   I agree with you, Mr. Martin, that for a protracted journey,
the train is preferable.

SCOTT (to KELLY, triumphant)   What'd I tell you?

SPIVEY   My unbiased opinion -

SCOTT   Listen to that! "Unbiased opinion!" The man's got learnin',
hasn't he?

SPIVEY (to JESS)   If you don't mind ... I have had a strenuous
day and I am nearly exhausted! Could we -

SUSAN (offstage)   Good evening!

(JESS makes a dash for the door. SPIVEY slumps.)

May I speak to Mrs. Shepherd?

KELLY (loud whisper to JESS)   Who is it?

JESS   An anomaly!

KELLY   Lord help, is it full-growed?

JESS   Of an age to consent!

(KELLY goes out to talk to the girls. JESS crosses to GARLAND who
is sitting on the cot, staring at the TV.)

Here's beauty distracted! She's torn her clothes, tangled her hair,
scratched her face on a briar -

GARLAND (morose)   Brace yourself.

JESS   For a man to think he's impervious!

SPIVEY (crossing to JESS)   Couldn't we -

JESS (to SPIVEY)   I say feed the flesh, and the spirit grows fat
and well-feathered!   Starve it, (Gesture to GARLAND.) and the sad
bony soul grows cynical.

GARLAND (morose)   Hogwash.

SPIVEY (desperate)   Couldn't we -

KELLY (at the door)   Listen at me a-goin' on!   Come in here.   Come
in the house.

(ANN and SUSAN follow her into the kitchen.)

Lord, if you aren't a sight in this world!   Looks like you'd rambled
all over hell and half of Georgia.   This here is Mr. Spivey ...
Scott Martin ...   And this here is Ann and ...   (Looks inquiringly
at SUSAN.)

SUSAN   Susan.

JESS (crossing to the jug)   What they need is a drink.

KELLY   That's my boy Jess.

SPIVEY (following JESS)   Mr. Shepherd!   I must -

KELLY   Poor things, they've been in a mess of trouble.   Lost their
way in the woods, had nothin' to eat, torn up their clothes, no
doubt got a skinful of chiggers and poison oak!   Law, I shouldn't
wonder tomorrow they'll be a-itchin' and a-scratchin' and a-hobblin'
round here all crippled up!   (Urging the girls toward the bedroom.)

JESS   What's the rush?

KELLY   Right in here.

JESS   Why the high pressure?

KELLY (to the girls)   You can freshen up a bit and I'll make supper
and afterwards I'll fix you a bed for the night.

(Pushing SUSAN ahead of her.   GARLAND stands up, staring at SUSAN.)

This here's Garland's room.   He has his programs in here, but I don't
guess he'll bother you none in the night.   (Boisterous.)   Whoops!
What am I sayin'?

SUSAN   Thank you, but I don't believe we can spend the night.

JESS (to ANN)   Look here, does my Adam's apple look psychopathic?

ANN   A little.

JESS   You know me well. You can sleep with my mother.

KELLY   Jess Shepherd, hush!

(Herding ANN into the bedroom.)

What was you doin' in them woods? Hikin'?

SUSAN   We were flying.

KELLY   Flyin'...? You hear that, Garland? (To the girls.)   Lord
now, was anyone killed?

SUSAN   There were only the two of us.

ANN   We had to bail out.

KELLY   In one of them parachutes...? You hear that, Garland?
(To the girls.) Where's your plane?

ANN   It crashed.

KELLY   Garland, you hear?

(GARLAND bolts for the kitchen.)

SCOTT (to GARLAND)   Looks like they'd want to know about trains.

JESS (to GARLAND)   Damned if that girl doesn't look like Barbara
Logan.

GARLAND   What if she does?

JESS   What if she does? What if she is! A bolt from the blue!
My chimney's struck! I'm afire! (Singing.)
She's my lily-of-the-valley,
My bright and morning star ...

(Giving SPIVEY a square-dance whirl.)

SPIVEY (protesting)   Mr. Shepherd! I -

KELLY   Land, Mr. Spivey, I know you're plumb worried with Jess
here rarin' round like a bull! Go on now, you boys!

JESS   Don't rush me.

KELLY   Get on out to that automobile! I declare -

(Shooing him out. GARLAND follows.)

JESS (at the door)   Hang on to that angel if you have to clip her!

KELLY   Looks like you're the one that's aimin' to clip her!   (Singing.)
If you kill a chicken,
Save me the wing.
You think I'm workin' -

SCOTT   Kelly, you mean to order any more chicks?

KELLY   Costs me twenty cents more a hundred if'n they come by your
railroad express.

SCOTT (incensed)   I told you that's gov'ment tax!

KELLY   Parcel's post I don't pay no tax.

SCOTT (heavily)   I can't figger it out. I just can't figger it
out. Railroad's money in your orchards out there--John's money
he made at railroadin'--and you stand there, Kelly, tellin' me you
mean to order them chicks by parcel post! (Indignant.) Huffman
over there in his post office will plumb overgrow his breeches!

KELLY (conciliatory)   Have a drink, why don't you, Scott?

(The girls, having managed in a desultory way with bowl and pitcher
at the washstand, appear.)

Set right down.

SCOTT (eagerly, to the girls)   Over to the station I've got whole
books of schedules! Nothin' in 'em at all, only schedules. Reckon
anyone had a mind to go there, I could sell 'em a ticket clean to
Los Angeles!

KELLY (hooting)   On that punkin vine?

SCOTT (ignoring her)   Got a train out a here first thing in the
mornin'. Four o'clock.

ANN (appalled)   Four o'clock?

SUSAN   Is there some other train?

SCOTT   Course'n the Southern's got trains over to Charlottesville ...
but there's no ways to get there tonight exceptin' by bus. (In-
gratiating.) Time you was to do that, you'd as well stay here until
mornin'. 4:06 A.M. Every mornin' but Sunday.

KELLY (triumphant)   Sunday? Well, tomorrow's Sunday!

SCOTT (defeated)   Sure enough, that's what it is, Sunday. I hadn't
thought of that.

KELLY   If they was to wait until Monday, we could do some visitin'.

SUSAN   Monday...?

SCOTT (brightening)   That's right. Send your folks a telegram!
I got some paper here ... (Fumbling in his pocket) ... and a pencil ...
Office is closed as you might say, but I can stop in there this
evenin' yet.

ANN (to SUSAN)   I could let Father know what's happened. (She
begins writing.)

KELLY (to SUSAN)   Reckon you'll stay the night?

SUSAN   If it's convenient.

KELLY   It's convenient or I wouldn't have as't you. But mind you
look out for Jess! Since't he was knee-high he's been reachin' for
skirts! Says you're his mornin' star!

SUSAN (amused)   He does?

KELLY   Says, "I'm afire! A bolt from the blue!"

SUSAN   He does?

KELLY   Yes and you whip him good. Lord, he's a mess! Do you know
what he done? Garland and me rarin' round here all winter workin'
ourselves to death and Jess up there in Pittsburgh -

ANN   Pittsburgh?

KELLY   Paintin' women as naked as jaybirds!

ANN (interested)   Painting...?

KELLY   Course he don't paint so good as a photograph. But he paints
right smart!

ANN   Jess is an artist?

KELLY   Garland don't care for women.

SUSAN   No?

KELLY   Just sets there at the television moonin' over that Barbara
Logan.

SUSAN   Barbara Logan...? The folk singer?

KELLY   Lord he'd walk in from the fields to listen to that fool
girl. Can't hardly eat nor sleep. I declare I worry over him.
You know it ain't right for a man to be.... It ain't natural!

Maybe now you girls is here he'll take an interest. It ain't natural
to do like he does. It's like he's sparkin' a ghost! (Double take.)
Maybe he is. Bein' the poor child is missin'!

SUSAN   She is? What happened?

KELLY   Haven't you heard? She was flyin' in one of them little
planes and there was storms in the mountains and her plane ... (She
trails off, staring at SUSAN.)

SCOTT (to ANN)   These words'll cost you extry.

KELLY (still looking thoughtfully at SUSAN)   How much is the extry,
Scott?

SCOTT   Forty-eight cents.

KELLY   I declare that seems mighty high.

SCOTT (to ANN)   A dollar ninety-five and forty-eight'll be -

KELLY   Lord help, telegrams is extravagant!

SCOTT   Now, Kelly.

ANN (handing him the paper)   Will you send it collect?

SCOTT (sadly)   Collect?... Reckon I'd best be gettin' along.

KELLY   No need to rush off.

SCOTT   Old lady'll be pitchin' a fit.

KELLY   She had the rest of them teeth out?

SCOTT   No, she told the dentist he don't pull none while the signs
is wrong. Her blood's in her head. She'd best wait till the sign's
in her feet. Pleased to meet you ladies. If you's to stay over
till Monday, I'll be proud to sell you them tickets. (He goes out
right.)

KELLY (following)   Well, good night!... Hurry back!

(She goes out after him. The girls look at each other and laugh.)

SUSAN   Did you see how she looked at me?

ANN   She thinks she knows who you are!

SUSAN   She knows she knows! Did you see her face?

ANN   You're the ghost of Barbara Logan! No wonder Garland stared when you walked into his room.

SUSAN   I've never been so stared at in my life.

ANN (laughing)   That's because he "don't care for women.   Just sets
there moonin' over the television!"

SUSAN   He doesn't look like a farmer.

ANN   He probably butchers hogs.

SUSAN   Don't you know he was "rarin' round here all winter?   Workin'
hisself to death?   While Jess was up there in Pittsburgh paintin'
women as naked as jaybirds?   He paints right smart!"   (Laughing.
Then breaks off.)   You don't suppose he's the one...?

SUSAN   What one?

ANN   Anyhow, I wasn't naked as a jaybird, and his name wasn't Jess.

SUSAN   What are you talking about?

ANN   Father's artist.   Didn't you know he buys them and brings them
home as if a man were a pair of skis or a dog?   They're supposed to
paint my portrait.   Father has a whole room full of me.   Once a year
since I was two.   Isn't that gruesome?   This time I left Father a
note: No more portraits or no more daughter!   (Laughing.)

SUSAN   Don't you know it's dangerous to run from Fate?   The faster
you run, the sooner you're caught!   You'll probably marry an artist.

ANN   You marry him!

SUSAN   Oh no!   If it's Love, I'm not having any.   What's love?
Kiss me quick, I'm off to the wars!   There's a customer waiting
to buy a new Ford, so off with your clothes, my dear!   I've a plane
to fly, an engine to drive, a case to try, a man to fire, so quickly,
my dear, into the bed and I'll write you, love, from Chicago!...
I'd as soon be a hen.

KELLY (singing offstage)
If you kill a chicken,
Save me the head.
You think I'm workin',
I'm layin' up in bed -
(Entering.)   Lucky it's moonbright for them boys out there.   Looks
like they're pickin' that car to its bare bones.   (To SUSAN at the
window.)   Can't see nothin' out there but them orchards.

SUSAN (dreamy)   Are they in bloom?...   Or is it the moon that makes
them so white?

KELLY (snorting) Apple trees is a mess of trouble! Full of worms.
And you'd best not trifle none in the April moon. Unless you mean
it.

(JESS and GARLAND enter, carrying suitcase, taperecorder, etc., and
followed by SPIVEY.)

SPIVEY (indignantly) I had the car checked. Only last week. I gave
him five dollars.

JESS (crossing upstage) Fuel pump.

GARLAND Needs a new gasket.

(They go out upstage with SPIVEY's gear.)

SPIVEY I hope, Mrs. Shepherd, that you can accomodate me for the
night.

KELLY (lewdly) Land now, Mr. Spivey!

SPIVEY (innocent) I'd be happy to pay you whatever -

KELLY Pay me! Whoops! (Seeing his bewilderment.) You sure won't
be happy to sleep on a couch, but you're welcome to do it. (Bustling
over to the pie-safe.) Now, why didn't I think to offer you girls
some wine! It's real mild. I made it myself.... Mr. Spivey?

SPIVEY I don't believe that I -

JESS (appearing to take his glass) Man, your toes aren't wet.

SPIVEY Really I ... (Backing toward the checkerboard.) Well ...
(Taking the glass and looking at it helplessly.)

KELLY (to GARLAND who is on his way to the TV) Land, Garland, it's
not time for your program! Why don't you give Mr. Spivey there a
game of checkers?

SPIVEY (alarmed) No thank you! (He crosses hastily to the chair
down right. GARLAND hesitates, staring at SUSAN. She looks up.)

GARLAND Shall we play?

(SUSAN moves to the stool right of the checkerboard. GARLAND takes
a box of checkers from his pocket, sits on the left stool. They
begin setting up the game.)

JESS (to ANN) Look. I'm a farmer. I know a crop when I see one.

ANN (amused) Have you guessed my yield to the acre?

KELLY (interrupting with a glass of wine for ANN)   Jess, you'd
ought to tell -

JESS   Am I at a loss for words?

KELLY   Jess, you'd ought to tell Ann here how Mr. Stuart -

ANN (interested)   Stuart...?

KELLY   J. D. Stuart. Reckon you've heard of him!

ANN (to JESS)   Do you know him?

JESS   He's an old man, angel. Forget him. What if he has got
money? I love you. I'm threadbare but clean.

KELLY (in high gear)   Mind I don't say it was right of Jess, but
Jess is the sort to say what he thinks no matter if a man wears
his collar buttoned. Land, they was pourin' it on! They was pitchin'
it! Old man Stuart--Mr. Stuart, I should say--with his tail in an
uproar, prancin' and swearin' all over his highkaflutin' office.
and Jess here ... "None of your style," says! "I'd as soon paint
clamshells! "

SUSAN (amused, to ANN)   Clamshells!

KELLY   "Your daughter," says--only chick nor child he's got--"Your
daughter," says, "is a filly!"

SUSAN (to ANN)   Filly!

KELLY   Course Jess don't know her from Adam. Never laid eyes on
her. But "your daughter," says - Oh, he talked up a storm!

JESS (to ANN)   Old man asked me to paint her.

KELLY (handing ANN the paper)   Here. It's all wrote up in the
paper. (Pointing it out.)

ANN (reading)   "Hall Shepherd awarded art fellowship!" (To JESS.)
But your name isn't Hall.

KELLY (explaining)   My brother named Pete we called him Bob.   And
my brother named Leroy we called him Pete. And Jess here -

JESS (to ANN)   I turned him down cold.

KELLY   You'd ought to go through with it, Jess, if she is one of
them glamor girls.

JESS   She's a long-stemmed job, raised in a flowerpot. With rings
on her fingers, bells on her ...(Gesture.)

KELLY   Whoops! I'd better go make up that couch! It's gettin'
too hot around here! (She goes out upstage.)

JESS (to ANN, his usual play)   I'd like to paint you.

ANN (amused)   Would you?... Suppose my father's a tycoon--like
Mr. Stuart?

JESS   I don't care if he's elk, mongoose, or octogenarian. You've
got bones in your face.

ANN   If my eyes were bright as stars ...

JESS   As snow in the moonlight.

ANN   All right, as -

JESS   Your mouth's a love song. Your breasts -

ANN   Let's just say I've been compared to a summer's day, but my
father has money. Like Mr. Stuart.

JESS   I'm a man of principles.

ANN   Prejudices, even.

JESS   Pure bigotry, in fact. I'd swear you are beautiful.

ANN (moving away)   Sheer ignorance.

JESS (following)   I swear I'll make love to you.

ANN   Rank superstition.

(He follows her out right.)

GARLAND   Your play ... Susan.

SUSAN (picks up a checker, hesitates)   But if I do that, you will ...
(She puts it down and tries another.) But then you would ... What
can I do? I believe in free will!

GARLAND   You could douse the lights and make a break for it.

SUSAN (laughing)   Shall we play again?

TV (coming on strong with country music)
At my heart you are my darlin',
At my door you're welcome in,
At my gate ...

GARLAND (turning the TV down)   TV's like a pig in the parlor. It crowds you.

SPIVEY (rousing)   Pigs? In the parlor?   (Alarmed.)   That is, if
I am to sleep on the couch...?

GARLAND   I said television -

SPIVEY   Aha!   (Drunk and sociological.)   What is your favorite
program?

GARLAND   I'm a poet. I like the commercials.

SPIVEY (pained)   Seriously ...

KELLY (sticking her head around the corner upstage)   Seriously,
Mr. Spivey, Garland's just crazy over Barbara Logan! Says he's in
love!   (She ducks out again.)

SPIVEY (shocked)   In love...?

GARLAND (baiting him)   Gutted with passion!

SPIVEY   Good heavens!

GARLAND   No vines grow on my charred facade. My shell's unfurnished
with vegetables.

SPIVEY   You're a farmer, aren't you?

GARLAND   Are you a sociologist?

SPIVEY   We can't pigeon-hole People, can we?   (Academic.)   Now.
As a member of the Rural Audience, wouldn't you say that Barbara
Logan is too sophisticated for ...

(He has crossed to the jug and is trying to imitate JESS's way of
pouring, crooked elbow and all. But it doesn't work. He gets his
hands crossed, etc. GARLAND watches in fascination.)

GARLAND   Too sophisticated for...?

SPIVEY   Well ...   (In sudden defeat, sneakily pours behind the table.)
for a farmer.

GARLAND   I'd say she's ...   (Looking at SUSAN.)   subversive.

SUSAN   Subversive!

GARLAND   As termites! My flooring's eaten away! I'm sick!

SPIVEY (earnest)   Do you write fan letters?

GARLAND   By the dozen.

SUSAN   You' do?

GARLAND   And throw them away.

SUSAN (laughing)   If you love her, say so!

GARLAND   How?... (Poetic, quoting Elizabethans.)   Can I say she's "fair, fair, and twice so fair, as fair as any may be"?   That she "hangs upon the cheek of night like a rich jewel in an Ethiope's ear"?...   Our age is **laconic**.   Serenading taboo.   Our metaphors are for propaganda, not for love.

SUSAN   Lord, must you make love in metaphors!   A woman wants facts and figures!...   When did you first know you loved me?   What day? How often each hour do you think of me?...   Be **simple**.

GARLAND   Love is ornate.

SUSAN   Be sincere.   No purple!

GARLAND   Love is baroque.

SUSAN   Be specific!

GARLAND   Love's ambiguous.

SUSAN   Avoid clichés!

GARLAND   Love is the greatest cliché of all.

SUSAN   Are you really in love with Barbara Logan?

GARLAND   Furiously.

SUSAN   If you met her -

GARLAND   God forbid!   I don't want to meet her!

SUSAN   No...?

GARLAND   What would I do?   Embrace my love through a window?   Chase her in taxicabs?   Love's unattainable!

SPIVEY (rousing)   In the interest of accuracy, I should think -

GARLAND   I have no interest in accuracy.

SPIVEY (shocked)   Good heavens!

GARLAND   Have you?

SPIVEY (crossing to them)   As a matter of fact, I am interested, almost exclusively, shall we say, in Love.

GARLAND   Love...? My dear Spivey, women -

SPIVEY   I don't care in the least about women. I care about Love.

GARLAND   You're drunk.

SPIVEY (earnestly) It's always hard to explain to the layman.
I'm a specialist on virginity. And ... uh ... related fields.
(Drunk and pompous.) I am making a survey.

(He returns to his chair down right. SUSAN and GARLAND are convulsed.)

SUSAN (rising, with a gesture that includes both men)   What talents
men have for Abstraction! (Crossing to GARLAND.) Has this Barbara
a mind of her own?

GARLAND   Wild as a duck.

SUSAN   That's orthodox for an alter-ego. But if you're making a
woman, don't make her clever! She'll cavil on the ninth part of a
hair! Give her a small brain and she'll do.

GARLAND (amused)   My love has a gentle wit.

SUSAN   Her wit's like a game in an alley!

GARLAND (amused)   At least she's honest.

SUSAN   No woman is honest!

GARLAND   No woman is perfect, and yet one dreams of perfection.

SUSAN   So you love a bunch of amorphous bones!

GARLAND (rise)   I borrow the rose. And leave the briars. (Circling
her.) A woman's finite. She can be put on file. Indexed, licensed
to drive, weighed, measured. Age? Sex? Color? There's no metamorphosis! Fortunately art protects me. I landscape the women I
meet.

SUSAN   Landscape them? Do you ...(Showing off her figure.) follow
the natural contours? (Turning.) If I were your Barbara ...

GARLAND   You can't be.

SUSAN   Why not?

GARLAND   Your eyes are brown.

SUSAN   What's wrong with brown?

GARLAND   Nothing. But could I prefer it to grey? Or green or blue
or hazel? A woman's eyes should be green in April, grey in December,
lyric by moonlight, rowdy at dawn! Brown is brown. You see? There's
no choice.

SUSAN   Poor man! So you think love should be perfect! Shall I
prove you wrong?

GARLAND   You might try.

SUSAN (crossing to him)   In perfect love is one satisfied?

GARLAND   Obviously.

SUSAN (staring at him)   Being satisfied ... he wants nothing more?

GARLAND (dreamy)   No.

SUSAN (archly)   Is he sated then?

GARLAND   You might say so.

SUSAN (moving away)   Being sated ... he no longer feels pleasure?

GARLAND (morose)   Possibly not.

SUSAN (farther away)   Can one love without pleasure?

GARLAND (wry)   No.

SUSAN (turning and crossing back to him)   Then perfect love is not
love! And love is -

TV   We interrupt this program to bring you the latest bulletin on
Barbara Logan, missing since noon when she left St. Louis by private
plane -

(SUSAN clicks it off.)

GARLAND (following)   What are you doing?

SUSAN   News is a habit. It's dangerous.

GARLAND   What is this? (Clicking the TV on again.)

TV   ... wreckage of a plane spotted in the mountains of Virginia,
northwest of Charlottesville ...

(SUSAN tips over the checkerboard, gets down on her knees, absorbed
in picking up the pieces.)

GARLAND   The man says Charlottesville. (Turning off the TV, crossing to her.) I should have known. (Also on his knees hunting checkers.)

SUSAN   Do you think you're psychic? Or is it her horoscope?
(Punctuating with checkers piled on the stool.) Taurus and Mars
in conjunction!

GARLAND (adding more pieces)   She was on her way to New York.

SUSAN (a few more)   They all are.

GARLAND   From St. Louis.

SUSAN   You tempt me!   (Standing up.)   If I said I were this Barbara ...

GARLAND (standing)   I wouldn't believe you ... Susan.

SUSAN   No?

GARLAND   Do you think I believe in miracles?

SUSAN   Does any man? He turns and runs, clutching his hat!

GARLAND   Figure the odds.

SUSAN   On a miracle?

GARLAND   On the distance between New York and St. Louis. Speed
of the plane, population, millions of acres, miles of road, trees
in the wood, rocks in the field ... What are the chances?

SUSAN   Chance is for scientists! (Crossing to him.) I knew a girl
who missed the bus to Teaneck. And went to Peru.

GARLAND   Why Peru?

SUSAN   Because that's where he was going.

GARLAND   Who?

SUSAN   The man she met when the taxi broke down.

GARLAND   I suppose she married him.

SUSAN   Oh, yes.   When they got to Peru.

SPIVEY (breaking in, drunk and solemn)   You people think your concerns are individual! I assure you they are not. You can all be
reduced to essential terms. (He looks at them earnestly.) We will
perceive them. Formulate them. From minutiae! (Dizzy at his own
profundity, he is weaving a bit.)

GARLAND   You couldn't do better, Spivey, if you'd run head on into
a post.

SPIVEY (coldly)   You may not realize how painstakingly from the
aggregate we discern social principles. How tediously, in fact,
we amass Truth!

(He pauses for full effect, looks masterfully around, and passes
out cold. KELLY enters from upstage.)

KELLY   Land, I should have give him supper!...   Jess! Garland!
Take Mr. Spivey there and put him on the couch. Minds me of John,
bein' Saturday night and all and him ...

(JESS enters right. He and GARLAND carry SPIVEY out upstage.)

You'd best take off his shoes!

(KELLY follows them out. In the silence, the TV is audible. SUSAN
is alone.)

TV   The time now is ten o'clock. Each Saturday evening at this
time, SPARKLE presents one of America's brightest stars ... Barbara
Logan!

(Guitar music. SUSAN sits on the cot watching. GARLAND enters from
upstage, followed by JESS.)

JESS (to GARLAND, looking from the TV to SUSAN)   Can the girl be
here?

GARLAND   She's canned!...   That's progress, isn't it?

JESS   What's wrong with you? Why didn't you recognize her?

(GARLAND doesn't answer. Stares straight ahead. JESS claps him on
the shoulder.)

Or did you? (Hilarious.) Man, you're sunk! Flat on the bottom!
You'll never come up alive!

                              ACT TWO

(Next morning, the first of May. KELLY is fixing a bowl of salad.
JESS is playing the guitar. His talk is punctuated with guitar runs,
etc.)

KELLY   Sunday or no Sunday, on the first day of May we got to plant
watermelon! And them girls had ought to've been up early washin'
their face in the dew! That's what my grandmother always said and
I swear -

JESS   They can sleep. I like them frisky.

KELLY   Mind you don't frisk around here too quick on the draw!

3

JESS   You overestimate me.

KELLY   Do I now! Didn't I see you here in this very room last
night? Law, you was burnin'!

JESS   My plans for today are quite innocent.

KELLY   Are they now!

JESS   Mountain climbing, a picnic, the simple country pleasures.

KELLY   Now look here, Jess, it's a pleasure all right. And simple
enough in the country or anywheres else! But I'll not have you
abusin' our hospitality to strangers.

JESS   I don't intend to abuse her.

KELLY   Nor wishin' her joy of her bargain, hear?

JESS   Damn strait-laced, aren't you?

KELLY   Do you think I'd approve of what's immoral? And you needn't
to think, Jess Shepherd, you're distractin' me! "Mountain climbing,"
says! "Picnic!" Do you think I don't know what you aim to do with
that poor little innocent -

JESS   Innocent, hell. Do you know who Susan is?

KELLY (exuberant)   She's Barbara Logan! That's who! And Garland's
beginnin' to rare. But it scares him, her fallin' from the sky right
out'n his television! Reckon he thought he was safe here in the
country. Ain't no man safe! (Suddenly serious.) You can leave
the girl alone. You hear?

JESS (a few runs on the guitar)   Why should I?

KELLY   You got to give Garland his chance.

JESS   What is this?

KELLY   Give him a chance, Jess!

JESS (stops playing)   Do you know what you're asking? I'm an experience no woman should miss.

KELLY   Jess Shepherd, you'll not stir a step from this house with
that girl! A little loose talk don't hurt no one, but the trouble
with you is you aim to do more'n talk!

JESS (guitar flourish)   I'm no damn theorist.

KELLY   You can just keep it all in your head! It's time you was
gettin' some morals. Mind what I said now. None of your prankin'!

(JESS is beating the guitar. She shouts at him.)

You get out here now and plant them melons!

(KELLY goes out right. GARLAND enters from upstage.)

GARLAND   What was that all about?

JESS   Morals. You've got too many. I haven't got enough. What dreams I had.

GARLAND (hunting a coffee cup)   You're worse than a dog.

JESS   You tossed a bit too.

GARLAND (pouring coffee)   Why not? I'm repressed. I'm supposed to dream.

JESS   Are you supposed to talk?

GARLAND (sitting down at the table)   Did I?

JESS (strumming the guitar as punctuation)   You strung off all the four-letter words like a valentine. Then you'd say "Barbara, Barbara ..." and curse awhile.

GARLAND   Interesting, though Freud might say -

JESS   Freud, hell! Why don't you poke me one?

GARLAND (affably)   Because you're a liar.

JESS   Better for you if I weren't. You don't know what a woman looks like enough to dream about one.

GARLAND   And you know too damn well what all women look like to dream about one!

JESS   Why so tragic? If you burn ... why not fiddle? (Extravagant run on the guitar.)

GARLAND (disgusted)   Oh my God!

JESS   The girl's ripe.

GARLAND   Who says so?

JESS   She's golden. And I don't mean her voice.

GARLAND   I suppose you would know.

JESS (exasperated)   Look, boy, if you want her, take her, but for God's sake, make up your mind! Because if you don't, I sure as hell will

KELLY (calling outside)   Jess!... Jess!

JESS   Damned melons. Let's plant them and take to the woods with the women.

GARLAND   I have even less use for women in the woods than out of them.

JESS   Why fight it?

GARLAND   You can count me out.

JESS   Can a crow pass up a melon? (Singing mockingly.)
I gave my love a cherry that had no stone,
I gave my love a chicken that had no bone,
I gave my love a ring that had no end,
I gave my love a baby with no crying.

(He laughs, goes on singing the next verse, and goes out right.
GARLAND picks a tomato from the salad bowl and fires it out after
him. The singing stops. Raucous laughter from JESS. GARLAND goes
out. ANN and SUSAN enter upstage. ANN, making an entrance, finds
the room empty.)

ANN (disappointed)   I thought I heard Jess.

SUSAN (carrying a bunch of apple blossoms and singing)
One morning, one morning, one morning in May,
I spied a fair couple a-making their way ...

ANN (looking for coffee)   You must be in love.

SUSAN   And sing? I'd cry salt tears! (Singing.)
I'm goin' a-walking because it is spring,
For to see the waters flowing,
Hear the nightingales sing ...
(Speaking.) Do you know where I found these? (The blossoms.)
On the way to the privy! (Laughing.) Nature's great! (Singing
and dancing.)
Good morrow, good morrow, good morrow to thee,
Oh, where be thou going, my pretty lady?...
(Laughing and giving ANN some flowers.)

ANN (holding the blossoms like a bridal bouquet and doing a mock
procession as SUSAN follows)   You can be married out there in the
orchard! With the apple trees as bridesmaids! And the sun to give
you away!

(They process. Then SUSAN breaks it off.)

SUSAN (big sigh, wide gesture)   Oh love, love, love ... (Suddenly
sitting on a stool.) I ache in a thousand places!

ANN (teasing)   Hussy, what were you doing?

SUSAN   Nothing! (Big sigh.) Oh, I shall die!

ANN (mocking)   Of course, if it's love, you're not having any!
You'd as soon be a hen. So off with your clothes and -

SUSAN   Garland isn't like that.

ANN (laughing)   I've noticed.

SUSAN   He hasn't even touched me! We've been here all this time
and he hasn't even (Woebegone.) touched me!... What's wrong?

ANN   With him?

SUSAN   With me!

ANN   He's certainly different.

SUSAN   What do you mean--different?

ANN   From Jess. (Abruptly.) Look. Why don't we go?

SUSAN (appalled)   Go?... Today?... This morning?... Now?

ANN   Someone can drive us to the nearest town. We can find a plane
somewhere.

SUSAN   Why would we do that?

ANN   I want a bath!

SUSAN   Find a pond.

ANN   Nature is great but I've had it.

SUSAN   Don't be a priss.

ANN   Anyhow Jess is an opportunist. He thinks opportunity strikes
again and again!... Why don't we go?

SUSAN   Why don't we wait until.... (Dreamy.)

ANN   Until you're through playing games?

SUSAN   It's all very well to play games, but how am I going to
get out of this one?... Do you think I'm dreadful?

ANN (mocking)   Sickening!

SUSAN (troubled)   I mean really heartless? To pretend to be someone he loves?

ANN   Don't we all?

SUSAN   But someone on television?... Some star who sings every Saturday night, and has millions of fans? Garland will hate me!

ANN   Do you think he's a moron?

SUSAN   It's not his fault he's neurotic.

ANN   So he's not a moron?

SUSAN   Of course not!

ANN   So who's playing games?

SUSAN (shaken)   You mean he's been putting me on?... What shall I do?

ANN   Tell him the truth.

SUSAN   But he has to discover some things first.

ANN   He sure does.

SUSAN   I mean about himself.

ANN   I could see last night that he thinks you.... (Sip of coffee.)

SUSAN   I what?

ANN   Of course he doesn't know what it's all about, so he thinks you.... (Another sip.)

SUSAN (frantic)   I what?

ANN   Do you think Jess will ever love anyone?

SUSAN (impatient)   Jess...!

ANN   Anyhow he adores you.

SUSAN (amazed)   Jess?

ANN   Garland!

SUSAN   Do you think so?

ANN   Of course he'll never marry.

SUSAN   Garland...?

ANN   Jess! Do you think he'll ever love anyone?

SUSAN (exasperated)   I hope I die before I'm so cracked! Sitting around mooning over my coffee! (With coffee cup.) Can he love me?...

Will he love me?... Does he love me?... I'd take these flowers
and drown myself!

(KELLY comes in from outside.)

KELLY   Mornin'! Well, look at them apple blossoms!

SUSAN   I hope you don't mind. I couldn't resist them.

KELLY   Be that many less apples, come harvest.

SUSAN   Oh! I didn't think -

KELLY   Reckon not. (Relenting.) Reckon you was thinkin' of something
else maybe, goin' round here with flowers in your hair! Them boys
is out to plant melons, and nothin' must do but I come in and fix
up some things for a picnic.

SUSAN   It's a wonderful day!

KELLY   Listen at her admirin' nature! You run along now. You'll
see a road out there by the smokehouse goes off to the new ground.

ANN   Smokehouse?

KELLY   Next the cowbarn. That smokehouse is where John and me set
up housekeepin'. Course'n it wasn't no smokehouse then! That's
how it is! One minute you're courtin' all innocent-like. Next thing
I knew, Jess was born!

(The girls are poised for flight, but she goes on.)

Doctor never did get there in time, bein' it was my first, you know,
and thinkin' was no hurry, he stopped to go rabbit-huntin'!

(The girls try to leave, but she is still at it.)

Time the doctor come, says, Miz Shepherd, you're fine. You don't
need a thing in the world but some Brunswick stew! And I've brought
you the rabbits!

(The girls are off. SPIVEY appears upstage. Rumpled, woebegone,
hung-over.)

SPIVEY   Good morning.

KELLY (turning)   Law, Mr. Spivey! You give me a start! (Getting
a good look at him.) Lord, Mr. Spivey, if you aren't a sight! Sit
down there and I'll fix you something.

SPIVEY (moving miserably to the table)   Thank you. I do feel rather....

KELLY   Of course you do. I declare you put on a show last night!

Standin' there a-posin' and posturin' like a fightin' cock, scramblin'
them big words around so smart! Oh, you was talkin' up a storm, you
was, when down you goes, flat on your tail!

SPIVEY   I am mortified that I permitted myself to -

KELLY   You had nothin' to do with it! You just passed out! Like
a dad-blamed general, you was, oratin'! We'll deceive you, says!
You'll be perkipulatin'! And down you goes -

SPIVEY (pained)   Please.

KELLY   I says to the boys, it minds me of John to see him a-layin'
there with his shoes on. Saturdays it seemed John couldn't get by
on less'n a quart. But he'd always get home! He'd come in that
door there, a-lookin' so bright, and he'd go straight on to the couch,
and he'd fold right up! First time he done it I like to had a fit.
Him in his old overhauls and boots, a-layin' there in the parlor!
But I got me an old spread, and ever' Saturday night, whenever he'd
leave, I'd cover the couch.

SPIVEY   They say that alcohol ... that is, one hears of such dreadful
things. I am really quite anxious.

KELLY   Shucks. Best in the world for what ails you.

(She slaps him on the back. SPIVEY winces.)

SPIVEY   But when taken to excess, one doesn't know..... I don't
see very well this morning. It is quite alarming.

KELLY   Here's what'll fix you up. Hair-of-the-Dog. (Giving him
the glass she has fixed.) Used to make it for John, Sundays. I
declare in no time he'd be chasin' me all over the house!... Not
as I had to be chased very hard! (A nudge.) What am I sayin'!
(She picks up the salad bowl, and sits across from him at the
table, slicing cucumber.)

SPIVEY (sipping cautiously)   I suppose every profession involves
a certain amount of discomfort. Particularly science. I should not
otherwise have demeaned myself. No. Obviously. One must do what
is expected. Acquiesce in the social pattern. Disregard the personal
cost.

KELLY   The boys is off to plant watermelon. Them switchy-tail girls
is off after them.

SPIVEY   Good.

KELLY   Now, Mr. Spivey, you don't fool me none. For all you're
so polite and full of learnin', you'd as soon be off with them girls
as the next one.

SPIVEY   I am not particularly interested in those two young women.

KELLY   Aren't you now!

SPIVEY   No.' They are outside the culture pattern.

KELLY   Listen to the man!

SPIVEY (leaning across the table)   That is, I should say that you
are a far more significant type.   I quite welcome this opportunity
of being alone with you for awhile.

KELLY (getting up)   What a mess of talk!   (Crossing to the chair
down right.)   That drink's sure set you to runnin' off at the mouth!

SPIVEY   Seriously, Mrs. Shepherd, I hope to learn a great deal from
you.

KELLY   Well, I ain't sayin' I don't know a thing or two!   If I had
a mind to teach you!

SPIVEY (innocent)   I am sure of it.   I shall be most gratified if
you will cooperate.

KELLY (whooping)   I declare you're a caution!

SPIVEY   Perhaps ... that is, if you are willing ... I should like
to try you out ... on my recording machine.

KELLY   Whoops!   (Roaring with laughter.)

SPIVEY (earnest)   I don't see ... it is really quite simple.

KELLY (more laughter)   Is it now!

SPIVEY   Indeed, yes.   You will find it no trick at all.

(More laughter from her, bewilderment from him.)

I assure you that with a machine there is less wasted motion -

KELLY (doubling up)   I declare!

SPIVEY   You have no idea how many people will be interested.   Indeed,
if everything goes well, I shall perhaps send a copy to the Library
of Congress!

KELLY (weak with laughter, shaking her head)   You'd best get on with
them questions.

SPIVEY   Well, well.   I suppose, Mrs. Shepherd, that in the days
of your courtship, young people remained in their own communities?

KELLY (flyswatter in hand, watching a fly)   Lord, yes.   We had no
cars to go roamin' round.   We had to take to the bushes.

SPIVEY   The ... uh ... the bushes?

KELLY   Do you think we was turtles to lay around in the fields?
(She swats a fly.)   Nights when the weather was bad, we like to
tore down my daddy's old couch!   Such creakin' and squeakin' and
jouncin' about!   Them springs was wore out with -

SPIVEY   Yes, yes.   This ... uh ... behavior was ... uh ... common
in young couples engaged to be married?

KELLY   Lord, there wasn't no talk of marryin' or not marryin'!
Everyone done it!

SPIVEY   Good heavens!   This may be revolutionary!   It contradicts
the principal tenets of Eubanks' work.   But even if it proves to
be only a cultural island, it gives me a place at the annual meeting!
Perhaps a job with Morse at Wisconsin!...   I must keep my head.   As
Eubanks points out, folk language is often misleading.   He suggests
reducing such doubtful expressions to strict scientific terms.   Ask
the subject -

KELLY   I declare, Mr. Spivey, I told you that drink would set you
to prancin' round here like a horse fresh out'n a stable.   You'd best
go hunt you some pretty girl to cool down your temperature.

SPIVEY   Mrs. Shepherd, I have a professional interest in you.   Just
as much, let us say, as a doctor.

KELLY (backing away from him)   Never did like no doctor messin'
with me.

SPIVEY (following)   What I should like to know ... that is, what
I ...   This is purely scientific, you understand....   Entirely
disinterested.   (Burst of courage.)   Would you say that intercourse
was common before marriage?

(He waits.   KELLY stares at him.)

KELLY   Law, Mr. Spivey!   What's that?   (She turns, smacks a fly.)

SPIVEY (in a tizzy)   Come now, Mrs. Shepherd.   You surely must
know ...

KELLY   Whatever'n it is, it don't sound very pleasant.   (She brushes
the fly off the table with the swatter.)

SPIVEY (feverish)   Good heavens!   It's the same as ... that is,
the same as ...   (He gives up.)

KELLY   I never could make a go with them highkaflutin' words, not
havin' no learnin'.   (She sits down at the table.)   I reckon you'll
just have to explain it to me the best ways you can.

SPIVEY   Good heavens!

KELLY   Simple-like, you know? And I'll see can't I get the hang
of it?

(She waits. SPIVEY looks miserable.)

Like I told you, I aim to cooperate!

SPIVEY (firmly)   Well.... (He turns away, then tries again.) Of
course.... (Goes on past her.)

KELLY (to his retreating back)   I reckon you think I'm right stupid.
Is it something to do with education?

SPIVEY (turning)   Good heavens!

KELLY   Or public work, like John had a job before we -

SPIVEY (frustrated)   It is simply a scientific term! After all we
are both mature human beings, and it is a scientific term for ...
that is, you might say, for ... a certain type of love-making! (He
is limp. He sinks into a chair.)

KELLY   Lord help my time! "Education," I says! Says, "public work!"
And all the time you was talkin' about sparkin'!

SPIVEY (harried)   I don't believe the word "sparking" is quite
accurate for -

(He is interrupted by GARLAND's entrance from outside.)

KELLY (to GARLAND)   Don't tell me you're through! Even Mr. Spivey's
talkin' about sparkin'! And he's got a string of words you never
heard tell of!

SPIVEY   Please, Mrs. Shepherd!

(But GARLAND is on his way to the TV. SUSAN enters from outside.
KELLY beams. Her disappointment has vanished.)

KELLY (to SUSAN, knowingly)   It's a good thing Susan come in here.
I need someone to mix up this dressin'. (Setting vinegar, oil, salt,
etc., on the table.) I've got to get out to them hens! If they've
started hatchin', they'll be a-killin' their young!

SUSAN   The hens? I thought only roosters -

KELLY   Law, them old hens don't do it on purpose! They're so stupid
they get to stumblin' around their nests, tramplin' them biddies to
death. It's plumb aggravatin'.

GARLAND   The females are stupid. The males jealous. Why marry?

KELLY   Like they say, it's better to marry than burn! Law, they'll
burn anyway! Look at John! Half blind he was and up in years and

me doin' the man's work round here. Lord, John, I says to him, I
can't be the work horse and the ridin' mare both!...
You interested in hens, Mr. Spivey?

SPIVEY   No, thank you.

KELLY (motioning to him to come outside)   You'd best come out in
the air!

(SPIVEY is oblivious. GARLAND is at the TV. KELLY turns to SUSAN.)

You can take them eggs and devil them. I packed your picnic basket
so's you all can run along! (She goes out.)

SPIVEY (crossing to GARLAND)   As a matter of fact, I am eager to ask
you..... But first I should explain that I am making a survey of
marriage customs here in the valley, including patterns of courtship. I should like to ask you--please understand I am not interested
in moral judgments. Moral judgments operate within particular cul-
tures. That is, certain types of behavior may be natural to your
mother, for example, which would not, shall we say, be natural to me.

GARLAND   I'm sure of it.

SPIVEY   Shall we...?   (Edging away from SUSAN.) That is, this
question is rather ... delicate.

GARLAND   Of course. (He follows SPIVEY left of the cot.)

SPIVEY   You see, your mother talked with the utmost candor of ...
that is, at first I was doubtful I understood her correctly.

GARLAND   I shouldn't wonder.

SPIVEY   You see, I understand the common meaning of "sparking"
but I began to think ... indeed I felt quite certain that....
Just what would you say she meant?

GARLAND   Just what did she say?

SPIVEY   She described, shall I say graphically, her youthful ...
that is, her premarital..... And said that she had ... in fact she
left no reasonable doubt that not only she, but all the young women
in this community had ... that is, a number of times!... Well, in
her usage the word apparently has an extended meaning.

GARLAND (dry)   An apt way of putting it.

SPIVEY (excited)   I am right then in thinking that to your mother
"sparking" is synonymous with ...

GARLAND (baiting him)   With?

SPIVEY   Uh ... (Desperate whisper.)

GARLAND   It means what you think it means.

SPIVEY   Shepherd, what you tell me places more than one scholarly
reputation in jeopardy! (Feverish.) Indeed, those reputations will
soon show certain disfiguring cracks that will quite impair their
solidity! Really, it makes me quite nervous to think ... that is, the
responsibility! (Pacing.) My field work must be meticulous. And
the tabulating ... I think I shall use Hobson on that. You'll excuse
me now? I must look at my recording machine. I think that after
awhile, perhaps, your mother,... (He goes out upstage in a flutter.)

SUSAN (laughing)   What did you tell him?

GARLAND   He answered himself. Poor devil, he can't read the big
books of life. So he lives like a worm in the bindings and chews
out a word here and there.

SUSAN   I suppose he was never in love.

GARLAND   Hell, no.

SUSAN   So he's making a survey. Would you call him a pervert?

GARLAND   I'd call him a pip-squeak!

SUSAN   Perhaps he's one of these clever men who know love's a poor
idea?

GARLAND   Is that what you think?

SUSAN   What else can you say! It's been so poorly planned! The
flesh is preposterous. Men and women as style are incongruous!
As number and symbol--insoluble. (She goes on mixing salad. Silence.)
Do you know what I think? I think you're a coward.

GARLAND   If you intend to reform me -

SUSAN   I intend to cure you! How does it feel to come face to face
with your Barbara?

GARLAND   If you're struggling to destroy my illusions, I'll struggle
to keep them intact. I have to! Or....

SUSAN   Or...?

GARLAND   Make love to my own projections!

SUSAN   Isn't that how it all begins?

GARLAND   With self?

SUSAN   Of course.

GARLAND   Then why bother!

SUSAN   Because we need each other.

GARLAND   Sure. So I learned you can make an ass of yourself like
Jess. Or give it up!

SUSAN   But it's not some thing! It's some one!

GARLAND (abruptly)   You think I'm a fool. I am one. (Going to the
TV.)   I'm staying at home. (Sits on the cot.)

SUSAN   Why shouldn't you? After all, the country's your business!
What are violets to you? Judas in flower? Dogwood in bloom? Let
Ann and Jess go.

(She goes to the table, begins furiously mixing salad dressing, reck-
lessly pouring in oil, and vinegar.)

GARLAND   Ann and Jess...?

SUSAN   We can't all go and leave you!

GARLAND (crossing to her)   I can't allow you to stay. Think of the
dogwood.

SUSAN   There are trees in the park at home.

GARLAND   The violets -

SUSAN   And violets for sale in push-carts.

GARLAND   The Judas -

SUSAN   Who cares? You can show me the cows'

(She is pouring salt in a steady stream into the salad. GARLAND
stops her by taking her hand.)

GARLAND   Isn't that enough salt...?

SUSAN   Salt...?

(A long look. He is about to kiss her.)

GARLAND (letting her go, and walking away)   As you say, the flesh
is preposterous.

(He sits on the cot, turns to the TV. SUSAN stands there, staring
at him. JESS comes in from outside.)

JESS (conversational)   Down with the rich.

SUSAN (turning to him)   I've heard money's more often decried than
despised.

JESS (on the make)   Those that aren't with us are against us. (Putting an apron over her head.) Have you ever been in a kitchen before?

SUSAN (clowning, putting the apron over her hair)   When I was nine years old I left school, cut off my hair -

JESS   And took the veil?

SUSAN   And sold newspapers. (Piteously.) I had to support my father.

JESS   A dead-end kid?

SUSAN   Yes, and no more than a stone's throw from the carriage trade. (Using the apron as a costume.) I used to watch them go out soignée! (Using the apron as a stole, fashion pose.) And come home stinko! (A pose.) There was one girl who kept a small black pig on a leash. (Using the apron string.)

JESS   A pig?

SUSAN   With a diamond collar. (Leading the pig.) She took him to cocktail parties.

JESS   And you're still not a revolutionary?

SUSAN   No, but she was.

JESS   The hell she was.

SUSAN   The whole bit. Denims from Saks, a farm in Vermont -

JESS   And about as much use as a blue-ribboned bitch in a dogshow.

SUSAN   Who liked to romp with the mongrels. (Cosying up to him.)

JESS (pleased)   Mongrels?

SUSAN (tossing the words toward GARLAND)   Rat-catching practical dogs! Moth-eaten mutts with spotty eyes!

JESS   Thank God, angel, you belong to the proletariat. (Pulling her by the apron strings away from GARLAND and toward the table.) Here.

SUSAN   What are you doing?

JESS   A woman should work. (Pointing to the saucepan of eggs.)

SUSAN (dubious)   You mean, I'm to ... cook them?

JESS   They're already boiled. You can peel them.

SUSAN (picking one up)   Peel them?... I have a psychosis about eggs.

JESS   You mean allergy.

SUSAN   No. A psychosis. When I was small, my mother called my
father an egg. I hated to eat one.

JESS   Quit stalling.

SUSAN   When I break an egg, I think of my father.

JESS   These are boiled.

SUSAN   So was my father! (They laugh together.)

JESS (pointing to the eggs)   Those who don't work, don't eat.

(SUSAN gingerly tries cracking the egg. Looks dubious.)

Perhaps it's not ripe.

SUSAN (looking at the egg)   Ripe?

JESS   Did you ever shell a green walnut? (Taking the egg, tossing
it in the air, and catching it.) This one was picked too soon.
(He drops it in the pan.) I thought you knew how to cook. In that
apron you have more class than mass.

(SUSAN strikes a pose.)

Looking at you I believe the old saw about form. All the artist
should do is uncover it.

SUSAN (evading)   Your manner scarcely persuades me.

JESS   What's wrong with my manner?

SUSAN   For one thing, it's too confident. And being too confident
it's either a pose or insensitive. And being a pose, can it be love?
And being insensitive, can it be Art?

JESS (his line)   I'd like to paint you.

SUSAN (amused)   Would you? Or is painting a means to: One - flatter
me. Two - undress me. (Peeling off the apron.)   And three -

JESS   Look here, I'm a country boy.

SUSAN   You're a gentleman.

JESS   Oh no.

SUSAN   Why else did you interrupt me?

JESS   Damned if I know. In the country we call a spade a spade.
And a bull a male cow. (Laughing.) Don't trust science, gal, get

religion.

SUSAN   Are you trying to proselyte?

JESS   Damn right.

SUSAN   What's your doctrine?

JESS   Love conquers all!

SUSAN (glancing at GARLAND)   Then come on!   (Tossing the apron on
the chair and picking up the picnic basket.)

JESS   Look here, do you know what you're doing?   Lady, you asked for
it!   (Grabbing the jug, he follows.)   Alleluia!

(They leave. GARLAND gets up from TV, crosses right as if to follow
them, hesitates, turns as SPIVEY enters upstage carrying his tape
recorder.)

GARLAND (wildly)   Jess has flamboyant ideas!   He fancies himself in
league with my radical flesh!

SPIVEY   Good heavens!

GARLAND (pacing)   All day he's seen my city beseiged.   Now he hopes
a thousand devils will pour into my streets, reach the utmost palisade
of the brain and -

(KELLY enters, breathless, followed by ANN.)

KELLY (yelling)   Garland, get off there now after Jess!   Don't
let him out of your sight!   (Desperate.)   Well, don't just stand
there!   Take Ann here and go after them!

GARLAND (on his way to the TV)   Ann can go if she wants to.

ANN (following him)   But I can't just ... go after them!

GARLAND (sitting on the cot)   Do as you please.

ANN (a wail)   How can I?   (She sits on the cot.)

KELLY (picking up the salad bowl which is still on the table)   "Picnic," says!   Don't guess they care if they eat or not!   They'll
come back here with their eyes poppin' out!

SPIVEY   You mean they...?   (Arrested at the thought.)   Good heavens!
(He stands there holding the tape recorder.)

Scene 2

(Late that night. SPIVEY is working at his machine, which he has set up on the table. KELLY waits anxiously. She has taken off her hat and apron, straightened her hair for the occasion. GARLAND and ANN are no longer on stage.)

KELLY   Ain't it fixed yet? It's near midnight!

SPIVEY (microphone in hand)   Good evening ... Good evening ... One, two, three, four ... Good evening. How are you?

KELLY   Real well, thank you.

SPIVEY (hushing her)   Please.

KELLY   I declare, Mr. Spivey, I keep forgettin'.

SPIVEY (briskly)   Well, well, Mrs. Shepherd, I believe we are ready. If you will sit here.... (Indicating a stool by the checker-board.)

KELLY (crossing)   What must I do? I declare I'm plumb nervous. I'm afraid I won't suit you. (Sitting and smoothing her hair.)

SPIVEY   We might begin as we did this morning.

(Turning on the machine, crossing to her, mike in hand, and more or less tangled in the wires, he sits on the stool opposite her and begins the "interview.")

I understand, Mrs. Shepherd, that in the days of your courtship, young people remained in their own communities?

KELLY (a deep breath, then deliberately, in a high unnatural voice) Lord, yes. We had no cars to go roamin' around. We had to - (Break-ing off.) It ain't natural!

SPIVEY (agitated, taking the mike from her)   Please! (He scrambles to the machine, turns it off.) Once we have started, be good enough to continue.

KELLY   But who am I talkin' to?

SPIVEY   You're talking to me. I ask a question. You answer me.

KELLY   Land, Mr. Spivey, you asked me them questions this mornin'! You know the answers as well as me!

SPIVEY   Perhaps if I rephrase my question? (He turns on the machine, returns with mike in hand to the stool, gets tangled in the wires,

etc.) Would you say that in those days the social code was less
rigid? (Passing her the mike.)

KELLY   I don't know nothin' about no code. We was just enjoyin'
ourselves!

SPIVEY (with mike)   There was no necessity then to be clandestine?

KELLY   There you go with them big words! "Education," says! Says,
"public work."

(She whoops, crashing the mike. SPIVEY draws it back in alarm.)

SPIVEY (with mike)   That is, Mrs. Shepherd, no one thought it immoral?
(Holding the mike toward her.)

KELLY (rising furiously)   Immoral! Would I do what was immoral?
I or my friends or kin-people? "Immoral," says! As if -

SPIVEY (following, mike in hand)   I didn't intend -

KELLY (furiously)   Mr. Spivey! You're a guest in my house and I'll
not ask you to leave it. But there's no cause I can see for a man
insultin' a woman unless'n he means to make somethin' of it! For
you to sit there so polite and full of learnin' and thinkin' such--
lechery!

SPIVEY   Good heavens, Mrs. Shepherd, did you think - (Excitedly
wrapping himself up in the wire.) Do you imagine that I ... that is,
that I wanted to ... (He realizes he is talking into the mike.)
Good heavens! (Flustered, he struggles to turn off the machine.)

KELLY (following and pouring it on)   Looks like a man with your
learnin' and all would have more sense as to ... Immoral? It's
nature! That's what it is!

SPIVEY   Please, Mrs. Shepherd, if I unwittingly said something
offensive, I apologize.

KELLY (sniffing)   Well!

SPIVEY   I assure you I meant no criticism. On the contrary, I
think very highly of you, indeed I do.

KELLY (sniffing)   Well!

SPIVEY   Your candor and good humor seem to me admirable, and I
assure you I am not one to indulge in narrow-minded old-fashioned
prejudice. Indeed, if my hypothesis is confirmed, you may someday
find yourself famous in the annals of anthropology.

KELLY (moving away)   You'd best soak your head in a tub of water!

SPIVEY (following)   Seriously, Mrs. Shepherd, I intend to print -

KELLY   Print? You mean to put me in the paper?

SPIVEY   No, no, in the Journal of Anthropology. That is a ... uh ...

KELLY   A magazine! Sure to God you're out of your head! What could you find to say about old Kelly Shepherd?

SPIVEY   I shall quote you--accurately, mind you, there is no carelessness in my work. I shall use your own words on "sparking."

KELLY   Have you taken leave of your senses?

SPIVEY   As students of American culture -

KELLY   Students? You mean boys and girls at their books?

SPIVEY   These are no mere boys and girls at their books, Mrs. Shepherd! They are serious scholars!

KELLY   What has scholars to do with such foolishness? (Going for her apron.)

SPIVEY (following)   Mrs. Shepherd, as I told you, my field is rural sociology. My special study is culture patterns in courtship, marriage, and childbirth here in this county.

KELLY (putting on her apron)   Is it now!

SPIVEY   Yes, you see, I have a small grant-in-aid and I had hoped -

KELLY   Is that the truth!

SPIVEY   I am a student of custom. Of--that is, of what is customary. There are many customs. Hundreds, in fact, thousands of customs.

KELLY (putting on her old hat)   Such as what?

SPIVEY   Such as ... such as weddings! (Singing.) Here comes the bride, here comes the bride! You see? Rice! Tin cans! Honeymoon! Why, Mrs. Shepherd, why? Custom! Think of Santa Claus, Easter eggs, Turkeys, Firecrackers, Pumpkins, Whistles, Confetti! Why, why, Mrs. Shepherd? Custom!

KELLY   Looks like anyone knows them things without goin' to school.

SPIVEY   But there are others. Old, very old. Almost forgotten.

KELLY   Then who cares?

SPIVEY   I do, Mrs. Shepherd. Suppose I were to learn of some rare, almost forgotten ritual. Can you imagine the consequences? My contribution would be invaluable. My position would be unique!

KELLY (dubious)   It would?

SPIVEY   I should be the envy of ... that is, I should be extremely
happy. Take May Day, for example. For a genuine instance of May
Day custom preserved in oral tradition--that is, passed down from
generation to generation--I would, Mrs. Shepherd, I would do almost
anything!

KELLY (sly)   You would?

SPIVEY   Literally anything, Mrs. Shepherd.

KELLY (improvising)   You know ... my grandmother used to talk about
first day of May. Would that be...?

SPIVEY   May Day! Indeed it would! What did she say?

KELLY   Well now ... if I recollect ... I declare there's somethin'
there at the back of my mind.... Would it be somethin' about ...
girls?

SPIVEY   Yes, yes.

KELLY   And ... boys, maybe?... Would that be right?

SPIVEY   Indeed yes!

KELLY   It's all comin' back to me how we.... It was some kind
of ... of ...

SPIVEY (eagerly)   Ceremony?

KELLY   That's right! That's what it was! A ceremony! There was ...
well, there was certain things us girls had to say.... A song, maybe?

SPIVEY (enthusiastic)   A song!

KELLY (rising)   Yes! And then we done certain steps ... well, like
them play-parties...?

SPIVEY (ecstatic)   Play-party!

KELLY   Just to show you there's no hard feelin's, would you like
it if I was to go through with it?

SPIVEY   Mrs. Shepherd, I ... (Emotional.) It would be stupendous!
Absolutely stupendous!

KELLY (thoughtful)   I reckon if I was to hide you....

SPIVEY   Hide me?

KELLY   It'd be seven years bad luck if them girls was to see you.

SPIVEY   Girls?

4

KELLY   We got to have girls. We'll go to their room -

SPIVEY   Their ... room?

KELLY   Now don't fret. I'll hide you under the bed!

SPIVEY   The bed?... No, no, I couldn't!

KELLY   You can have your machine under there.

SPIVEY   I couldn't think of it!

KELLY   Lord, Mr. Spivey, what harm would there be?

SPIVEY   But ... my position? Under the bed! In a young woman's
room? Good heavens!

KELLY (persuasive)   Who's to know the difference? You'll be hid
under there before they come in. And afterwards I'll bring them
in here so's you can slip out!

SPIVEY (dubious)   Well.... No, no, it's impossible! (Walking
away.) Absolutely impossible! (Turning back.) Can't you arrange
some other way to -

KELLY (firmly)   Them words is a charm! If I was to say them just
anywheres and anyhow, them two girls would die old maids, that's a
fact!

SPIVEY (hesitating)   Perhaps in the interest of science.... (A few
steps.) You are convinced that it is all right for me to.... (He
stares hypnotically at the cot.)

KELLY (sly)   If it wasn't, would I have as't you?

SPIVEY (bolting)   But under the bed? It is so ... so ignominious!
(Desperate.) What would Eubanks do!

KELLY   Lord help, I hear someone! They's aways off yet but if
you're goin' to set up your machine under there ...

SPIVEY (looking at the tape recorder)   As a man I ought to refuse ...
But as a scholar ...

(He picks up the tape recorder and starts for the cot. KELLY follows
him, gathering up the wires.)

I want you to understand that I am not accustomed to ... (At the cot.)
to concealing myself under beds, and that only my devotion to scholarship could conquer my reluctance to ... (Staring at the cot.) to
undertake such an enterprise! A scientist cannot turn his eyes from
the truth. (He leans over to put the tape recorder under the bed.)

KELLY (to his rear)   Leastways not if it's naked!

SPIVEY (straightening up)   Please, Mrs. Shepherd.   This is no time
for vulgarity.

KELLY   You'd best hurry and get under that bed!

SPIVEY (on his knees)   I must confess this seems to me a highly
dubious undertaking. (Heavy sigh.) To what a pass science brings
us! We follow knowledge like a ... sinking star! (As he disappears
under the cot.)

KELLY (needling him)   Course'n if them fool girls was to catch
you under there, they might not understand, bein' flighty and all,
that it was--like you say--for scholarship! But don't you fret now!
No one's goin' to catch you! Not with Kelly Shepherd runnin' the
show! (Convulsed at her own joke.)

SPIVEY (sticking his head out)   For any other cause -

KELLY   Go on now and get under there!

SPIVEY (head out again)   You do realize, don't you, that I ...
that otherwise I wouldn't consider such an enterprise?

KELLY   Lord, Mr. Spivey, I reckon I can tell a Peepin' Tom when I
see one! Like you say, only a scholar!

(SPIVEY retreats under the bed. KELLY, convulsed, takes the water
pitcher from the washstand and goes out upstage.)

SPIVEY (struggling to find a comfortable position)   Discipline,
yes. And self-sacrifice.

(ANN and GARLAND enter from outside.)

ANN   Where can they be!

GARLAND   Jess likes games. Murder. Jealousy. Insanity! Any
number can play!

ANN   If he's only playing a game -

GARLAND (savage)   What's any game but a killing?

ANN   You mean...?

GARLAND   Jess has neither morals nor constancy! He's always in
love!

ANN   But -

GARLAND   Permanently.

ANN   Oh...!

GARLAND   He says he's never met the woman who could resist him.

ANN   Oh!

GARLAND   Nature, he says, is promiscuous.

ANN   How could I -

GARLAND   All women, he says, are young and fair. He's forever afire. They forever must quench him. Good God! I'll kill him! (Controlled.) What time is it?

ANN   A little after one.... Jess was talking about Susan all morning.

GARLAND   What did he say?

ANN   Do you think he was teasing?

GARLAND (violent)   How do I know!

ANN   Is something wrong?

GARLAND   No!

(Sounds of laughter outside.)

If Jess thinks I'm in a sweat.... Come on!

(He draws ANN quickly off upstage. SUSAN and JESS enter from outside. SUSAN is wearing his jacket.)

SUSAN (laughing)   Don't look so innocent. Haven't you just declared your evil intentions?

JESS   Have I?

SUSAN   Don't you know?

JESS   Not always. Let's be charitable. Charity begins here ... (Kissing her.) and goes on (Drawing her toward the bedroom.) by a direct route -

SUSAN (stopping him)   This road is legally closed.

JESS   I proceed at my own risk.

SUSAN (evading)   But you don't love me.

JESS   What's that got to do with it?

SUSAN   You don't think I...?

JESS   Damned if I know. You never finish your sentences. (Closing in again.)

SUSAN (evading)   Have you ever made love before? You're too precipi-tate! Men have no palates. No sense of pace.

(JESS is stalking her as she crosses to look outside.)

No poetry! See how the stars drift out the doors of the west!
(She is swept off her feet.) Put me down!

JESS   Flat on your back! (Striding toward the cot.)

SUSAN (kicking)   Oh!

JESS   Why don't you bite my ear?

SUSAN (kicking)   Let me go!

JESS   Struggle, angel. Beat on my chest.

(Laughing, he carries her toward the cot where SPIVEY looks out in
terror. JESS drops SUSAN on the cot. SPIVEY's hands shoot out
frog-like. He cowers.)

SUSAN   How can you be so ... so practical!

JESS (laughing)   What else did you have in mind?

(GARLAND rushes in from the hall, grabs JESS, spins him around and
slugs him. SUSAN screams. JESS does a flip backwards onto the floor.
GARLAND rushes out right as JESS struggles to his knees and leans
groggily on the edge of the cot. SPIVEY has squirmed farther into
the corner.)

SUSAN (leaning over JESS)   Did he hurt you?... Isn't it wonderful!

JESS (feeling his jaw)   Wonderful?

SUSAN   Oh you poor dear! Is it broken?

JESS (rubbing his jaw)   What in hell was that all about?

SUSAN   Poor dear, is there a lump? (Feeling the jaw.) He loves
me!

(Exuberantly she kisses him as ANN enters from upstage.)

ANN   Beasts! Both of you! I hate you!

(JESS moves toward her.)

Go away!

JESS   Damn right!   (He goes out upstage.)

SUSAN   Ann, darling, forgive mé.

ANN   Go away!

SUSAN   But don't you see? He loves me.

ANN   How can you think so!   (Throwing herself on the cot, banging SPIVEY's head.)

SUSAN   Because I'm immodest. I can't be quiet. I want to shout-- he loves me!

ANN   He doesn't love you. He can't.

SUSAN (quiet)   Why?

ANN   Because he loves me!   (Throwing herself on the bed again.)

SUSAN   Has he said so?

ANN   Of course he's said so!

SUSAN   This evening?

ANN   This evening, this morning -

SUSAN   He touched my hand when I was pouring the salt.

ANN (indignant)   Your hand? Weren't you just now in bed?

SUSAN (turning)   Darling, are you talking about Jess?

ANN   Of course I'm talking about Jess!

SUSAN   But it's Garland!

ANN   Garland?

SUSAN   Poor Jess! His jaw's nearly broken.

ANN   What!

SUSAN   Garland hit him.

ANN (outraged)   Hit him!

SUSAN   That's how I know Garland loves me!...   What shall I do?

ANN   Tell him the truth!

SUSAN   He'll think I tricked him.

ANN   Didn't you?

SUSAN   Doesn't a woman always? Don't they want us to? They're
indignant. They reproach us. We're forced to an alibi! We say
we love them. Could we have said so at first?... Poor Jess!
(Laughing.)

ANN (starting upstage)   Why didn't you tell me?

(On her way she is confronted by KELLY who enters carrying the water
pitcher and a couple of bath towels.)

KELLY   Reckon you'd like a bath. I've brought you some water.
(Backing ANN into the room.)

ANN   I wanted to see Jess.

KELLY   Lord, child, this ain't no hour of the night to be gaddin'.
Get off your things while the water's hot.

ANN (trying to get rid of her)   Thank you, we -

KELLY   You must be plumb filthy. (To SUSAN.)   All that climbin'
and hikin'.

SUSAN   Please don't bother.

KELLY   Lord, it's no bother.

ANN   I'm sure we can manage.

KELLY   You girls ain't used to the likes of this, and I aim to
help you. Get off your things.

(ANN takes off her sweater.)

I tell you I had a day here with Mr. Spivey! Him and his machine!
Poor man was worryin' hisself to death over a mess of foolishness.
He seemed so fevered and all that I.... You'd as well take off
your shoes.

(ANN sits at the head of the cot, SUSAN at the foot. SPIVEY cowers
between them. As KELLY talks, the girls take off their shoes, their
legs dangling near his nose.)

Here he was carryin' on about custom this and custom that! I told
him my grandmother had a charm for the first day of May. That's
today! First day of May, says, we done steps! Says, we made songs!
On I talked up a storm! Poor man, I done it to please him and he
taken it in so serious! I reckon he'll put it in one of them books.
And you know ... (Long pause for SPIVEY's benefit.) there ain't
a word of truth in none of it!

(She roars with laughter. SPIVEY wrings his hands.)

Get off your shirt now.

(ANN starts to unbutton her shirt. SPIVEY covers his eyes.)

What was that!

ANN   What?

KELLY   You know, it wouldn't surprise me none if Jess was under that
bed!

ANN   Jess! (Both girls get up.)

KELLY   Look at her grab her shirt! Well, I only said it to fret
you. But it wouldn't surprise me none. I wish 't Jess was more
refined. Like Mr. Spivey!

(She sits heavily on the bed, legs wide apart. SPIVEY cowers between
her ankles.)

There's a gentleman for you. He talks nice, he don't curse none,
and he keeps his hands to hisself. You don't catch him skulkin'
round under beds! Hidin' in ladies' chambers expectin' - (Rising
up.) I declare someone's under that bed! You got Jess under there?

ANN   Of course not!

KELLY   Land, I was young! That moon, that old lady up there ridin'
so high, she'll fire your blood till it melts down your bones and
you ain't got a scruple left! (Addressing the bed.)   Jess?...
You hear?

ANN   There's no one -

KELLY   Jess Shepherd, you don't fool me none! You come out a there
before I grab you out by the ear!

ANN   But look -

KELLY   No. Let him come out hisself. Like a man!

(She waits. SPIVEY is paralyzed.)

Jess Shepherd, I'm ashamed! You ain't no man, you're - (She looks
under the bed. Screams.) It ain't Jess! (Running upstage.) Jess!...
Garland!... Garland!... Jess!

(SPIVEY wriggles out from the bed.)

ANN   Mr. Spivey!

SPIVEY (on his way)   I didn't intend - that is, you see -

(JESS roars in upstage.)

JESS   Spivey!

(SPIVEY turns frantically, heads for the outside as GARLAND enters
right. SPIVEY wheels, dashes back , stumbles up and over the cot. JESS
grabs for him, falls prone on the cot. SPIVEY escapes left.)

KELLY (looking off after him)   He runs like a deer! He's took to
the air like a flyin' squirrel!   Look at them elbows a-thrashin',
them heels a-flyin'! (Turning back, severe.) He ought to be tore
to pieces. Under that bed he was! Like a Peeping Tom! And these
girls ready to bathe! Him and his talk. Him and his delicate manners.
Oh, he was dainty he was! Too nice to be clean!

(JESS has discovered the tape recorder.)

JESS   What in hell's all this? (Pulling it out.) He's got a tape
on here.

SUSAN   What!

JESS   Half-run. (Turning it on.)

SUSAN'S VOICE   ...I had to. I love him!

SUSAN (trying to turn it off) Really!

GARLAND (holding her back) No censorship.

ANN'S VOICE   Garland?

SUSAN'S VOICE   Yes, Garland. What shall I do? Tell me.

ANN'S VOICE   Tell him....

(Silence. The reel turns soundlessly. KELLY is staring at it in
fascination. GARLAND is kissing SUSAN. JESS and ANN have faded
upstage.)

SUSAN (in GARLAND'S arms) Is love a game? I used to say so. But
love's a wild wind blowing up spring!

GARLAND   I loved you before I saw you.

SUSAN   And now?

GARLAND   I'm consumed. I have chills and fevers.

SUSAN   Then you're not disillusioned? You said -

GARLAND   I said flesh was poorer than fantasy, God help me.

SUSAN   A woman's finite.

GARLAND   She's worlds upon worlds.

SUSAN   But there's no metamorphosis!

GARLAND   Why should she change?

SUSAN   She can be weighed, measured -

GARLAND   Who'd add an inch to perfection!

SUSAN   Perfection? Poor man, to think love should be perfect!
Shall I prove -

SPIVEY (outside, left, stage whisper)   Mrs. Shepherd!

KELLY   Lord, if it ain't Mr. Spivey again!

SPIVEY (fearful and desperate)   The machine! It belongs to the University!

KELLY   Land, Mr. Spivey, I don't know what got into me to do you
like that! You was little Cupid hisself!

SPIVEY (dazed)   Cupid...?

KELLY (indicating SUSAN and GARLAND)   Them tapes of yours! I was
plumb out of my head.

SPIVEY   I'm afraid I ... I insulted you.

KELLY (warmly)   We was both fools!... You'd best get the **brandy**.

SPIVEY   Brandy?

KELLY   Peach brandy! To celebrate! John buried it the summer afore
he died. You see that bank out there? With them vines on it? You
take a spade from the shed and dig down a piece and you'll find it!

(No one notices SCOTT MARTIN when he appears from the outside right.)

SCOTT   Anyone home?

KELLY   Lord, Scott! You give me a turn!

SCOTT   I hollered two-three times.

KELLY   What in the world you doin' here this time of night? Is
your wife took sick?

SCOTT   I got a message here for Ann. She here?

KELLY   At two o'clock in the mornin' you come round here with a
message? I declare, Scott, you ain't got good sense, but bein'
you're here you'd as well sit down.

(SCOTT pulls a chair out from the table, sits as if ready to make
an announcement.)

Ann!... Ann!... Come in here.

(ANN and JESS enter upstage.)

SCOTT (importantly) Well, I talked to him.

KELLY   Talked to who?

SCOTT (to ANN)   Your daddy.

ANN   Father?

SCOTT   Mr. Martin, he says, this is J. D. Stuart.

KELLY   J. D. (To ANN.) Your daddy...?   Jess, you hear?...   Scott,
you never!

SCOTT (proud)   That's right. That's what I did.

ANN   Where is he?

SCOTT   Reckon he's on his way here. Mr. Martin, says, I'm indebted
to you. Indebted, he says. To me! The reward is yours.

ANN   What reward?

SCOTT   Mr. Stuart, I says, I'm a railroader. I railroaded the most
of my life, and I aim to railroad with what's left of it. You'd
as well keep the money.

KELLY   Now, Scott, don't get foolish!

SCOTT   But, I says ... since you insist ... I'd be grateful for the
money to buy my old lady a set of teeth.

JESS   Look here, Scott, I don't understand a damn word you've been
saying!

SCOTT   Ann, there, give me a telegram for her father, see? Time
I remembered to send it, I knew he'd be pitchin' a fit on account
of that girl on TV bein' killed and he -

KELLY (startled)   Killed! (Looking at SUSAN.)   Barbara Logan?...
Was she killed?

SCOTT   Course she was.

KELLY   You hear that, Garland?

(GARLAND is staring at SUSAN.)

SCOTT   Somewheres in Kentucky.

GARLAND (looking at SUSAN)   Kentucky...?

SCOTT   That's what it says on TV. And you know what that half-wit
Hugo done? He told the police he seen these girls on the mountain,
and of course the plane was spotted from the air, and you'd a had
300 newspapermen here lookin' for Barbara Logan if I hadn't of called
Mr. Stuart.

GARLAND (to SUSAN)   Do you think I believe in miracles?

SUSAN   Does any man?

GARLAND   I suppose she married him.

SUSAN   Oh yes ... when they got to Peru.

(SPIVEY enters right, carrying a dirty bottle at arm's length.)

SPIVEY   Mrs. Shepherd, is this the brandy?

JESS   You Peeping Tom -

KELLY (between him and SPIVEY, taking the bottle)   Now Jess, it
wasn't Mr. Spivey's fault! I told him -

JESS   I suppose you told him to get under the bed!

KELLY   Well ...

SPIVEY   As a matter of fact -

(JESS roars with laughter. KELLY passes the brandy to GARLAND and SUSAN,
who pour out glasses for everyone and pass them.)

KELLY   If it wasn't for Mr. Spivey and them tapes ... I declare
he's little Cupid hisself!

SCOTT   Cupid?

KELLY (handing him a glass)   Have a drink!   (Offering one to SPIVEY.)
Mr. Spivey?

SPIVEY (dubious)   Thank you I....   (He is stuck with it.)

GARLAND (raising his glass)   Cupid!

(All raise their glasses. SPIVEY hesitates, then clinks his glass against KELLY's.)

SPIVEY   Cupid--eh, Mrs. Shepherd?

HUGO (entering)   Never pass by, I say, never pass by!   You can sell
a man right into a weddin'!   You wouldn't believe what a mess it
takes to get married!

(He opens the suitcase, tosses out rice, garters, flowers to the
couples, finally pacifiers and rattles.)

BIRDWATCHERS

By Barbara Allan Hite

CHARACTERS

He
She

SCENE

A forest clearing.

(HE comes in with much equipment--folding chair, binoculars, two
cameras, safari hat, and thermos of martinis--sets up his stuff,
pours a drink, begins scanning the area with binoculars. SHE comes
in, sets up her stuff--campstool, binoculars, camera, large purse--
begins scanning the area with binoculars. They discover each other
through the binoculars.)

SHE   Hi ... there.

HE   Hi....

(Pause.)

SHE   Are you by any chance doing the same thing I'm doing?

(HE looks, smiles, doesn't know what to say.)

Does that sound like a silly question? (Slight awkward pause.)
But one doesn't expect to find another ... one sitting in a certain
spot in the forest ... (Pause.) ... Someone who's not fishing
or ... picknicking.... So I was merely wondering if -

HE (cutting in)   I'm hoping to catch a glimpse of a certain ivory-
billed woodpecker, almost extinct, rumored to be building -

SHE   That's it! Imagine. Yes. The ivory-billed woodpecker is
supposed to be building its nest right here in this very area, according to the Audubon Guide.

HE   Well, I'm sure glad for the confirmation.

SHE   Then you must be my partner.

HE   I didn't know we were supposed to have partners.

SHE   Oh, yes, for verification.

HE   Oh, verification. I don't know. Maybe I am, then.

SHE   Good. Right. (Rises.) Let's set up our station. (Crosses to shake hands.) I'm Alice Wren.

HE (extending hand)   Martin Foglesong.

SHE   I'm so happy to meet you. Now, we just want to move our things together just a little bit. We'll confine our area more that way. (Going to get purse.) Of course, this is not what you'd call a legitimate field station, but for lack of anything else to call it, I always call it that.

HE   I don't have any objections to calling it that, really.

SHE   Right. Good. There, that's fine. Now, out with the equipment. (Goes to her spot, gets stuff. Pause, watching him.) You were assigned to this spot?

HE   Well, no, not that I know of. It just seemed like a likely spot. Shady, not too shady. Quiet. It wasn't that I had any particular kind of spot in mind beforehand. It's just that as I came along, I was looking for a spot and when I got here, I thought this seemed like a good one.

SHE   But you do have your card?

HE   My card?

SHE   Your Audubon card, for identification.

HE   No. No, I don't. I just heard, you know ... through the grapevine.

SHE (standing, laughs a bit)   Oh, that's never very dependable, is it? Well, it looks like you were fortunate today. (Setting up.) I don't suppose it matters this time about the card. (Pause, watches, then:) I'll bet this is your first experience.

HE   Yeah.

SHE   Well, you're going to really enjoy it, I'm sure. (Goes to sit.)

HE   I didn't know what to bring along in the way of equipment, you know. First time and everything as it is. (Indicating all his stuff. Sits.)

SHE   Right. I think we always feel so much more at home with some of our own things around us. (Pause. She gets tissue for nose.)

HE   Are you native to this area, Miss ... Finch?

SHE   Wren ... No, Alice Wren.

HE (laughing, overlapping her correction)   Oh, I'm sorry.

SHE (also laughing)   It's all right. People often get it confused.
Yes, I was born 'n raised ... just down the road there. (Pause.
She gets book out, marks page.)

HE   What's that book you have there?

SHE   Oh, this? Oh, it's just my official Audubon Field Guide. I'm
afraid not to use it. On the only occasion I ever used something
else, I had a terrible time getting confirmation.

HE (after a pause).   What ... uh ... what kind of confirmation do
you get?

SHE   Well, you confirm that you've actually seen the bird you think
you've seen.

HE   Oh, yeah, yeah.

(SHE gets camera out. Loads it.)

HE   What kind of film do you use?

SHE   Kodak ... color. You know, I once got a shot of a flycatcher·
actually ...   (Indicates, opens mouth, etc.)

HE   Catching a fly?

SHE   Right. It was a little bleary because I was so excited, but
you could see that fly just about to be ... chomped.

(Pause.)

HE   I hope you don't feel embarrassed that I'm here, too.

SHE   Oh, no, not at all. I'm used to it really.

HE   I could move to the other side of that tree.

SHE   Now don't be silly. This is a pastime that one thinks of as
being secluded or, well, solitary. Secluded is not a word that
seems to fit with pastime, is it? A secluded pastime sounds odd .
Or rather a solitary sort of activity. You yourself made reference
to that fact before when you spoke of the quiet. Yes, one does
expect to be quiet at a time like this. (Rises, goes left.) But
according to the regulations, two are necessary for verification and,
actually, to be perfectly honest, I wouldn't know what to think if
I were alone. (Looks down and up.) Although I've never been paired
with a man before.

HE   I was afraid of that. I was afraid I'd make you nervous.

SHE   You're not making me nervous.

HE   Maybe you think I'm peculiar then?

SHE   No, no, I think it's wonderful of you men to take an interest.

HE   You don't think it's queer?

SHE   No, no, it seems perfectly ... normal to me.

HE (rising)   But it's never happened before?

SHE   If we're partners, I don't think we should question it. No
one wants to feel out of place and no one is. I think you just have
to accept that. You can question anything, you know.

HE   Who belongs and who might not?

SHE   We want to remember why we're here.

HE   Then you're not concerned about the matter of the card?

SHE   Of course I'm concerned about the matter of the card, but I'm
sure you have an explanation for that. (She waits.)

HE (pause)   Have you been interested in birds long?

SHE   I've always loved all living things really. I always had a
little turtle or a fish around. (Awkward pause.) Well ... and
what about you? Were you, too, an animal-lover from the very first?

HE   Oh, I'm a writer.

SHE   Really, how exciting. (Moving to sit.)

HE   I exaggerate my interests.

SHE (sits with anticipation next to him)   Oh, through imagination!
That's wonderful. (Awkward pause. She gets camera, rises.) Well,
let's see. I'm just going to try to get my bearings. I like to
take a few shots of the general area before things start ... happening.
(Clicking, turning camera.)

HE   The setting. That's a good idea, background material.

SHE (clicking, unconsciously posing as she turns)   I knew a man
once who took pictures of the woods and mountains on his vacation
and blew them up, you know, enlarged them to cover his entire living
room walls when he got home. Isn't that unusual? It was quite an
unusual effect.

HE (in one of his ways of speaking)   I can imagine ... he said with a curious inflection.

SHE   He only turned them on for parties or when they had a few friends over.   Such a novel idea.

HE (pause, then:)   A woman is very lovely in the woods.

SHE (pause)   Are you saying that deliberately to make me nervous?

HE   No, no, it just seemed like a perfectly likely thing to say. (Pause.)   Have you studied much on the passenger pigeon?

SHE   What?

HE   The passenger pigeon.   It became extinct around 1931.

SHE   Oh.   Oh, yes.   (Recovering.)   You know, we've been having a series of programs on already extinct birds and animals.   We read the reports from Congress at the time of that occurrence.   (Moving back to him.)   It was a tragic thing, and the thing most tragic about it was the lack of concern on the part of our lawmakers and elected officials.

HE   Is that what you think?

SHE   Well ... well, yes.   I do.   It was.   Don't you think it was?

HE   It still is.

SHE   Yes, you're right.   In many instances.

HE   Nothing has changed since 1931.

SHE   Well, a lot of things have changed ...

HE   In the realm of official attitudes, I mean.

SHE   It's an involved process.   I mean, we can't expect change to occur overnight.

HE   My father was a member of the Senate in 1931.

SHE   Oh.

HE   A man of conscious opinion.

SHE   Oh, well, not all the lawmakers -

HE   I'm just kidding.

SHE (turning away)   We're partners, you know, but that doesn't mean we have to be friends.   We don't even have to talk, if you'd rather not.

HE (stands, goes right)   You mean there are couples of strangers
sitting in awkward degrees of comradeship and intimacy all through
this entire ... place? Like this?

SHE   I don't think you're ready to sympathize with the situation.

HE   I don't believe it. Listen, I don't want to believe it. I've
got my values and so forth. I think you're making it up.

SHE   Oh, no, no, it's according to the regulations.

HE   But then, you seem to be a person who's very careful to know
what's going on and to do the right thing. (Calms down, sits.)
I don't want to cause any commotion, but the idea makes me want to
climb a tree. Just how many ... "partners" ... do you suppose there
are sitting here and there throughout the area in various official
positions?

SHE   I see what you mean. You miss the spontaneity.

HE   The seclusion ...

SHE   The spirit of primitive discovery ...

HE   Yeah ... that spirit....

SHE   But you see, there are people who want to abuse the Natural Resources.

HE (putting her on a bit)   Listen, it all has to do with the deliber-
ate, manipulated simultaneous destruction of the authority figure
by radical forces. You spit on your police, your Armed Forces, your
coaches and umpires, and you've got people who are going to spit on
your Natural Resources. It stands to reason. And you're going to
have it rub off on people like me who, subsequently, don't know where
they stand.

SHE (rising)   No, no, no. As I understand it, it's the people who
are spitting on the President and the Army who want to save the
Natural Resources.

HE   Ah, but where does that leave a person like me?

SHE   Well, you writers are alone so much of the time ...

HE   That's no excuse for ignoring the social situation as it exists.
You're being polite. Knock it all down and you don't have a leg to
stand on.

SHE   I think it's mainly a matter of concern.

HE   It's also a question of priorities to some degree.

SHE   Right. You feel concerned and you put that concern first.

HE   People before profit.

SHE   You come out and you look around and you see what needs to be
said. (Pause.) But I don't think you usually say it ...

HE   Or else everyone says it ...

SHE   Exactly. Just the same.

(They get amused at the whole thing.)

HE   People before profit. You know.

SHE   It's a matter of concern ...

HE   Or a question of priorities....

SHE   Oh, it's true. Do you know, do you know what's happened to me?
Well, you know what it's like to be driving along on the highway, and
you see a sign that says "Caution, Mowing Operations Ahead, Speed
Limit 45 mph," so you slow down and, after a while, you come to a
sign that says, "End of Mowing Operations, Thank you, Resume Speed,"
but in the meantime, the thing is, you haven't seen one mowing machine
in operation.... Well, this has happened to me, I don't know how
many times. The other day I saw a sign that said "Slow, Men Working,
Speed Limit 25 mph," and I didn't believe it, I simply didn't believe
what it said. When I realized what had happened, of course, I slowed
down to 40 mph, just in case, but it didn't change my mind. Once
that has happened ... I mean, it's not easy to know what needs to be
said....

HE   You should talk to some of my friends. (Goes back, sits.)

SHE (following)   If we were at a cocktail party, we'd never meet
each other.

HE   I don't know.

SHE (sitting)   Yes, you'd be talking with people in dark glasses
and raised eyebrows.

HE   Ha, that's good. The women who have very few eyebrows and find
it easy to know what needs to be said.

(Pause.)

When I was sixteen, I used to imagine I was locked in a prison cell
for being a spy. I was locked in there with another spy who turned
out to be a girl in disguise. A nice girl, hardly talked at all,
quiet, very attractive and pure. Very dedicated to the purpose of
our mission. We were both scheduled to die for treason. Naturally,
we fell in love. It was the only time I saw her reserve break down.
Sometimes I saved her and sometimes I saved us both. Sometimes we

died together. Prior to that we shared a brief but meaningful ...
relationship.

SHE   I used to imagine in bed at night. I imagined I was a wounded
nurse in the war, left for dead in the forest. This sensitive soldier
finds me and waits with me for help to arrive. He never spoke to me
or touched me in an aggressive manner. He was in uniform and mindful
of his duty. But of course, we fell in love, too. I was facinating,
even wounded--in my mind I was. It was difficult for him to main-
tain his duty. It called for terrific restraint.

HE   It's funny when you're younger.

SHE   Imagination is much easier when you're younger.

HE   Just the opposite for me.

SHE   For you, I guess you're right. Well, it's never easy.

IIE   And you never want to come out of that prison cell.

SHE   To see help arrive and wake up in the hospital with everyone
else. (Pause.) You know, I think it's stupid to have pictures of
woods and mountains all over your living room walls.

HE   It is, he said with raised eyebrows.... Wait!

SHE   What?

HE   Shhh. Don't move. Shhh.

(HE rises, and, looking up, slowly creeps to the side of the stage.
SHE follows.)

SHE   What? Do you see it?

HE   Shhh. Don't move.

SHE   Where? Where is it?

HE (crawls down right, looks, runs around upstage)   I thought I saw
it. We've got to be careful. We're making entirely too much noise.

(They move back toward chairs.)

SHE   I just had a thought. Do you know what I think? I think we're
really exposing ourselves entirely too much. I think perhaps we should
move our positions.

HE   You've got a point there. We have to be careful. We should
seclude ourselves more carefully.

SHE   Right. Let's move our things. (Picks up stool and chair, stops.)

Where do you suggest we put them?

HE   Listen, you've had more experience at this than I have.

SHE   Well, under cover of a tree might not be a bad idea. I don't think it could hurt.

HE   Provided we can see clearly enough.... (Checks around.) Here?

SHE   Right. I'll just give you a hand with some of your things. This is so cozy.

(Pause as they get settled.)

HE   Say, uh, what happens if you have to, you know ... go to the bathroom?

SHE   Oh. Well. There's a rest room in the Information Center at the entrance.

HE   How far is that?

SHE   Didn't you see it?

HE   No.

SHE   Well, it's not far.... (Pause.) Do you...?

HE   Oh, no, no. I was just curious.

(HE begins to look through binoculars. Pause.)

SHE (whisper)   You know, a man has a certain appeal when he's doing the same thing you are.... He has even more appeal when he's not, if you want to know the truth.

HE   Well, I'm probably not. I'm probably much more serious about this than you are.

SHE   What do you mean "serious"?

HE   Serious. My life's work. This may even be a sort of bread and butter to me.

SHE   Oh, you're a professional?

HE   This may be a matter of my livelihood, whereas for you, some woman's club probably. "Girls, Alice Wren is going to devote her entire day next Saturday all day looking for ... getting a glimpse of our ivory-billed double-breasted woodpecker. What about that, girls?"

SHE   Double-breasted woodpecker. How serious is that?

HE   It's just an attitude.

SHE (standing, crossing behind him)   Logically, I wouldn't want to disturb you if it meant your livelihood, but on the other hand, I hate to be insulted.

HE   My work is very relevant to the World, he said with a careless shrug.

SHE   I bet you're writing a book.

HE   It must be done with the utmost accuracy.

SHE   Men have such a special feeling for pages. Moistened and flipped. Confronting the world from between the covers. Man speaks to Nature. Nature speaks to Man.

HE   It's not a book.

SHE   Oh, no, I know what it is! You're doing the movie script first. Right. That's it.

HE   I shouldn't have insulted you.

SHE (crossing to him)   Wait. I can see a TV series. Backwoods social renegade, perhaps widowed with small, adorable child, battles poachers and politicians to protect the bird he loves. Each episode takes us deeper into the world of real man as he pits himself against the elements of nature. You could have a hurricane one time and a flood, swamp poison, alligators, Spanish moss....

HE   And a woman who wants him to go to Washington to save the swamp. "But Mary, I'd be like a fish out of water in Washington. The swamp is my home; it's all I've ever known...."

(SHE giggles.)

Shhh.

SHE   What?

HE   Don't move.

SHE   What? Again? Where?

HE   Shhh.

(HE moves to try to see it. SHE follows.)

I feel sure I saw a large object ... moving.... It is a large bird, isn't it? How large a bird is it?

SHE   Oh, about so long. I have my book here. (Crosses to chair, right.) Let's see. "Length 18 inches. Red crested head plumage."

HE   I feel sure I saw something of that nature. There....

SHE   Well....

HE   I don't see it now.

SHE   Hmm.

HE   Maybe we should.... (Indicates chairs.)

BOTH Move ... over there....

SHE   Maybe you're right. At least it wouldn't hurt.

(They move.)

HE   Would you like a drink?

SHE   What?

HE   A drink. I, uh....

SHE   You really have come prepared! I always thought it would be
nice to fix up a little iced tea or lemonade or even just some good
old plain water to bring, but I never have done it.

HE   Martini, dry martini.

SHE   I don't believe it!

HE   Now I guess I'll feel embarrassed about it.

SHE   Oh, no, please, really....

HE   I, uh, I thought it would help to, uh, pass the time....

SHE   Please don't feel you have to explain it.

HE   Not only do you get paired with a man, but then he turns out
to be a drunkard....

SHE   I'm sure you know what you're doing.

HE   I wish you'd just go ahead and say what you think.

SHE   I am, really. I think we've built up quite an open relationship really.

HE   Then why won't you have a little drink?

SHE   You're not an ornithologist, are you?

HE   I write stories, or articles--whatever you want to call them--

on various topics, whatever strikes my fancy or, most likely, whatever is available at the time. Lots of times I have to do a little
research, if something comes up that I'm not familiar with. Last
year I did a little piece on canoeing for the Free Sportsman, and
I watched these guys make their own canoe and try it out.

SHE   I see.

HE   As a matter of fact, I don't need to actually see the bird to
write the story. You know, it's the human-interest angle. Or, for
that matter, I can invent the bird in my mind if it comes to that.

SHE   Well, would that be fact or fiction you're writing?

HE   Frankly, you see, there's very little distinction in your popular mags these days. You know, everybody wants his facts jazzed up--
turn 'em into an adventure story. When I first started out, I didn't
know how to do that, but it really isn't hard once you get the hang
of it. Say, for instance, you're doing a thing on infection, pretty
scientific, you know. But you would never start off saying something
like "Infection results from the presence of certain poisonous micro-
organisms in the body ... or so forth. You see, you'd want to grab
'em up with something like "There's a battle being fought in the
bloodstream at this very moment, ... in the darkest recesses of the
veins...."

SHE   That is much more involving, isn't it? I see what you mean.

HE   Now, at the same time, if you're writing fiction, you want to
get it to come very down to earth and close to home. Say your main
character is a psychopath who's set on destroying an entire city
by poisoning the water supply. Well, you want to make him very much
like the guy next door, a family man--empties the trash, cuts the
lawn, plays catch with the neighborhood kids. You know.

SHE   A surprise ending. I never thought of it like that.

HE   There's a longing for realistic sensationalism in the air ...
at the breakfast table ... orange juice that tastes more like oranges
than oranges themselves do. That sort of thing.

SHE   Oh. I think I see what you mean. (Thinking, moving away.)
I was just thinking then, how are you going to do this story.

HE   Well....

SHE   "There was a mysterious air about the forest that morning...."

HE   Hey, good, very good!

SHE   Then what?

HE (thinking)   I'll describe the forest glen, in detail....

5

SHE   And then...?

HE   I'll build up suspense by describing a few of the more common
birds of the area....

SHE   Which?

HE   Which?

SHE (by him)   Which birds? Which of the more common birds?

HE   Well, I don't know. I'll have to work that out.

SHE   Maybe you could invent them too?

HE   Of course not. I can just look around here - What's the matter
with you?

SHE   There we are in the mist of the mysterious early morning air,
watching the robin hop-hop-hopping along when suddenly we're going
to feel the power and glory of the mighty wings winging ... schooom!
Dipping! And there we all are, stunned, in the midst of the great
hoax!

HE   That's not true.

SHE   No, it's not. What is it then...?

HE   It goes beyond that, when you read it, beyond truth ... as you
describe it.

SHE   An extraodinary lie.

HE   Art.

SHE (Pause, then closing in)   Do you know what I bet? I'll bet you
don't even have an Audubon Card.

HE   Aha! That's it, is it? I knew it. I knew you were getting
at something, trying to wheedle it out. No, I wouldn't have one,
wouldn't take it if someone gave it to me, paid me for it. I don't
believe in cards like that. I never would, I'd never take it!

SHE   It's a matter of assuming responsibility for your actions.
Being held accountable, that's all. (Looking for her card.)

HE   I don't want any part of it.

SHE   This is an Audubon-protected forest.

HE   I know all about that kind of protection. And you sign a special
register, time of entering, time of departure, largest bird observed -

SHE   There are people who take advantage.... I can't find it, can't find my card.

HE   Oho!

SHE   I thought it was right here with my Sears Chargaplate.

HE   Driver's license, social security, Blue Cross and Shield, Gulf,
Exxon, Master Charge, Bank America -

SHE   I can't find it.

HE   Illegal! Both illegal! Illegal in the "Audubon-protected forest."

SHE   I hate not to know where something is.

HE   We knew it was wrong, but fate seemed to compel us, held us in
a tenacious grip.

SHE   I was supposed to return my Master Charge last January....
"Kindly cut your card in half and return to us...."

HE   We're both in this thing together, he whispered. Let's neither
of us forget that fact for even an instant.

SHE   I charged a living room of furniture on it last December, $999,
and that plus Christmas sent it way over the $500 limit. No, I can't
find it.

HE   Early American?

SHE   What? I just don't see it....

HE   Your living room, Early American?

SHE   Spanish revival. That really upsets me.

HE   Oh. Cha cha cha.

SHE (realizing) Well, that's it, is it? That really makes it clear.
I know what you're doing, trying to pull me down. You didn't want
to be partners in the first place.

HE (angry) No, I came to look for a bird!

SHE   Oh, that's what you say, that's what you think, but you didn't
come to see a bird. You're pretending, you're filling your pad there
with pretense, that's the truth! And you're not so much better for it.

HE   I hope to see that bird. I hope to see the bird, not carry on
a conversation about some imitation living room furniture. (Angrily
moving his chair away from hers.) I have to get a feeling ... I came
to get a feeling for my story....

(Long pause.)

SHE   But what are you going to do about me? What will you do with
me? In your story. What will you do?

HE (sees her problem)   Oh.

SHE   I'd like to know.

HE (looks at her. Long pause, then:)   Would you want to be in there?

SHE   I don't know.

HE   Would you want to be in there ... as you are?

SHE (smiles)   Ah. Well....

HE   Or....

SHE   I could be something more ... sensational. (Pause.) Once upon
a time ... I imagined an enchanted forest.... Flowers bloom at the
foot of the trees even though the sun never reaches them. (Change.)
The thing is--could you put me in there the way I am?

HE (smiles)   Well, I can see possibilities - (He looks up, sees
the bird.) Wait! Don't move! Slowly ... on that oak between the
three pines and the maple, on the trunk between the third and fourth
branches on the left. See it?

SHE   Yes, yes!... It's beautiful, beautiful ... big....

HE (whispering)   Is it an ivory-billed woodpecker?

SHE (also whispering)   Oh. I have my confirmation guide ... here ...
(Gets book.)

HE   Slowly, slowly.

SHE   I have the page marked ... here ... oh, yes....

HE   Okay. What?

SHE   That must be it.

HE   What does it say?

SHE   "Extensive white on wing, folded and in flight, and white bill
are diagnostic."--that means distinguishes it from the pileated
woodpecker -

HE   Let's see that thing. Yeah. Yeah. That looks like it. I'll
be damned! (Getting camera, shooting, etc.)

SHE   Oh, it's really exciting. (Noticing him.) My camera! My camera's over there!

HE (taking pictures)   Never mind. Don't move. I'll send you what I have. (Kneeling, getting different shots.)

SHE   Well. It's funny, but I don't know what to do. I mean I feel so silly in a way, standing here.

HE   Commit to memory, remember.

SHE   I feel ridiculous, just looking this way, not doing anything.

HE (gives her a piece of paper)   Describe it, what it's doing.

(HE begins to write.)

SHE   Beautiful. Just imagine.

HE   What do you usually do on these occasions? After all, you're experienced at this sort of thing. You ought to be right at home.

SHE   Well, it's never been this ... important before. Usually it's not so crucial. I don't remember. Just to see it ... so special. (Change.) What are you doing?

HE   Writing, making the most of my time.

SHE   Poor bird.

HE   I wonder if that stuff sticking out of that hole is the nest? Do you have any information on that?

SHE   Oh. (Stands to look, then stops.)

HE   Not very neat, is it? All those sticks. Hardly room for the bird.

SHE   Somehow, I hate to think of you ... using that bird.

HE   I hate to think of you wasting it.

SHE (louder, rising)   It's not a waste to let something alone!

HE   Shhh. Let it alone, then. Be quiet.

SHE   It's not a waste to sit and watch.

HE   Sit Sat Sat. I call it a waste.

SHE   A liar and exploiter makes that kind of statement, and that is a waste. (Poking the pad with her **foot.**) That's what's a waste!

6

HE   I hate to think of a person doing nothing, going to club meetings!...
Look at that! (Kicks purse.) That is nothing. Means nothing.
Nothing. No thing. Not a thing. Waste. Vanity. Trivia. Bobby-
pins and mosaic pillboxes.

SHE   My bird book was in there.

HE   Hateful, shameful waste, pollution, rigamarole, rot. Using some
poor animal's hide to carry around a lot of Nothing!

SHE   Oh, you and your judgments and your observations, scraping and
picking away at the seams. (Tearing pages out of the pad.) And your
notations, your deceiving descriptions ... inventions!...

(Silence. They know the bird is gone. They look at each other for
a count of five or six, then look up for a count of four or five
and back at each other.)

He   Well.

(HE collects some of his papers. Hands her her purse. SHE gives
him some papers. SHE gets her purse back in order. Pause.)

I guess partners aren't supposed to act like that.

SHE (weak smile)   No, they never do.

HE   She said with an enigmatic smile.

SHE   Well.

HE   I don't suppose it'll come back any time soon?

SHE   Well, according to ... (Changes, stops.) I wouldn't think so ...
no.

HE (getting his stuff together. SHE helps him.)   It's on the tip
of my tongue to say that I enjoyed meeting you, sharing this morning's
activities with you.

SHE   That's the usual thing to say.

HE   I'll have to think of something ... more ... sensational.

(SHE nods.)

I'll work that out. Well, listen, so long.

SHE   So long.

(HE goes. SHE waits, then calls after him.)

I'm sorry.

(SHE goes and·picks up the campstool, turns, sees some of his papers
still on the ground, picks them up and almost puts them, unread, in
her purse. But the idea of reading them occurs to her and SHE begins
to read, coming upon one that SHE reads aloud quietly.)

"Miss Wren enchants the forest."

(But the problem comes up again, and SHE says, more loudly toward
where HE has gone:)

You! How can anyone believe you?

(SHE puts the paper in her purse, or begins to, then starts to go,
looks back, begins to smile; and looking up where the bird was, then
where he left, repeats half-seriously:)

"... enchants the forest...."

(SHE looks up quickly again to where the bird was, smiles, and leaves.)

A MERRY DEATH

By Nicolai Evreinov

Translated by Christopher Collins

CHARACTERS

Pierrot
Harlequin
The Doctor
Columbine
Death

SCENE

Harlequin's house.

(Doors to the right and left. Center stage is a bed; a large clock
over it shows eight o'clock; below the clock to the right is a large
indoor thermometer and to the left a lute. At right downstage is a
small table with a lamp on it and two stools nearby. At left downstage is a glass-doored cupboard with bottles, wine glasses, bread,
and fruit. If the third stool by the bed were mentioned, then one
would have to acknowledge the description of the stage as complete.
As the curtain rises HARLEQUIN is asleep with his head facing upward
and his arms straight at his sides. His hair is gray; as for the
rest of him, HARLEQUIN looks like a harlequin. Flies are buzzing.
PIERROT shoos them off HARLEQUIN's face, with the cuffs of his long
sleeves, of course, and brushes the sleeper's nose in the process,
of course. Then he walks over to the audience and waves his hands
at it.)

PIERROT   Shh.... Quiet! Take your seats as noiselessly as possible
and try to keep any talking and shifting in your chair to a minimum,
because if any of you were dragged along by one of your uncultured
friends, and you're too serious to take any interest in some harlequinade, then there's no point in your bringing it to the attention
of the rest of the audience. who, after all, are not concerned with
your personal tastes. Furthermore, Harlequin is asleep.... You
see! Shh.... I'll explain everything later! In the meantime, don't
wake him up, please! And when Columbine shows up, don't applaud
like mad, just to show your friends that you had an affair with her
and know how to appreciate real talent! I beg you earnestly! This
is no laughing matter: Harlequin is gravely ill! Just think, he's
delirious over Columbine, although she doesn't pay him the slightest
attention, since Columbine is my wife, and that, naturally, settles
it. I strongly suspect Harlequin will not survive the night; a
fortuneteller once predicted that the day he slept more than he drank,

he would die at the stroke of midnight. You can see it is now eight
o'clock in the evening and he's still sleeping. I can even say more--
I know, perhaps for certain, that Harlequin will soon die, but what
decent actor would tell his audience the end of the play before it
begins! I'm not one to let the management down, and I understand
quite well that an audience comes to the theater not because of some
meaning or other or for the masterful dialogue, but simply to find
out how it all turns out in the end; and nevertheless I find myself
unable to hold back a sigh and to say, crying on my long sleeve
(Does so.): "Poor, poor Harlequin, who would have supposed." I
loved him very much! He was my first friend, which, by the way,
never hindered me from envying him a little, because as everyone
knows, if I am Pierrot, it is only because I am a harlequin who has
not succeeded like the madly popular Harlequin. No matter what you
might think, I'm not so simple as my costume, and, I assure you,
I've already run for the Doctor, useless as it may be, since Harlequin will die perfectly well without the Doctor, but ... that's the
way decent people handle these things, and I'm not one to be uncon-
ventional; after all, if I didn't behave like everybody else then
I'd be the bold, merry Harlequin, for whom laws don't exist, but
I ... I'm merely the stupid, cowardly Pierrot, whose character, in-
cidentally, will become quite clear to you during the subsequent
development of the play, if you will only stay till the end of the
performance and don't clear out right away because of all my babbling.
So I'll stop, informing you only of the following plan which came
to mind without any outside assistance whatsoever: if Harlequin
is fated to die at the stroke of twelve by this clock, then wouldn't
it be a friendly gesture on my part to set the hands back, even if
only two hours! I've always enjoyed swindling people and so, when
it comes to swindling Death and Harlequin into the bargain, to the
disadvantage of the former and the advantage of the latter--I would
say that you can't call the plan anything other than sheer genius.
And so, to work! The play begins! (He climbs up on a stool and,
balancing precariously over the bed, sets the clock back exactly
two hours.) Poor, poor Harle ... (Falls with a crash on the floor.)
Poor Pierrot!

(On his knees, he rubs his back with a tearful expression on his face.
HARLEQUIN awakes, smiles, pulls PIERROT by the chin toward him and
kisses him tenderly.)

PIERROT (innocently)   It seems I woke you up?

HARLEQUIN   Why didn't you do it sooner?

PIERROT   What for?

HARLEQUIN   My hours are numbered.

PIERROT   Oh stop it!

HARLEQUIN   I want to live them.

PIERROT   You will.

HARLEQUIN   And you almost let me sleep right through them.

PIERROT   I thought....

HARLEQUIN   What time is it?

PIERROT   Six.

HARLEQUIN   Is that all?

PIERROT   Yes. How do you feel?

HARLEQUIN   Like I'm dying.

PIERROT   The way you worry about your health makes me laugh.   (He cries.)

HARLEQUIN   Stop it! I am alive. What have you been doing? The clock isn't lying?

PIERROT   I went for the Doctor. Try to rest! I've got to take your temperature. (Takes the thermometer from the wall.)

HARLEQUIN   For the Doctor. (Laughs.) Well, after all, he might amuse me....

PIERROT   Move your arm! Like that. (Places the thermometer in HARLEQUIN's armpit.) Sounds like someone coming. (He runs off left and immediately returns. The thermometer has burst into flames.) What happened to the thermometer?

HARLEQUIN   It shows the exact temperature.

(PIERROT hastily removes the thermometer, puts out the fire, and hangs the thermometer back in its place. HARLEQUIN leaps up and twirls around, snapping his fingers.)

Oh ho! Harlequin's not dead yet!

PIERROT (sounding dissatisfied)   Only you wrecked the thermometer!

HARLEQUIN (approaching the lute)   It's true, I haven't long to live, but.... (Takes down the lute.) Just look how many strings are broken and the rest are worn! But is that anything to keep me from playing the introduction to a serenade?

(He plays.* Steps are heard left.)

PIERROT   Do you hear that? The Doctor. Stop playing and lie down
quick. It's him. I can recognize people instantly by their footsteps.
Only people hurrying to the aid of those near and dear sound like
that.

HARLEQUIN (stops playing and hangs the lute up)   Hurrying after
the money.

(A knock at the door; HARLEQUIN lies down.)

PIERROT   Come in!

THE DOCTOR (in an enormous pair of glasses, bald, with a large red
nose, with a pump under his arm, enters left, stops, and sings to
the audience:)
The minute that they call for me
The sick to see, the sick to see,
I'm off to patients day and night
And strive to heal with all my might.
      Millionaires and proletarians
      I come flying to care for 'em
      And yet all the pink pills 'n mess
      Never cure any illness.

And soak a ragged invalid,
Why, God forbid, God forbid!
When the patient's poor, what can you ask?
You ask a kopeck, his very last.
      Millionaires and proletarians, etc.
(Speaking.) How do you do, my dear Harlequin! What seems to be
the problem?

HARLEQUIN   That's for you to say.

THE DOCTOR   You're quite right. (He turns to PIERROT. In his ear.)
You should never contradict a sick person. (To HARLEQUIN.)   Did you
take your temperature? (Sits on a stool near the bed; PIERROT is to
his left.)

PIERROT (after waving his hand)   Don't ask.

THE DOCTOR (to HARLEQUIN)   Do you feel something coming on?

---

*The harlequinade music must be a plainly simple arrangement so as
to sound pleasantly child-like, to remind the old folks of some
poorly done balagan. --N.E.
(A balagan is a folk theatrical presentation built upon farcical
situations and circus acts. --Translator's note.)

HARLEQUIN   An attack.

THE DOCTOR   Of coughing?

HARLEQUIN   Laughing.

THE DOCTOR   What's so funny?

HARLEQUIN   You are! (Laughs merrily.)

THE DOCTOR (to PIERROT)   Doesn't he believe in medicine?

PIERROT   No, only in you, it seems.

THE DOCTOR   Strange patient, all right. (To HARLEQUIN.) Let me take your pulse. (With his right hand takes out his watch, with left grabs the foot presented by HARLEQUIN.) Oh ho! Never count that! (Releases the foot.) Stick out your tongue.

HARLEQUIN   At who?

THE DOCTOR   Me!

HARLEQUIN   Oh, you? (Sticks out his tongue and makes a face at the DOCTOR.)

THE DOCTOR   Thank you.

HARLEQUIN   You're welcome! (Sticks out his tongue again.)

THE DOCTOR   That's enough now!

HARLEQUIN   For God's sake, don't be shy!   (Sticks it out again.)

THE DOCTOR   I already saw it.

HARLEQUIN   That's nice! (Pulls his tongue back in his mouth and hides it.)

THE DOCTOR   Now I've got to listen to you.

HARLEQUIN   What should I talk about?

THE DOCTOR   You don't understand me.

HARLEQUIN   Don't understand you? The hell I don't! People like me see right through people like you, but people like you--you can bet your life on it--will never understand people like me.

THE DOCTOR (to PIERROT)   Delirious. (To HARLEQUIN.) All right! But allow me to put my head on your chest! I have to do that, so....

HARLEQUIN   Your wife isn't jealous?

7

THE DOCTOR (listens to all sides of the patient; to PIERROT)   He
has quite a fever. It'll be a miracle if my ear and cheek don't
burn up. (To HARLEQUIN.) Yes, yes, you're a sick man, all right,
but let's hope you'll recover shortly. (To PIERROT.) Hopeless,
the mechanism's completely broken down. (To HARLEQUIN.) You did
the right thing to send for me. (To PIERROT.) You'd have done better
to send for the undertaker. (To HARLEQUIN.) You've got a healthy
organism. (To PIERROT.) But it won't live. (To HARLEQUIN.)
Proper care is all you need. (To PIERROT.) It's no use.

HARLEQUIN   What do you advise?

THE DOCTOR   You must go to bed early. No excitement. Absolutely
no drinking. No spicy, salty, greasy, sweet, sour, or rich foods,
nothing too hot, too cold, or too filling. Move around very gently;
don't get emotional over anything. Constantly guard against drafts.
Stay well clear of any commotion.

HARLEQUIN   So that's it! But is such a life worth living?

THE DOCTOR   That, sir, is for you to say.

HARLEQUIN   What's your diagnosis?

THE DOCTOR   Old age.

HARLEQUIN   But I could be your son.

THE DOCTOR   You're much too rude for that. Good-bye. (Takes his
leave and goes over to PIERROT; quietly.) And who's paying for the
call?

(PIERROT nods in HARLEQUIN's direction. The DOCTOR again takes his
leave of HARLEQUIN.)

Good-bye.

HARLEQUIN   Good-bye.

(The DOCTOR walks off indecisively, then stops.)

Did you forget something?

THE DOCTOR   Didn't you forget something?

HARLEQUIN   Nope, not a thing; I remember all your instructions
perfectly. Don't worry!

THE DOCTOR   No, no, that's not the problem.

HARLEQUIN   What is, then?

THE DOCTOR   Hm.... Between the two of us--you forgot to pay me for
the call.

HARLEQUIN   Odd!   How could that have happened?

THE DOCTOR   I do hope you won't be angry at me!

HARLEQUIN   Of course not, for goodness' sake!

THE DOCTOR (once more taking his leave)   Well, good-bye.

HARLEQUIN (shakes his hand with feeling)   Good-bye, Doctor, good-bye.

THE DOCTOR   Hm.... You've again lapsed into forgetfulness.

HARLEQUIN   Yes, yes! So I did! You're so right! It'd be rude of
me to deny it.

THE DOCTOR   And so I'm reminding you.

HARLEQUIN   I'm so grateful.

THE DOCTOR   It was nothing, really.

HARLEQUIN   Oh no, it wasn't! For goodness' sake!

THE DOCTOR   And so ... the money?

HARLEQUIN   You'll get it as soon as I recover, as soon as you cure
me.

THE DOCTOR   Yes, but ... I should warn you that I endeavor to cure
all diseases except incurable ones; and yours....

HARLEQUIN   Well, when I get a little better, when your advice starts
to work. But who knows? Maybe you lied to me; why should I pay then?

THE DOCTOR   But when you're dead, who's going to pay me then?

HARLEQUIN   Pay for what, if I may ask?

THE DOCTOR   What do you mean, for what?

HARLEQUIN   If I really die today, what is your art worth if it can't
save me from death! And if I live, then it's not worth anything either
if it can't predict any better than some illiterate fortuneteller!

THE DOCTOR   I didn't come here to philosophize.

HARLEQUIN   I know why you came.

THE DOCTOR   Without the innuendoes, if you please.

HARLEQUIN (to PIERROT)   He calls that an innuendo. (Takes some money
from under his pillow.) Here's why you came! (He goes over to the
door right and offers the DOCTOR the money.)

THE DOCTOR (reaches for the money)   Thank you!

(HARLEQUIN disappears with a laugh behind the door and instantly
appears in another; the DOCTOR rushes over to him. PIERROT doubles
up with laughter, and HARLEQUIN has already run out the opposite
door and whirled around the DOCTOR; he whirls, disappears left,
reappears right, and repeats the whole performance again, then stops
in front of the DOCTOR and gives him the money.)

HARLEQUIN   Pretty frisky, wouldn't you say?

(A hammering sound, similar to a heartbeat, is heard.)

THE DOCTOR   You know, sir, may the Good Lord bring you fortune in
the next world--the first time I've seen a dying man like this. But
what's that noise?

HARLEQUIN   That's my heart beating.

(A locomotive's puffing is heard.)

THE DOCTOR   And that?

HARLEQUIN   That's my breathing.

THE DOCTOR   And you're still on your feet?

HARLEQUIN   Yes indeed; and I've preserved enough good spirits to
welcome death.

THE DOCTOR   How do you mean, welcome?

HARLEQUIN   Oh, it happens to be coming right on time. The man who
has lived wisely will always welcome death.

THE DOCTOR   You speak in riddles.

HARLEQUIN   But for people like you.... (He laughs.)

THE DOCTOR   How do you know?

HARLEQUIN   Would you like me to show you how you're going to die?

THE DOCTOR   Be interesting.

HARLEQUIN (lies down on the bed, trembles all over, then moans)   Ach!
Och! O-och! I'm still so young ... I haven't really lived yet....
Why have I been so virtuous all my life?... I"m still full of all
sorts of desires.... Turn me toward the window.... I'm not tired
of looking at this world yet.... Save me!... I haven't done half
what I wanted.... I was in no rush to live, because I kept forgetting
about death. Save me! Save me!... I haven't had any fun yet, I
was always preserving my health, my strength, my money, for the morrow.

I loaded it down with the most wonderful hopes and rolled it along
like a snowball getting bigger all the time! That morrow has rolled
clear off the edge of the possible! Right off the cliff of my worldly
wisdom!... Ach! Och! O-och!

(He stretches one last time, trembles, and goes limp. The DOCTOR
cries. HARLEQUIN gets up with a laugh and claps his hands.)

No! That's not how Harlequin will die.

THE DOCTOR (tearfully)   What must I do?

HARLEQUIN (extends his hand)   Something for the advice! From now
on I'm charging you.

THE DOCTOR   How much?

HARLEQUIN   Same as you.

THE DOCTOR (returns the money)   Well then?

HARLEQUIN (with an air of importance)   Go and live. That's all.

THE DOCTOR   What does that mean?

HARLEQUIN   Well, if you don't understand, you are incurable. I say
to you: "Go and live, but live, not as if you were immortal, but as
if you might die tomorrow."

THE DOCTOR (nods his head distrustfully)   Hm.... I'll try. (Wipes
his eyes. Good-bye, Mr. Harlequin.

HARLEQUIN   Good-bye, Mr. Doctor.

(The DOCTOR puts a finger to his forehead, and meditatively swaying
in time with the same music that was heard at his entrance, he leaves
left.)

HARLEQUIN (to PIERROT)   What have you got to say about him, Pierrot?

PIERROT   Nothing good.

(It is growing dark.)

HARLEQUIN   The old fool supposes I can't sense death coming! As
if a man who spent more time sleeping than drinking could still
doubt the approach of death. By the way, what time is it?

(The clock shows eight.)

My clock isn't slow? It was always right in step with me, but now....

PIERROT   You're too suspicious.

HARLEQUIN   Not everybody ought to be like you.

PIERROT   I.e., like what?

HARLEQUIN   You'll soon see. Help me set the table for supper.

PIERROT (running toward the cupboard)   With great pleasure.

HARLEQUIN   We'll need to set three places.

PIERROT   Three?

HARLEQUIN   Yes.

PIERROT   Who's the third for?

HARLEQUIN   For Death.

PIERROT   It'll sit at the table with us?

HARLEQUIN   If you're not afraid of it.

PIERROT   Two glasses should be enough; I won't be eating with you.

HARLEQUIN   Come, come! I was joking! Death will be feasting on me.
That will be enough for it. But set three places anyway. (Lights
an oil lamp.)

PIERROT   But who's the third place for?

(At left is heard COLUMBINE's singing:)
My wifely honor disregarding,
When nights I hear a distant lute,
By moon I run to meet my darling,
My doubly sweet forbidden fruit.
    Heart thumping, ears ringing,
    And fearing perdition,
    Just what if my husband
    Were hiding and listenin'.

PIERROT   What's this? The voice of Columbine.... The voice of my
wife!...

HARLEQUIN   Now you know who the third place is for....

PIERROT (tragically) Ahh! Treachery!... Ahh! Perfidy! So that's
your idea of friendship!...

HARLEQUIN   Calm down, nothing's happened yet!

PIERROT   That's all I need!

HARLEQUIN   That's all I need!

PIERROT   And I'm supposed to be your friend!

HARLEQUIN   You're both my friends. But you want to be the only one, so you're jealous?

PIERROT   You know **very** well why I'm jealous and who's to blame.

HARLEQUIN   Be sensible. If you really love me and love Columbine, you ought to be very happy for both of us. What's more, you know both of us love you. So why complain? Set the third place!

PIERROT   No, I'm not that simple. Nice people don't behave that way and the only thing for me to do is to avenge my honor.

HARLEQUIN   By?...

PIERROT   Killing you.

HARLEQUIN   But I'm going to die very shortly anyway; my hours are numbered. What's to stop you from telling everybody that you did it?

PIERROT   You're right....

HARLEQUIN   Then there's nothing to talk about! Set the third place.

PIERROT (meditatively)   How can I?

HARLEQUIN   Come on! We're wasting time.

(PIERROT hesitates for another second, then goes for the third place-setting, but on the way back stumbles and drops the plate.)

Clumsy! Going around breaking things!

PIERROT (with pathos)   A fine one to talk! You destroyed my happiness.

HARLEQUIN (setting the third place)   Skip the rhetoric, thank you! You lost interest in Columbine a long time ago, and the only reason you're jealous is because it's the conventional thing to do.... But shh....

(Again COLUMBINE's singing is heard.)
Behind a mask we find our Columbine,
And dressed so fine from head to toe.
She has to see her darling Harlequin.
She dreads to meet her spouse Pierrot.
     Heart thumping, ears ringing,
     And fearing perdition,
     Just what if my husband
     Were hiding and listenin'.

HARLEQUIN   I'll meet Columbine, and you fix the lamp.

(He runs off left. PIERROT stands lost in thought.)

PIERROT   Hm.... "Fix the lamp!" (Suddenly claps himself on the
forehead.) I'd do better to fix the clock! (Leaps on the bed and
takes hold of the clock hands.) If Harlequin's death must be my
doing, so be it! Ladies and gentlemen, you are my witnesses! Such
things cannot go unavenged: I'll set the hands ahead two hours!
(Does so.) Ah! Harlequin, it's plain no one can excape his fate.
(Leaps from the bed.) Now my mind's at ease: I have been avenged.

(Paces around the room, wrings his hands. At left is heard the
"Columbine theme.")

I wonder how she'll react. (He stands near the door, feet wide apart,
body leaning forward and hands on hips.) Come right in, Mrs. Unfaithful!...

HARLEQUIN (offstage left)   Don't worry, Columbine! Walk right in.
I persuaded him and, honest to God, he agreed with me.

COLUMBINE (enters, eyes flashing, pounces on PIERROT)   You agreed?
So that's it! Agreed!... So, you good-for-nothing, you value your
wife so little! Her betrayal doesn't mean a thing! Nothing? Answer
me! (Beats PIERROT.)

PIERROT (distraught)   But listen, Columbine....

COLUMBINE   What? I have to listen to you? Listen to the most
worthless husband of all worthless husbands...?

PIERROT   But Columbine....

COLUMBINE   You blockhead....

PIERROT   You won't let me get a word in....

COLUMBINE (beats PIERROT)   No excuses!... And I, unhappy woman,
married a scoundrel like you! Gave him the best years of my life!
And he won't even stand up for his wife's honor! (Beats him.) Take
that! And that! And that, you fathead!

PIERROT   You're going too far! Harlequin, defend me!

HARLEQUIN (backing up)   But it's strictly a family affair.

PIERROT   But dear friend....

HARLEQUIN   I wasn't brought up to interfere in the married lives of
other people.

COLUMBINE (to PIERROT)   So that's how you love me! That's how jealous
you are! What about your vows, you atheist?

PIERROT (recovering)   God damn it, this is unheard of! You brazen
hussy, you're the one who came here for a tryst and you still have

8

the gall to accuse me -

COLUMBINE   Enough! Shut up! I know very well how scoundrels like you weasel out of things: when they're guilty, then they try to defend themselves by attacking the innocent. But you won't fool me, you good-for-nothing.

HARLEQUIN (stepping between them)   My friends, let's not waste precious time! When the supper is on the table, why spoil the appetite!

COLUMBINE and PIERROT   But this is outrageous!

HARLEQUIN   I don't care for long drawn-out quarrels.

PIERROT and COLUMBINE   It's not my fault.

HARLEQUIN   It's time to make up! The path of true love never runs smooth.

PIERROT and COLUMBINE   Not for anything.

HARLEQUIN   Stubborn as hell.

PIERROT and COLUMBINE   My deepest feelings have been outraged!

HARLEQUIN   That's enough!

PIERROT and COLUMBINE   No.

COLUMBINE   First, he's got to be punished.

HARLEQUIN   How?

COLUMBINE   Kiss me, Harlequin! My dear, sweet Harlequin!

HARLEQUIN   So as not to give offense by refusing.... (Kisses her.) I was always a kind lover. (Kisses her.) Besides that, I have a tender heart. (Kisses her.) Even children know about it. (Kisses her.) What's more, as master of the house (Kisses her.), I must be polite to my guests (Kisses her.), especially when it concerns (Kisses her.) the fair sex (Kisses her.).

PIERROT (to the audience)   Poor people! They haven't the faintest suspicion that I've already avenged myself and so my mind's completely at ease.

COLUMBINE (to HARLEQUIN) Kiss me harder, passionately, make it hurt, bite me, don't hold back! (They kiss as she desires.)

PIERROT (coolly, even sneering a little, to the audience)   They imagine they've mortally wounded me.

COLUMBINE (to HARLEQUIN)   More! More! (To PIERROT.) Ach, you insensitive oaf.

PIERROT (to COLUMBINE)   Go right ahead, help yourself! (To the
audience.) My conscience is clear, I stood up for my honor and
there's nothing for me to get excited about.

COLUMBINE (to HARLEQUIN)   Kiss my eyes, my forehead, cheeks, chin,
temples! (HARLEQUIN doesn't have to be asked twice.)

PIERROT (to the audience)   Ladies and gentlemen, you are my witnesses,
I have been avenged.

COLUMBINE   Kiss my neck where the hair stops, where I tremble when
you kiss me.   (HARLEQUIN is as kind as ever.)

PIERROT   It's all the same to me, They can do anything they please.
I have done my duty as an outraged husband, and I feel great.

COLUMBINE (stamping her foot on PIERROT's)   So, you scoundrel! It
doesn't mean a thing to you!

PIERROT (to the audience; smiling blissfully)   I'll drive them crazy
with my utter calm.

COLUMBINE (to HARLEQUIN)   Well, let's treat him to our Dance of Love!

HARLEQUIN   I wouldn't think of refusing you, but....

COLUMBINE   But what?

HARLEQUIN   But suppose Pierrot isn't enough of a choreography-lover
to forget everything else?

PIERROT (to COLUMBINE and HARLEQUIN)   Go ahead, don't be shy! (To
the audience.) I've avenged myself in advance for everything, and
there's no reason to get upset about the past.

HARLEQUIN (handing PIERROT the lute)   Perhaps you'd like to do the
accompaniment?

COLUMBINE   Of course! He ought to be doing something during the
dance!

PIERROT (takes the lute and sits down)   With the greatest pleasure,
if that is what you desire. (To the audience.) I hope you do understand how indifferent a husband can be, once he has properly avenged
his outraged honor.

COLUMBINE   Play!

PIERROT (to the audience)   My God, how easy is the heart after one
has avenged oneself, and so no one has any right to laugh.

(Plays with feeling as HARLEQUIN and COLUMBINE enthusiastically do the Dance of Love. Suddenly HARLEQUIN stops, staggers, and hardly breathing, flops on the bed. PIERROT breaks off the music.)

COLUMBINE   What's the matter? What happened?

HARLEQUIN (clutching at his heart)   No.... nothing, nothing at all.

(Again a heart is heard beating, like cannons going off, and the furious puffing of a locomotive is heard.)

COLUMBINE (horrified)   Your heartbeat is deafening! Such terrible wheezing!

PIERROT (to the audience, joyfully)   Harlequin's giving in! Harlequin's getting weaker! Rejoice with me, you poor husbands! You, whose wives are in danger!

COLUMBINE (to HARLEQUIN)   Nothing like this ever happened to you before.

PIERROT (to the audience)   On the other hand, don't! Grieve with me, because when all is said and done, Harlequin is my friend and that's all there is to it. Don't quarrel with him over some slut! And if Columbine does find him more to her taste than me, blame not him, but Columbine, who's always had such abominable taste. But that's not fair of me. (Becomes quite meditative.)

HARLEQUIN (gets up and laughs)   Did I scare you? (Kisses COLUMBINE.) Forgive me! (Looks at the clock, which shows twelve o'clock.) Soon you'll know the real reason.

COLUMBINE   What's the matter?

HARLEQUIN   Let's have some supper. The Dance has given me an appetite and I feel wonderful.

(They sit down, drink, and eat.)

COLUMBINE   What are you keeping from me?

HARLEQUIN   Drink, Columbine, drink! When there's good wine on the table, there's nothing to worry about.

(They drink, kiss each other, laugh softly.)

PIERROT (to the audience)   Oh God, what unbelievable pangs of conscience I'm experiencing. Think of what I've done to Harlequin! And for what? For what? I can't eat a bite, and I can't look Harlequin in the face. I'd be only too happy to confess my evil deed to them! But alas! I can't do that, because what would then become of my vengeance! And not to avenge is impossible: I am the deceived husband and had to avenge myself, because that's the way decent people handle these things. Ach, how awful I feel, how I want to cry! (Waves his

fist at the audience.) Nasty, evil people! You're the ones that
dreamed up these stupid rules! It's because of you I had to shorten
the life of my best friend. (Turns his back on the audience.)

HARLEQUIN (to COLUMBINE)   Why are you late today?

COLUMBINE   The Doctor held me up--I met him not far from here.

(The "Doctor theme" is heard in the distance.)

He was limping along, drunk, and stopping all the girls.

HARLEQUIN   And so?

COLUMBINE   He begged me to make him happy. He assured me he was
full of strength and had been very handsome thirty years ago. By the
time I convinced him I wasn't a historian fascinated by the past,
time went by and so I was late.

HARLEQUIN (to the audience)   The poor doctor! Why, oh why didn't
he come to me for advice sooner!

COLUMBINE   I felt very sorry for him.

HARLEQUIN (to the audience)   So near and yet so far.

COLUMBINE   He cried and kept saying, "Why the hell did I save my
strength!"   And I answered, "Your wrinkles inspire in me respect,
but not passion."

HARLEQUIN   But you know, Columbine, he's younger than I am, even
though in years he's twice my age.

COLUMBINE   I don't understand.

HARLEQUIN   Because you haven't given any thought to true old age.
(Claps PIERROT on the shoulder.) But, my friend, you're not drinking
anything, or eating or participating in the conversation?

COLUMBINE   He's trying to depress us, but a good-for-nothing never
succeeds.

PIERROT (crying)   Unhappy woman, it would never occur to you that
Harlequin is dying.

COLUMBINE   What do you mean "is dying"? May your tongue rot off!
Or did you slip some poison in the wine? No, no (Disdainfully.),
people like you are incapable of that.

PIERROT (still crying)   Poor Harlequin, your minutes are numbered.

COLUMBINE   What's he talking about? What rubbish is this?

HARLEQUIN (turning to the clock)   Yes, Columbine, it's true. It's
time you knew.... I feel certain I'm going to die soon.

COLUMBINE (mournfully)   Harlequin!... My love! (She cries.)

HARLEQUIN   Don't cry, Columbine! I'm leaving here with a smile on
my lips. I want to die, the way I want to sleep when it's late and
time to rest. I've sung all my songs! I've danced up all my joy!
I've used up all my laughter!... I've joyfully squandered my strength
and my health along with my money. I was never stingy and so I was
eternally happy and carefree. I, Harlequin, will die as Harlequin.
Don't weep, Columbine! Rather rejoice that I am dying, not like
the others, but surfeited with pleasure, happy with my fate and
with the life I've lived. Or would you rather see me desperately
hanging on to life, with a prayer on my lips! No, that's not Harlequin. He has fulfilled his destiny and dies happy! And that's the
truth! Didn't I give my kisses to whomever needed them! Didn't I
lavish my soul on the good of others! And how much I comforted the
wives of ugly husbands! And how many times I fooled people who thought
they were **smart**! How many people I aroused with a passionate song
or a nasty crack! How many did I set a good example for! And now
I've lived up my life! And all Death gets is the shell! "Seize
the moment"--that's my motto! And I wasn't lazy about seizing it!
I seized so many I don't need any more. Well, one more kiss, a swallow
of wine, a burst of merry laughter--and that'll do it!

COLUMBINE   How can you not be afraid?

HARLEQUIN   Being born was scarier! Now I'm going back!

COLUMBINE   To sink into non-being, into nothing!

HARLEQUIN   And if it's "nothing," then how can I be afraid of it?

COLUMBINE   Well, I'm afraid!

HARLEQUIN   Your cup is not yet empty, you're afraid you won't finish.

COLUMBINE   But just imagine -

HARLEQUIN   Let's talk about the way the hours go by!... How swiftly
they pass! Abandon yourself, Columbine! Press the grapes of life!
Turn them into wine! Don't be slow with pleasure, be sure to get
enough before Death arrives! (Takes the lute in hand.) And you
abandon yourself, too, friend Pierrot, if you're capable of it.

(PIERROT sobs violently in reply. HARLEQUIN laughs.)

No, no! Not that way, you don't understand!

PIERROT   The lamp's going out....

HARLEQUIN (sadly)   And there's no oil in the house.

COLUMBINE   But it's still burning! Look!

HARLEQUIN (joyfully)   It's burning, Columbine! It's burning! (Plays
on the lute and sings.)
Oh listen to this **song** of mine!
All my friends, Pierrot, and sweet Columbine.
All my life I've sung this song of mine.
And so now I'll sing this song of love,
I'll sing this song of love ...

(The **strings** break off as does the song.)

COLUMBINE (sadly)   The strings broke!

HARLEQUIN (laughs)   My song is sung....

(A knock at the door.)

Who's there?

(Again a knock, left.)

Pierrot, go see who it is!

(PIERROT takes the lamp and opens the door. Enter DEATH*--a bright,
white skeleton dressed in a billowy transparent dress similar to
COLUMBINE's; there's some sort of triangle on the skull. DEATH
majestically extends a hand in HARLEQUIN's direction. PIERROT trembles,
causing the lamp to flicker agonizingly. COLUMBINE remains motionless on a stool, with her arms hanging weakly at her sides and her
eyes closed. PIERROT's eyes are also closed. HARLEQUIN rises to meet
DEATH. HARLEQUIN is very gracious.)

Welcome, **madam**, you're right on time. We were just talking about
you. So good of you not to keep us waiting. But why so tragic?
Look around, madam! You're in the house of Harlequin, where they
know how to laugh at the tragical, even at you.

(DEATH melodramatically approaches the clock and extends her hand to
it.)

Enough, madam, enough! True enough, if I weren't all laughed out, I'd
die laughing--literally. What? You want to stop the clock? There's
still time, madam. As far as I know, my time's not up yet. Or do
you expect a fight from me? No, no, I'm not a stupid, vulgar bourgeois.
I know how to treat a charming lady. I wouldn't contradict her,
I haven't even the strength, I've used it all up. But the traditional

---

*In Theater Wagon's production the figure of Death materializes only
to Harlequin, who sees her and acts with her. --F.C., Jr.

dance? The dance like they had in the good old days when people
still knew how to die, not like today. And Death herself was a
source of amusement. I beg you! Ach, you're surprised at the
request? Oh yes, Harlequin these days is nearly extinct!

(Pleasant violin music is heard, appetizingly mingled with the sharp
sounds of a xylophone and castanets. DEATH dances....)

HARLEQUIN   Columbine! Pierrot! Open your eyes, now! See how
wonderful it is!

(He claps his hands to the music, and then tenderly takes COLUMBINE's
by the waist and sits on the bed with her. The Dance is over. DEATH
stops in front of HARLEQUIN and puts her hand on his shoulder. PIERROT,
trembling all over, creeps to the door at right.)

HARLEQUIN (to DEATH)   One moment, my dear, one moment. Allow me to
part from the world in worldly fashion. One more, just one more kiss,
Columbine! Pierrot, where are you going, scaredy cat?... (Gets up.)
So you're not up to lighting the way for me? (Takes the lamp and
hands it to DEATH.) Light the way, Death, there's still a drop of
oil in the lamp.

(He returns to COLUMBINE; DEATH stands in front of the embracing
couple. Kisses and languorous sighs are heard. Somewhere far off,
the "Harlequin theme" is heard.)

COLUMBINE (as if in a dream)   Harlequin, my beloved!...

(The lamp goes out; the music dies with the last kiss. Several seconds
of silence and darkness. Then the stage is illuminated with beautiful,
deathly pale moonlight. The clock shows twelve. COLUMBINE is kneeling
by HARLEQUIN's deathbed. PIERROT appears at right.)

PIERROT (to the audience)   That's the situation! I haven't the
slightest idea what I ought to mourn first; the loss of Harlequin, the
loss of Columbine, my own bitter fate, or yours, dear audience, sub-
jected to a work so lacking in seriousness? And what is the author
of the play trying to say?... I don't understand. However, I'm the
stupid, cowardly Pierrot, and it's not up to me to judge the play in
which I played an unenviable role. But your surprise will be all the
greater once you learn what the culprit guilty of perpetrating this
strange--just between you and me--mockery on the public has commissioned
me to say by way of conclusion. Shh.... Listen! "When the great
Rabelais lay dying, the monks all clustered about his bed and tried
everything to get him to repent his sins. Rabelais merely replied
with a smile, and when his last moment had come, said merrily; 'Lower
the curtain, the farce is over ...' He said it, then died." Why
the unscrupulous playwright had to stick somebody else's words in the
mouth of one of the dramatis personae, I can't imagine--I'm not a free
agent; but, being a conscientious actor, I shall remain so till the
end, and so, implicitly subjecting myself to the author's will, I
merrily shout, "Lower the curtain! The farce is over!"

(The curtain descends; PIERROT remains in front of it.)

Ladies and gentlemen, I forgot to tell you that neither your applause
nor your hisses will be taken seriously by the author proclaiming
that nothing in life is worth taking seriously. And I might add that
if he's right, than I fail to see why anyone should take that author's
play seriously, especially since HARLEQUIN has no doubt already risen
from his deathbed and is now preening himself for the curtain call,
since--say anything you please--actors aren't responsible for the
wild ideas of the playwright. He leaves.)

ON THE CORNER OF CHERRY AND ELSEWHERE

A Play in Layers

By Jeannie Lee

CHARACTERS

Moon Mother
Suzie
Dr. Shade/Sol (pronounced "soul")
Cindy

SCENE

SUZIE's world.

ACT ONE

(The play may be performed with no break, or in two acts. The arrangement here indicates both possibilities.

The Set: Think in triangles! A schematic set is appropriate, as
the play takes place in SUZIE's head.

Left--SUZIE's Apartment: A small, round table, set for two, with a
chair at either side. In the center of the table, a mixing bowl,
a spoon, and an outsized box of Aunt Jemima's pancake mix. Beside
the bowl--one high-heeled shoe. Perhaps a glass slipper? Don't
overdo it.

Up right of the table, an easel, bearing an empty picture frame.
Painting paraphenalia is strewn hither and yon. Most noticeable
is a pot of red poster paint with a long-handled brush protruding
from the top.

Up Center--The Cage: In the cage is a swing of the sort found in
monkey houses; but it could be red velvet--with fringe. The bars
are bent, and some are missing--like teeth in an ancient mouth.

In addition to the swing, the cage contains a medley of colorful,
stylized props--scrub bucket, beat-up ukelele, umbrella, and huge
pink hat.

Right--DR. SHADE's Office: A throne. Behind the throne, an easel
sporting a large empty frame. A scattering of brushes and paints.

Offstage is heard a street call--the voice of an old woman:)

MOON MOTHER'S VOICE   Rags! Rags! Old rags to buy and sell! Old
rags to buy and sell.

(The lights come up on SUZIE, with the limp--standing up left in
front of the easel. The street call turns into a song--sung offstage during the suicide pantomime.)

MOON MOTHER'S VOICE (slow and sad)
I walk alone
      through the wreckage of my friends.
They say I am to blame
      for the way it always ends.
Their hearts go to rags,
        one after the other,
And the cloth of good-bye
      is the saddest color.

(The suicide pantomime: SUZIE crosses sadly to the pot of red paint,
takes a long-handled brush, slowly raises the brush, and paints
a long red slash across her left wrist, just as the first verse
of the song ends. Try for a dream-sequence effect where everything seems to happen underwater.

MOON MOTHER enters, continuing the second verse of the song on stage.
She is a hunchbacked hag, dressed in rags, and pulling a toy wagon
filled with rags.)

MOON MOTHER
The cloth of good-bye
      is the saddest color.
Death is red,
      but life is duller
Than the moon smoked out
      at the back of the sky.
Old rags to sell,
      Old rags to buy.

(DR. SHADE, wearing a white lab-coat and carrying a net, enters
right. He collides with MOON MOTHER head on. Getting a look at
MOON MOTHER, he decides she can't be true, and screams. MOON MOTHER
cackles good-naturedly; she is, after all, the kindest of hags.)

MOON MOTHER   I dreamed I stepped on a scream, and it didn't make
a sound!

DR. SHADE (recovering his composure)   I've got a rag for you, mother.
(He displays his net.)

MOON MOTHER (indignant)   Doctor, this rag is full of holes! (She
sticks her tongue through one of them.)

DR. SHADE   That's what makes it a rag.

MOON MOTHER   It looks like a net to me. A net for ... catching things. Tee hee! Eh, just what do you catch in your net, dearie?

DR. SHADE (pompously)   Schizophrenic artists and artistic schizophrenics. My men have set a net on the ceiling of every subway in this city. Schizophrenics travel around a lot, you know. They keep going from one self to the other self and back again. Consequently, they make great use of the subway.... What will you do with him, now that he's a rag?

MOON MOTHER   Polish the moon with him, of course.

DR. SHADE   Polish the moon! I would prefer that he be used to wipe up a puddle of piddle.

MOON MOTHER   Oh, no, no, dearie, my rags are for polishing the moon. All my rags. You see, the moon takes a great deal of polishing. (Dancing around DR. SHADE.)
Har dee har har,
And hee hee hee!
To keep him bright as he can be,
I rub, I scrub,
I dub-a-dub-dub!
It's the least I can do,
For when he's blue
The moon won't sleep in me.

(She leans toward DR. SHADE and whispers conspiratorially.) You see this hunch, here, on my old wreck of a back?... The moon ... he sleeps inside. (Taps her hunch, gives a low cackle.)

DR. SHADE   What?

MOON MOTHER   He sleeps inside.

DR. SHADE   No!

MOON MOTHER   Don't you say "No" to me, you impudent young man! I'll prove it. (Talking to the hunch over her shoulder.) Yoo hoo ... Lunus! Lunus, dear, yoo hoo ... are you in there? (She squirms.) Ooooh hee hee ha ha!... It tickles when he rolls over!

DR. SHADE   Mother ... (He takes her by the shoulders, looks into her eyes--tender, concerned.) You're mad, mother. (He turns to the audience.) An advanced form of schizophrenia, I'd venture, with an intricate delusionary system designed to protect the patient against.... (Turns back to her.) I'm going to have to insist that you come with me, Mrs. ... Lunus, to Saint Eugenia's Sanctuary for the Insane and

Getting There.

(He drops the net over her head, leads her struggling and hooting
offstage. SUZIE has been watching this scene. Alone now, she holds
out her wrist, inspects it carefully.)

SUZIE (talking to herself) It certainly is taking me a long time to
die! (She paints another slash across her wrist. To her wrist,
squeezing it.) Oh, come on, gush! Like you're supposed to. (She
sucks her wrist, spits out the blood. Pause. She looks up, sees
the others are gone.) Strange people ... Figments! Figments of my
mind.... I had a very repressed childhood. That rag woman looked
like some kind of a Mother Goose reject.... Mother Goose ... oh
my God! My childhood passing before me ... I am dying! Oh Wow ...
there isn't time to let my whole life wash over me in orderly little
episodes. I'll skip ... skip right to the end. To Sol. He was the
End, all right.... Especially before breakfast. The first time I
ever met Sol was before breakfast. I mean, Wow! In he walks--this
strange hulk, all uninvited--and, plunk, down he sits!

(Enter SOL, the artist--played by the same actor who plays DR. SHADE,
but minus the white coat. In he comes and, plunk, down he sits.
SUZIE limps over to join him.)

SOL   I'm hungry. Do something.

SUZIE   But ... but ... hey! I don't even know you.

SOL   I'm Solace St. Clair. I live on the floor above the floor
below. Now cook something.

SUZIE (incredulous) Hey, wait a minute. Just 'cause I live upstairs
and you happen to live downstairs doesn't mean you can ... I mean,
just walk in here and, I mean ... oh, what the hell. (Plunging in,
breathless.) My name's Suzie. How do you like your eggs?

SOL   I don't like them.

SUZIE   Oh. (Thinks a moment.) Sausage and sweet roll?

SOL   Ugh!

SUZIE   Didn't your mother ever tell you to eat it anyway?... Oh,
I know. How about some old left-over tuna-fish casserole? It's a
little bit burned on the bottom, but....

(He gives her a withering look.)

No, huh? Well, gee, I'm running out of ideas! (Happy, incredulous.)
Hey, how come you can do this to me? How come you can come barging
in here and make me feel all apologetic about my tuna-fish casserole
and all, when I don't even know you? How come?

SOL (holding up the box of Aunt Jemima mix) You could make pancakes.

SUZIE   Yeah, pancakes! (She gets the bowl and spoon, pantomimes pouring the batter in, beating.) They'll be ready in a jiffy.

SOL   There's a girl who lives on the floor below the floor below. I think her name is Cindy. I know you know her.

SUZIE   I'll say!

SOL   She bakes sunflower cakes and sings--all day. (Singing.) "Songs of the Sun and Saturday." Those cakes--honey and sesame seed-- I can't get them off my mind!

(SUZIE laughs.)

I'm an artist. I've got to work in the natural light--from eight in the morning until three in the afternoon. Unfortunately, that's when she bakes. How can I work? I can't work! The smell of them comes wafting up through the floor boards ... Oh!... But she's lovely. I couldn't go down there and ask her to feed me. I came to you instead. I knew you'd feed me.

SUZIE (dismayed)   Oh!... How can you be so rude?

SOL   I'm not rude, really, it's just that I lack tact.

SUZIE   "She's lovely. I couldn't go down there and ask her to feed me. I came to you instead." Like ... like I was so desperate for somebody to feed.

SOL   Well, aren't you?

(SUZIE, in a rage, dumps the bowl of imaginary pancake batter out all over the table.)

My pancakes! You dumped them out!

SUZIE   Yeah! (Pause. She walks away, then turns back.) What are you staring at?

SOL (pointing)   Your foot.

SUZIE   Do you think if I left the door open really wide, you might go out by mistake?

SOL   You've been leaving the door open really wide in hopes I might come in by mistake ever since puberty. So far, all you've managed is a rather prodigious collection of flies.

SUZIE   Oh ... oh! (She turns away, trying not to cry.)

SOL   I'm sorry. No, I ... I really am. I do that to people, I -

SUZIE (looking around wildly for something to change the subject with)   Please ... say something about something else.... My painting!

Look. (She displays the frame on the easel.) It's Cindy--the sun-
flower-cake-kid.

(He rises, looks at the painting for a long moment, impressed.)

SOL   It's beautiful.

SUZIE   Oh, that's just because she's beautiful.

SOL   No, it's beautiful beyond her. Who are you studying with?

SUZIE   Well, nobody right now. You see, I was at the academy.....

SOL (outraged)   And you quit?

SUZIE (nodding sheepishly)   At the academy they were doing all these
compositions like "Calves Liver and Carburetor," and the only thing
I wanted to paint was ... (She hangs her head in shame.) people.

SOL   People are "out" this year.

SUZIE   They are at the academy.

SOL   Never mind. From now on you'll study with me.

SUZIE   With you?

SOL   Yes. It's settled.

SUZIE   But I don't even know you! Hell, I said that already. Well ...
hey, what do you know about art?

SOL   I know what I don't like. "Calves Liver and -"

SUZIE   OK, OK, so I'll never serve it again!... Hey ... wait a
minute. What did you say your name was?... Solace Saint.... Hey,
you're not....

SOL (amused)   Yes.

SUZIE (terrifically excited)   Your painting? "Rorschach in Red and
Gold, Called What Do You See?" Yours? You? Oh, my God, I think I
gotta sit down. Solace St. Clair--where was my mind? Like somebody
comes to your door and says "I'm Leonardo Da Vinci. Feed me!" And
you don't even gotta sit down? Hey, wow, they're looking for you
everywhere. The cops and the curators ...

SOL   I know.

SUZIE   "Famous abstractionist Solace St. Clair absconded today
with one of his own...." Why did you do that? Just walk into the
Metropolitan and take it off the wall like that?

SOL   My Masterpiece! "What Do You See?" I called it "What Do You See? Rorschach in Red and Gold." I didn't like what they saw, so I -

SUZIE   Just walked into the Metropolitan and.... (She pantomimes lifting it off the wall and sneaking out.)

SOL (smiling, with a touch of pride)   Um-hum.

SUZIE   What was it they saw?

SOL   They saw themselves--seeing it--in their new hat. "Pink in profusion--just this side of sentimental." Finally, there she was-- the ultimate hat. Fearless and Forever! "Mr. St. Clair," she said, "it's so Now!" Then she kissed me--on the mouth.... Well, what could I do? I snatched it off the wall and rented a cold-water flat at the top of the world, where I could be anonymous and look down on everything but myself.

SUZIE   You're not anonymous anymore. I know it's you down there. (She indicates the floor.)

SOL (sheepish)   I hadn't planned to tell anyone.

(SUZIE laughs triumphantly.)

SUZIE   That woman--the one in the "pink and profuse" who kissed you. Did you know her?

SOL   Yes. She was my friend--hat and all.

SUZIE (puzzled)   So how come you couldn't let her feel a little affectionate? I mean, everybody's gotta have something to feel affectionate about--even if it is just a picture, and not a person, that's so "Now!" That's some little thing you could have done for her. Let her kiss you, and left the damn thing hanging on the wall.

SOL   Affection makes me ... claustrophobic. When she kissed me, the walls started closing in.

SUZIE   Hey, do you have it with you now? "Rorschach in Red and Gold," I mean.

SOL   It's downstairs, right over my bed.

SUZIE   Wow! And my bed is right over your bed! No wonder I have such talented dreams!... I don't guess ... I mean ... you wouldn't want to....

SOL   Take you down and show you?

(SUZIE nods eagerly.)

No.

SUZIE   Oh, please!

SOL   It's not finished.

SUZIE   Not finished? But you had it hanging in the Metropolitan!

SOL (agitated)   I thought it was finished, but it wasn't. "What
Do You See?", I called it "What Do You See?" If it had been finished
they would have seen something besides themselves seeing it. My
art didn't communicate. Don't you see? My God, I brought it here
to work on it, but I haven't been able to. My colors are like ghosts--
thin, intangible ... something I could walk through. "Pallid on
the palette," as it were. My God! (He laughs bitterly.) I ...
I can't get anything to look solid anymore. But you ... oh, I know,
your perspective is off, and your shading is unbalanced--but, Suzie ...
your work is alive.

(Lights dim out in the apartment. SOL fades. DR. SHADE and MOON
MOTHER enter from the opposite side. MOON MOTHER is calm now, holding on to his hand. She still has the net over her head.)

MOON MOTHER   How far is it to Saint Eugenia's Sanctuary for the
Insane and Getting There, dearie?

DR. SHADE   We'll be there before you know it, mother. You'll like
it at Saint Eugenia's; it's a place of ... rags.

MOON MOTHER   Oh, ragged hearts, yes. But my heart's not ragged,
lambie. What could you do at Saint Eugenia's for the likes of me?
(She lifts the net back off her face.)

DR. SHADE   We could ... operate. Remove the moon.

MOON MOTHER (terrified)   Oh, no! You mustn't, dearie, you mustn't!
Mercy! Oh, mercy ... he's all this wretched old woman has in the
world! (She cries, beats her fists against her head.)

DR. SHADE (comforting her)   We'll remove the moon and give you a
man.

MOON MOTHER   A ... a man?

DR. SHADE   A man is more than the moon. You'll see.

MOON MOTHER   Would you do that for me? An old witch of a woman
like me?

DR. SHADE   Yes.

MOON MOTHER   Why?

DR. SHADE (gripping her by the arms)   Because I ... (Turning away,
detached.) Because you interest me.

MOON MOTHER
The man began by saying he loved,
Then stood on his hands
To put his silly head
Above his heart.
"You interest me" was all he said,
To a hag,
Who pulls rags
In a little red cart.
But I know, lambie, I know. (She takes his arm, nestles up to him.)

DR. SHADE (brushing her away)   Don't you be affectionate with me,
old woman.

MOON MOTHER   So you're a-feared of love, are you? A-feared this
crazy old snaggle-tooth might want you to love her back? A-feared
you couldn't love me back, eh, dearie? Agh! Let love love itself
out. That's all it ever wants to do. Only open your heart and
breathe in the breath I blow you. You don't have to blow it back--
only receive it! Receiving is the best of giving, you silly slip
of a boy ... or didn't you know?

(DR. SHADE, angry, starts to put the net back over her face.)

Dearie ... do you really think we need the net?

(He considers for a moment, then he turns to her, smiles, removes
the net and tosses it away. They go off arm in arm. SUZIE crosses
to the table, begins ladling out the imaginary pancakes in the imaginary frying pan. SOL enters left, plunks himself down in his
usual chair.)

SOL   All right. Now let's get cracking. Today I want to see the
rest of your work. Everything you've done in the last couple of
years. Landscapes, abstracts, motion studies, everything.

(SUZIE runs to the easel, holds up an empty frame.)

SUZIE   Well ... there's this one.... (Looks at it.) Ugh! (She
puts down the frame, then holds the same one up again.) And there's
this one.... Ugh! (And a third time.) And there's this one....
Ugh!

SOL (angry)   "Ugh"? What do you mean "ugh"? Sheer genius! (Puzzled,
amazed.) But ... they're all of Cindy!

SUZIE   It's because she's beautiful.

SOL   Don't you paint anyone who isn't beautiful?

SUZIE   No. (Pause.) You're beautiful. I'd like to paint you.

SOL   I wouldn't like to have you paint me.

SUZIE   How come?

SOL   Because you're a Sol painter. You'd paint the Sol right out
of me.

(They laugh together.)

You think Cindy's beautiful, but is she really? How well do you
know her?

SUZIE   Oh, Cindy's my best friend! She comes up to borrow honey.
You know, for her little cakes? She's always running out of honey.
That's how I get her to sit. I trade her two ounces for two hours.
But really she just does it for me.

SOL (looking at the portrait)   Hmmm. I'll bet she smells just like
her little cakes. Maybe I can't get them off my mind, but I wouldn't
actually want to eat one. I came to you instead.

SUZIE   Oh! Then you know she's not real.

SOL   She's just a great big wishful think on somebody's part ...
probably mine.... Hell, I'm going to find you someone really beautiful to paint. After breakfast, we'll take a walk--to the corner
of Cherry and Elsewhere, where the most beautiful people in the
world wait for the el. We'll "abscond" with one of them. Yesterday
there was an old man waiting--with the world in his face. If he's
still there.... After breakfast we'll take a walk.

SUZIE   Oh, you go, Sol. I ... well, I don't like to walk much.

SOL   But I'll need you. I have an unfortunate way of putting things.
If I should unwittingly insult our quarry, I'll need you to counter
with a compliment. Otherwise he might just get on the train when
it comes--if it comes--which would be a great blow to art -

SUZIE   Sol, I want to go ... I really want to go, but....

SOL (angry)   But you won't. Why not?

SUZIE   Well ... because.... (She looks down at her foot, unconsciously moving it back and forth.)

SOL (scornfully)   Because you happen to have an infinitesimal limp?
You're afraid our old man with the world in his face won't talk to
your face, he'll talk to your foot, because that's where you think
the world is.

(Pause. She nods, ashamed. She won't look at him.)

He's old. What does he care?

(She winces, turns away.)

It's congenital, isn't it? A rather important little bone in your
ankle never developed.

SUZIE (whirling around on him defiantly)   So why do you have to
tell me about myself? Not "Is it congenital?" but "It's congenital."

SOL   Isn't it?

SUZIE   Yes!

SOL (one of his triumphant smiles)   Let's take a walk.

SUZIE (wanting to very much, but finally shaking her head)   Later
on--maybe. Can you wait till ... later on?

SOL   Maybe.

SUZIE (stopping short, sniffing)   Whooops! I think I smell ...
(A beeline for the frying pan.) Oh, I do! I do! They're ruined.
All black on the bottom!   (She is busy snatching out the imaginary
pancakes.)

SOL   Incompetent female. Begin over. (She does, feverishly.)
You cook like you paint like you act. Everything's overdone.

SUZIE   I'm sorry....

SOL   You have no excuse. You're not even good-looking, and you
don't even like to take walks.

(This is too much. She turns around and lets him have it.)

SUZIE   Every morning! You do it every morning! Rude, rude, you're
so (beginning to cry.) rude!

SOL (feeling bad)   Oh. (Pause, then wistfully.) Are you going to
throw me out without my pancakes?

SUZIE (complete reversal, laughing)   No! (Pause. She dishes up
more pancakes.) Maybe you're not rude at all. Maybe you're just
honest. Maybe ... maybe it's very attractive.

SOL   Maybe it's not. I've tried to change, tried to be polite.
My friends are all very polite. Once I even got so far as to say
"please." But "thank you" ... I'm afraid "thank you" is just beyond me.

SUZIE (loving him all the more)   Is it, really?

SOL   Maybe the first ones were black on the bottom, but in a moment
(She anxiously turns the pancakes.) you're going to hand me a second

plate of the fluffiest, most delicious-looking cakes--that are really
clouds--that a man ever saw, and I'll want to say it ... but I won't.
And then the moment for saying it will be gone.

(She carefully places a stack of pancakes before him. He digs in.
SUZIE is waiting. Nothing. She walks away center. He finishes.
Looks at her once and leaves. The lights dim on the apartment side
of the stage. SUZIE slowly kneels and covers herself with the net.
She looks at her wrist, begins to cry quietly. MOON MOTHER enters.)

MOON MOTHER   Dearie me, dearie, such tight little tears. That's
no way to weep--if you're going to weep, weep the weather! Hurri-
canes of heartache! Typhoons of tears!

SUZIE   Oh, Mother, you've seen me! (She hugs her.)

MOON MOTHER   I didn't see you before, because I didn't think you
deserved to be seen before.

SUZIE   No, I guess I didn't. But how did you escape from the Doctor?

MOON MOTHER   The Doctor? Oh, you mean that nice young man with a
problem. I gave him the slip on the corner of Cherry and Elsewhere.
Stepped down a manhole. I had to. He wouldn't hear of my coming
back for you; thought you were something I'd seen that wasn't. Humph!
Maybe you are for all I know!... But even if you are, I couldn't
just leave you here to dissolve in a pitiful little red puddle of
paint, now, could I?

(She rocks SUZIE in her arms.)

SUZIE   I'm so ashamed.

MOON MOTHER   There now, child, there now. Dearie me, I can't get
at you for all this net. (She lifts it off.) What are you doing
in this net, child, are you a schizophrenic?

SUZIE   I'm an artist. I mean, I was.

MOON MOTHER   An artist? Oh, whoop dee dee! I'm sure the Doctor
will find you ... "interesting."

SUZIE (wistful)   You think so?

MOON MOTHER   Yes! Why at Saint Eugenia's ... you do want to be
taken to Saint Eugenia's, don't you?

SUZIE   I ... I guess I do, or I wouldn't have crawled into the net.

MOON MOTHER   Well, come along then, child.

(She leads SUZIE to "Saint Eugenia's" and they end up over toward
stage right. During the walk and "song" DR. SHADE appears stage
right, at his easel with his back to them.)

There's a time for shade, a time for sun,
A time to do what can't be done,
A time to take a bit of fun
And put yourself in the loony bun!
Oh, no, no, I suppose I mean "bin."
I have been to the bun!
I have bun to the bin! Tee hee!

(They see DR. SHADE, fall down, begin to salaam. DR. SHADE whirls
on them.)

DR. SHADE   So! You escaped down a manhole, did you! I put every
man and mole--every ditch, every drain, every toilet bowl was being
watched. Do you hear me? Watched! You had to come up somewhere,
and when you did, my man would be right there to ... hmmmm....
Where did you come up?

MOON MOTHER   I didn't. I'm still down there!

DR. SHADE   Oh, no wonder. Well, you won't escape again, mother.
I'll see to that. I trusted you, let you walk beside me, free!
"We don't need the net." you said. Then you disappeared into the
ground!

MOON MOTHER   Poor lambie, all alone? No more hand to hold? Well,
I had to go. I forgot something. Her. (Pointing to SUZIE.)

DR. SHADE   I told you, she's a figment!

SUZIE   Oh! Could I be just a figment of my figment?

MOON MOTHER   Now, don't get defensive, lambie. I came back to
you, didn't I? Mother will always come back.

DR. SHADE   Well, she'll never come back again, because I'll never
let her go again. I'm going to put her in the cage!

MOON MOTHER   Dearie me, the cage! The cage is the forever version
of the net, I suppose.

DR. SHADE   Variations on a theme, mother. Now ... get in there!
(He swings open the door to the cage. MOON MOTHER gets in. The
door slams shut.)

MOON MOTHER
Was it his rage
Put me in a cage?
Or was it his cage
Put me in a rage?
Riddle me this and riddle me that,
I'd figure it out if I thought down and sat!

(She does. DR. SHADE, meanwhile, has returned to his painting. His back is to SUZIE.)

SUZIE   Uh ... excuse me, Sir....   (No reaction--louder)   Excuse me, Sir....

DR. SHADE (whirls on her)   I will not excuse you.   You think you want to be excused, but you don't.

(He turns back to painting. SUZIE waits a moment in anger. Then she gets up and gives him a swift kick in the ass.)

Owwww!

SUZIE (quickly)   Excuse me, Sir, is this the loony bin?

DR. SHADE (indignant)   This is the dark side of the moon.

SUZIE   Oh, that'll do. Could you ... could you put a band-aid on this? (She holds out her wrist.)

DR. SHADE (examining it)   So! Slashed your wrist, did you?... A very unoriginal way to go, if I do say so. And I do.

SUZIE   Oh. (She blushes, hides her wrist behind her.)

DR. SHADE   When I think of the repertory of really great deaths! My God, you might have climbed to the top of the clock in Times Square and impaled yourself on the hour hand at precisely two minutes of twelve.

SUZIE   Or I could have jumped off the roof of People's Drug--Ahhhhh.... (She does a fade-out scream and crumples onto the throne.) But half- way down I would have thought better of it.

DR. SHADE   Exactly. Let me see your wrist.

(Again she puts her hand behind her back, hangs her head.)

What are you ashamed of?

SUZIE (reluctantly bringing her hand forward)   I wanted you to see it before it got all dry. It doesn't look like it hurts any- more ... but it does.

DR. SHADE   That's not blood at all! It's ... (Puts her wrist to his mouth, sucks.) it's paint! (Spits it out.)

SUZIE   I'm an artist, Doctor. I was painting myself to death.

(Silence. He looks at her contemptuously.)

Well ... well ... don't you even want to know why?

9

DR. SHADE   I know why. Why do they all...? (He pantomimes three different suicides--hanging, stabbing, cutting his wrist.)

SUZIE   Oh ... I shouldn't have come here!

DR. SHADE   No. (He turns abruptly back to his painting.)

SUZIE (talking to his back)   Well, it was all because he had this adorable little fault. He couldn't say "thank you."

MOON MOTHER· (calling from her cage)   Adorable indeed! Women, women-- what's to be done with them?
They take the weed to be the flower,
And the flower to be the weed.
They feed his fault on sugar and salt--
While all his virtues go to seed!

DR. SHADE (talking with his back to her, still painting)   So. You found it endearing, did you? "His adorable little fault." "When he doesn't say thank you to me, I don't mind. Which makes me more kind than his mother and the others--who do mind." His fault made you feel superior. So much for it's being adorable.

SUZIE   Oh. But I thought I loved it--just because I loved it. (She runs to the cage.) Mother, Mother! Did you hear?

MOON MOTHER   Yes, yes. He's right, of course, child. A woman will always love a man who gives her something to forgive....
But fiddle dee dee
To the why and the who--
When the love itself
Is the only thing true!

SUZIE   Yeah! I loved his little fault. Who cares why? (She runs back to DR. SHADE, who still has his back to her.) You spoiled it by telling me why!... Oh, I want to get out of here. I don't want to know why anymore.

DR. SHADE (whirling around to face her)   Get out? There is no "out." There's only "in." You wanted to come in. The mad mother-- you came into her mind, all moon-muddled as it is. And you came into my mind, too. You wanted to come into my mind, and now I'll be go-to-hell if I'm going to let you out!

SUZIE   Oh ... you won't put me in the cage, will you, Doctor?

DR. SHADE   I should ... but no. I'll give you a ground card. You're free to run around the fringe of my thoughts. But so help me, if I try to think of you and find I can't, I'll lock you up so fast -

SUZIE   Yes, Sir.

DR. SHADE   And now--Out! I mean, "out" as far as you can go and still be "in." I've got work to do.

(She starts to leave.)

Suzie,... come here.

(She returns to him, trembling. He takes her wrist and very tenderly applies a band-aid.)

I almost forgot, you were bleeding to death.

(She looks at him, then bursts into tears. SUZIE moves to the cage area and sinks to the floor. Blackout in DR. SHADE's office. He leaves.)

MOON MOTHER   Now that's what I call "weeping the weather."
Fetch me a bucket and mop, say I,
And I'll scrub the floor with the tears you cry!

(MOON MOTHER opens the door of her cage, comes out with the scrub bucket, and puts it in SUZIE's lap to catch the tears.)

We mustn't let all that strong salt solution go to waste. Oh, my, no. Why it's just the thing for those stubborn yellow streaks and stains.

SUZIE   Oh! You got out!

MOON MOTHER   Why yes, dearie. To think he can keep moonlight in a cage. Fiddle dee dee! That young man takes himself much too seriously.

(SUZIE begins to laugh.)

Stop that! If you laugh, we shall never be able to wash the floor.

SUZIE (in a burst of false exuberance, imitates MOON MOTHER)   Fiddle dee dee! You can't catch me!

MOON MOTHER (setting the bucket aside)   Oh, well, I have no doubt he'll make you cry again soon enough.

(SUZIE's laughter stops suddenly.)

SUZIE   I was crying because he wouldn't let me tell him. I wanted to tell him so much! Why I.... (She looks at her wrist.) "Why do they all?" ... He wouldn't turn around and look at me.

MOON MOTHER   You could tell me, dearie.

SUZIE   Oh, could I?

MOON MOTHER   Of course, it wouldn't be like **talking** to him ...
but talking about him would be the next best thing, wouldn't it?
Silly scat of a girl, where does his name live, under your tongue,
I suppose?

SUZIE (crossing to the apartment)   His name was Solace--I called
him Sol--and he always came up in the morning.

(The lights come up on SUZIE's apartment. SUZIE is busy at the
table, as SOL enters.)

SOL   Are the hotcakes done?

SUZIE   This morning I'm making them in a shoe, see? To avoid that
feeling of sameness. (She proudly ladles batter from the bowl into
the shoe, which she then sets in the frying pan.) Oh, whimsy, whimsy!
There!

(She flips it. He laughs, she laughs, they look at each other.)

SOL (incredulous)   You made me laugh ... in the morning!

SUZIE (delighted)   And nobody else has ever made you laugh -

SOL (joining in)   Not since I was two and a half!

(SUZIE dumps the pancake on his plate.)

SUZIE   Here we go again!

(She ladles out another pancake. He falls to eating. She **quickly**
gets a brush and a **picture** frame, and begins painting his **portrait**
from behind. He turns and catches her.)

Ah ha! I'm stealing the soul of Sol--painting him with his mouth
foal!

(He is chasing her around the table.)

SOL   I told you....

(He catches her. Mimes painting a beg red X across the picture,
which exists, as usual, only to them within an empty frame.)

I will not be immortalized in the middle of a pancake.

SUZIE (suddenly serious)   You will not be immortalized at all....
Sol, I really, really want to paint you.

SOL   I'll have another cake.

(He sits down. Sulkily, SUZIE dumps the shoe out again.)

SUZIE   There. Now you have a plate of footprints--coming and going.

SOL (trying to recapture their former playful mood)   This one is just standing there.

SUZIE   Oh, would you rather it walked away? (Looking at it.) Yeah, I guess you would. It is kinda soggy looking ... damp around the edges ... Ugh.

SOL (smiling his know-it-all smile)   No, not this morning. I won't play.

SUZIE   Play what?

SOL   You know what. The soggy game. You say it's soggy, not because you really think it's soggy, but because you want me to say it isn't soggy. Well, have it your way. It's soggy.

(He eats. She looks at him--hurt.)

SUZIE (to herself)   Well, if he'd just say it! "Suzie, they're light as clouds this morning...." I wouldn't have to try and make him say it.

(A pause. He keeps eating--silently. She walks around the front of the table, limping more than usual. Suddenly he bangs his fork down.)

SOL   Look at you! Poor wounded bird, dragging your wing across the floor! Why do you limp more when your feelings are hurt?

SUZIE   You know why. You always know "why."

SOL (that smile again)   You want to hurt me by showing me how much I've hurt you.

SUZIE (softly)   Yeah.

SOL (conversational, smiling)   You're a bitch, Suzie.

SUZIE (silence, then the explosion)   Why do you always have to smile like that? Like a cheshire cat who knows "why." All the time detached--from everything! Even from your own smile. Just hanging there--teeth. Teeth in the dark. Oh, I wish I could make you mad one time!

SOL (still smiling)   Make me call you a bitch and mean it? (He screams.) Bitch!... Like that? Loud? What would that prove? I mean it, but I find the word more effective when employed in a conversational tone.

(He rises, crosses to the easel, stands looking at the painting.)

Here. (The brush to SUZIE.) We'll work with the bitch colors to-
day--red and gold.

(She paints.)

This is the last time I'm going to let you paint Cindy.

SUZIE (freezing)   Oh.

SOL   Today I'm going to find you a new face. Today I'm going to
take that walk to the corner of Cherry and Elsewhere. With you or
without you.

(She looks at him--afraid. Then:)

SUZIE   With me, Sol.

SOL   Good.

(He is standing behind her; she paints.)

Last night I dreamed somebody poured water on the sun and put it
out. The only sunlight left in the world was here. (Indicates the
painting.) So I walked into your painting, and I sat down here ...
to the left of the tree. Cindy was there. I've never met Cindy,
but she was there, and she said something to me.

(SUZIE has stopped painting, turns to him.)

She said ... "The sun is where you see it."

(He turns her to her painting again.)

This is where I see the sun.

(SUZIE is overwhelmed with love, pleasure. She lets her head fall
back against his shoulder. He holds her for a second, then moves
away.)

SUZIE (briskly, covering up)   You know my work so well you can
walk into it in your sleep. I can't walk into your work.

SOL   No.

SUZIE   Because I've never even seen your work. I ask and I ask -

SOL   I'm tired of your asking.

SUZIE (accusingly)   Is it getting done? Or is it just hanging
there over your bed, so you can dream it's getting done?

SOL   No. It's getting done.

SUZIE   Because of me! Because of me it's getting done! When you
came to me your colors were all dying, but now -

SOL   They're alive again. It's true.

SUZIE   So why can't I see it? "Rorschach in Red and Gold Called
What Do You See?" How can I tell you what I see when you won't even -

SOL   I don't want to know what you'd see.

SUZIE (puzzled, angry, frustrated)   Sol ... how come?

SOL   Because ... you'd see yourself ... feeling affectionate ...
about me. You'd see nothing but -

SUZIE   L, O, V, etcetera! How come you can't say it?

(He turns away.)

How come you can't let me say it?

SOL   Because the last woman who "said it" wore a "profusion of
pink."

SUZIE   "Just this side of sentimental."

(Pause. SOL quickly goes back to the easel. As she talks, he paints
here and there. SUZIE sits dejected at the table.)

SUZIE (wistful)   "I love you." Why is he afraid for me to say it?
Like I was asking for something. But I'm not asking for anything--
except to be able to say it. (Silence.)

SOL   Stop sulking and get over here. I want you to fix the light
in the foreground.

(She crosses silently, looking at the floor.)

SUZIE (sulking)   What light--I don't see any light.

SOL   Suzie -

SUZIE (screaming)   It's not worth fixing! It's Ugh!

SOL (screaming back)   OK, have it your way! It's Ugh! Ugh! Everything you do is Ugh! Soggy! Damp around the edges. Ugh!

(A knock on the door. CINDY enters with her basket of sunflower
cakes. What can you say about CINDY? She is delightful--mostly
because she is constantly delighted--with herself and everyone else.
She may have a guitar slung over her shoulder.)

SUZIE   Cindy! Oh--I'm so glad to see you!

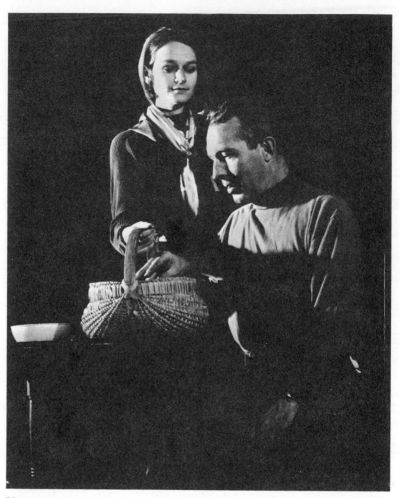

10

CINDY   Suzie, love!

(She gives SUZIE a warm little hug. Then catches sight of SOL.)

Oh, He's here! (Whispering.) The one you told me about? The
one who was bothered by the smell?

(She giggles impishly, gives SUZIE a wink, then comes forward to
meet SOL.)

Have one!

(She gives him a dazzling, completely genuine smile and holds out
her basket. He peeps inside, takes out an invisible sunflower cake,
pops it into his mouth, chews about twice and practically swoons
into the chair.)

Do you love my sunflower cakes, Mr. St. Clair? Everybody loves
my sunflower cakes because ... well, because they're so delicious!
(Another impish laugh.)

SOL (his eyes rolling)   My God, they're delicious!

SUZIE (aghast)   You said you wouldn't actually want to eat one!

CINDY   I bake the sun in a batter. The best batches happen around
noon. My cakes just rise and rise till they fill the whole room!
I often have to eat my way to the door.

SOL (completely smitten)   May I ... have another?

SUZIE   Sol!

CINDY   Oh, please!

(She holds out the basket; he takes one, reverently.)

Suzie?

SUZIE   No thanks. (To SOL.) You said she wasn't real!

SOL   I was wrong.

CINDY   Actually I just came up to borrow some honey. You know,
to dribble over the tops? Suzie's a love. She's always lending
me honey.

SOL   You live alone. Who is all your baking for? (Apprehensive.)
Do you have a lover?

CINDY   Oh, no! I bake for my friends at Saint Eugenia's. All
week long I go around white as a clown with the flour and the sugar
and the salt of it all. Don't I, Suzie? Then when Saturday comes

I fill up my basket with edible euphoria, and off I go!

SUZIE (wryly)   Off she goes.

CINDY   We sing a lot at Saint Eugenia's, and we eat a lot too.
"Songs of the Sun and Saturday." When I sing, they all sing, and
I don't care who says they're "insane and getting there."

(As CINDY sings, she moves to the cage and the lights come on it
and MOON MOTHER. SOL and SUZIE freeze, hearing and seeing it in
their minds.)

Only wait for the sun and Saturday!
It's a "tell me what's the matter?" day.
How can you be lonely
When I'm just a thought away?
So sing a song of the sun!
You can leave the rest undone!
Only wait for the sun and Saturday.

So sing a song of the sun with me,
And if he captures you,
It's only 'cause he wants to set you free.
You can't lock light in captivity.
So sing a song of the sun!
You can leave the rest undone!
Only wait for the sun and Saturday.

(On the last two lines, MOON MOTHER joins in exuberantly in her
ruined old voice. After CINDY stops, MOON MOTHER starts the song
over for a line or two. She holds out her hands through the bars.
CINDY takes a cake from her basket, presses it into MOON MOTHER's
hand. CINDY slowly leaves; they wave. CINDY crosses back to the
apartment. Lights go out on the cage.)

CINDY   Do you love my song, Mr. St. Clair? I love my song.

SOL (very tenderly, maybe reaching out to brush a strand of hair
from her eyes)   It's my song, too.

SUZIE   Little Red Riding Hood, with her basket of good intentions!
Don't you think maybe Grandmother resented the hell out of being
brought a bunch of those buttery things in bed? Like, there she
was, all schizophrenic and all and couldn't get up or out. And it
would seem the least Little Red Hiding Good could have done was to
catch it from her! I mean, how smug! To come in and eat buttery
things and go out, when all the other buttery-thing-eating people
can't ever go out again at all!

CINDY (hurt)   Suzie, that's not like you ... to see it that way....

Moon Mother--she always seemed so glad to see me.

SOL (glaring at SUZIE)   She was glad to see you. She was more
than glad. I heard her singing all the way from here.

SUZIE (a croaking, sarcastic imitation of MOON MOTHER)   "Only wait
for the sun and Saturday" -

(SOL reacts to this by whacking SUZIE across the bottom. He is not
being playful, he means it to hurt. SUZIE sees CINDY's face, is
full of remorse.)

Cindy, I'm sorry. I didn't mean to make fun of your song. 'Cause ...
hey, it's everybody's song--even mine.

(She smiles at her friend ruefully, holds out her hands. CINDY takes
her hands, gives them a squeeze.)

CINDY   Oh, Suzie, I've just got to keep singing at Saint Eugenia's,
even if I do look like "The Salvation Army with a straight face."
Because the only other thing would be not singing at Saint Eugenia's -

SOL   Because she was afraid of looking like "The Salvation Army
with a straight face." Mother needs someone to sing with.

(SUZIE nods slowly.)

CINDY   Besides ... I"m in love with the Doctor!

(She giggles.)

SOL (upset, his hand on her shoulder)   You can't be in love with
the Doctor, because -

SUZIE (thinking "let's break this up")   Hey, now that you're here,
I've got this great idea for the next portrait. I want to paint
you (Brush to SOL.) painting Cindy (Brush to CINDY.) painting me.
Now.... (She positions everyone in a triangle.) Look like you
mean it. Ready?

(The three of them paint frantically and move in a pattern.)

SOL (more and more drawn to CINDY, suddenly throws down the brush)
What am I doing? I told you you couldn't paint Cindy again.

SUZIE   Oh, Sol.

SOL (grabbing CINDY by the hands)   Cindy! Walk with me to the
corner of Cherry and Elsewhere! Help me find someone for Suzie
to paint the soul out of!

CINDY   But Sol, why don't you and Suzie -

SOL   Suzie's not much on walks. Come on! (He pulls her toward the door; she resists.)

CINDY (looking back over her shoulder)   Suzie...?

(SOL pulls her out the door. SUZIE stands, looking after them. At this point, there may be an intermission if desired. Or the play may continue with SUZIE's next speech.)

ACT TWO

(If there is an intermission, the lights come up on SUZIE in the same position as at the end of Act I. MOON MOTHER is moving out of the cage to stand near her.)

SUZIE   So that's how it was. He took her to our corner. Only I guess it wasn't our corner, 'cause we hadn't ever been there.... Oh, we had, too! I'd been seeing us there. Seeing how it would be with us--there. And the sound of the el, and the kind of hiss the cars make when they stop. "Suzie,... Suzie,... you watch the doors in the middle, and I'll watch the doors at the front. Some-body beautiful is bound to get off sometime." Then we'd be all day--just watching the doors. And maybe the wind would blow up cold on the corner and he'd have to put his hands in my pockets--'cause he didn't have any pockets.... And ... and then he took her.

MOON MOTHER   He took her where you wouldn't go--except in your mind.
Can you blame a man who isn't blind
If he find the beautiful to be the true
And leave a girl like you behind?

SUZIE   He said, "I wouldn't actually want to eat one." And then he gobbled! Ooooh! (Sad.) I gave him everything I was. I was art, I was breakfast, I was lots of **talk after** breakfast.... But what she was.... She was beautiful.

MOON MOTHER   Was beautiful. Of course that's worlds away from looked beautiful.

SUZIE   Oh no it's not! It should be, but it's not.

MOON MOTHER
If it's not--
Then it shouldn't be.
Tee hee!
Look **here,** child, he took her because he loved her. You **must** forgive him for that.

SUZIE   It's where he took her.

MOON MOTHER   To that special little corner--of your mind--where
he had promised to take you? Yes, that was insensitive of him.
Perhaps it was criminal! Were I judge, I should send him to the
stocks and, while he was thus positioned (She mimics a man in the
stocks.), I might even be persuaded to pelt him with a prune pit!
But you! You would have the poor man hanged. (She shakes her head
at SUZIE.) Tsk, tsk, tsk.

DR. SHADE's VOICE (offstage) Fee fi fo fum!

MOON MOTHER   The giant! At least he thinks he is. Oh, hide!
Hide!

(She scurries into the cage, slams the door. SUZIE crouches beside
the cage--her hands over head--air raid position. Offstage we hear
the barking of a really huge dog. A St. Bernard, perhaps, or a
Great Pyrenees. Then a dog does appear--but it is not the dog that
belonged to the bark. It is a Pekinese perhaps, or a Pomeranian.
Attached to the dog is a leash. Attached to the leash is DR. SHADE,
flourishing a long whip above his head.)

DR. SHADE   After it, Old Blue! We'll track it through the marshes,
we'll track it through the mire. The footprint--soggy, damp around
the edges. (To SUZIE.) You! (He taps her on the head with his
whip.) Have you seen it? Which way did it go?

SUZIE   It got cold. I'm afraid I ... threw it out.

DR. SHADE   But you can't have! That pancake was one of your "little
hurts." You don't throw out your hurts, not any of the little things
he "did to you." Oh, no. You lay them out lovingly in the larder
and wait for the mould to grow.

SUZIE (rising)   But I've got to save my hurts! They're all I've
got. I never asked him for anything else.

(Without warning, DR. SHADE grabs her by the hair and jerks her
head back--Valentino style.)

DR. SHADE   Will you go to bed with me?

SUZIE (flabbergasted)   Well ... I ... I mean, I.... Yeah!

DR. SHADE (releasing her, turning his back on her)   Maybe you never
asked for anything (Whirling around to face her again.), but you
sure asked to be asked for something.

SUZIE (backing away from him)   Oh! Is that what he thought? Sol...?
Is that what...? Oh, no! Please.... No!

DR. SHADE (advancing on her)   Yes! You asked to be asked.

SUZIE (covering her ears, screaming)   No! (Pause. She squares

her shoulders, drawing courage from somewhere, deciding to stand up
to him.) That doesn't count. If you know you're not going to be
asked, then the asking to be asked doesn't count.

DR. SHADE   Hmmm. Perhaps you're right.

SUZIE (incredulous)   You ... you think so?

MOON MOTHER (beating her head against the bars and wailing)   Let
me out! Ohhhhhhh! Let me out! Ohhhhhhh!

DR. SHADE (running to the cage, reacting with something halfway
between fury and compassion)   Stop that! I can't **bear** it.

MOON MOTHER
These bars around the moon are curled;
They're causing a striped eclipse!
And all around this room, the world
Is seeing the moon in strips.
Were there any doubt
About
The need to let me out
I'd shout,
"'Tis not the sun, 'tis the moon, you see!
'Tis not the moon, 'tis me!"

(She falls to her knees, takes DR. SHADE's hand, and kisses it through
the bars.)

DR. SHADE (all compassion now)   Mother, I haven't forgotten you,
mother. The operation will be soon, now, very soon. We'll remove
the moon from your hunch ... yes.... In the meantime, is there anything I can do for you?... A walk? You'd like to go for a walk,
wouldn't you?

MOON MOTHER   Oh, yes, dearie, a walk would be so nice.

DR. SHADE (getting the leash, opening the cage, putting MOON MOTHER
on the leash)   Of course, I'd have to take you on a leash....

MOON MOTHER   May I lift my leg on every other lamp post?

(DR. SHADE leads her off. She mimes lifting her leg on every other
lamp post as she goes. Again we hear the barking of the huge dog
offstage.)

SUZIE   "Let me out! Ohhhhhhh! Let me out!" Hell, she can get out
whenever she wants. She just did that to make Fee fi fo fum feel
more like Fee fi fo fum. (She begins to laugh.) "Let me out!"

(MOON MOTHER and DR. SHADE come in again. This time it is DR. SHADE
who is on the leash. He is down on all fours. She cracks the whip
above his head. Offstage we hear the barking of a tiny dog. SUZIE

laughs and laughs. MOON MOTHER steps back into the cage. DR. SHADE
locks the door and leaves, dragging the leash.)

SUZIE (running to the cage)   Oh, Mother, I love you! Now that he's
gone, can I tell you the end of it?

MOON MOTHER   The end of what, child?

SUZIE   The end of the story!

MOON MOTHER (musing on the quality of "ends" in general)   An end
is a beginning that goes on too long.

SUZIE   Oh. Am I boring you?

MOON MOTHER (patting her on the head)   No, no, dearie. In you I
am having a second spring. Go on, go on.

SUZIE (fading into the apartment as she talks. Lights go up in that
area)   Well ... it was five o'clock by the time they got back.
They came in with their faces all flushed with the wind ... and
with each other. And Cindy was singing ... and Sol was singing
too....

(SOL and CINDY enter singing; their arms are around each other.
SUZIE remains with her back to them.)

SOL and CINDY
So sing a song of the sun!
You can leave the rest undone!
Only wait for the sun and Saturday....

SOL   Suzie--we've found her! The most beautiful woman in the world.

(MOON MOTHER slowly comes out of the darkened cage, circling around
back to collect her wagon.)

MOON MOTHER   Rags! Rags! Old rags to buy and sell!

(She crosses to the apartment during her speech. By the end, she
has seated herself in one of the chairs. SOL and CINDY stand behind
her in tableau; each rests a hand possessively on her shoulder.
The tableau is a long one. They look at each other, but do not
move for the duration of MOON MOTHER's speech. The lights dim in
the apartment as MOON MOTHER is crossing toward them.)

And when the moon rises, he rises deep down in my womb. (Slowly,
rhythmically.) Up he comes--up and up, through the hollow of my
body. I can feel him, round, a little past the full. Up and still
up, until he reaches the height of my hunch. And there he sleeps
the sleep of the golden snore.... Indeed! I am the happiest whore!
The moon is mine, and who could ask for more?... And yet ... and
yet I could cry, when I think of the sky. The sky--so sad, and so

11

empty. When I 'think of the songsters! I've stolen their rhyme for
June!
For them I could cry
Tears out of tune.
I could cry--
When I think of the sky.
(She sits.) Agh! These astronauts are driving me mad! (She snatches
at the air around her hunch.) Like mosquitoes, swarming about....
(She swats her hunch.) Missed him again! Every time they blast off,
I itch.

(CINDY kindly helps her scratch her hunch. Slowly SUZIE turns to
face them. She is shocked, horrified.)

SUZIE   This?... This...! (She gestures to MOON MOTHER.)

SOL (proudly)   The most beautiful woman in the world.

(SUZIE begins to laugh--a laugh of horror.)

SUZIE (between gasping and laughing)   Oh, no!... She's an old man
you brought me back ... an old man!

SOL (angry)   She's a woman.

SUZIE (screaming)   She's a monstrosity! Something that got loose
out of a nightmare--something horrible, horrible!

(She is crying now--terrified, like a child, by the nightmare "thing."
SOL crosses to her, takes her arms and begins to shake her. CINDY
runs to MOON MOTHER, turns her with her back to SUZIE and SOL and
remains there, comforting her.)

SOL   Stop it!

CINDY   It's not true, love, don't listen.

SUZIE   I can't paint this! You and Cindy ... you can afford to
think she's beautiful, because you're beautiful. But you ... you
brought her here, to me! Oh....

SOL (shaking her harder)   Stop it!

(She quiets down.)

She--is beautiful.

SUZIE   Would you make love to her?

(Silence is the answer: SUZIE becomes very calm.)

OK.

(SOL releases her slowly.)

Then let me paint what "is beautiful." You and Cindy. (To MOON
MOTHER.) Could you put them under a spell? You look like you could.
A spell--so they couldn't move?

(MOON MOTHER nods and cackles; draws elaborate signs in the air.
SOL, now in a trance, holds out his arms to CINDY. She, in a like
trance, holds out her arms and sleepwalks toward him. They embrace--
slowly, like people in a dream. Then--within the embrace--they are
still. SUZIE takes an empty picture frame and her red paintbrush.
Inside the frame she repeats the same motions with the brush that
MOON MOTHER used to cast her spell. While she is painting, MOON
MOTHER is chanting.)

MOON MOTHER
You may paint the dark side of a dream,
And see the thing that's better left unseen,
But remember--
What you see
Will be.

SUZIE (after a pause, softly, tenderly)   There. It's done. (She
stares at the frame.) They're naked ... lying down, naked ... which
is funny because Sol has a hunchback. Looks ... all ... crippled.
(She touches the painting gently. Then:) Sol, why did you take her?

(Silence. Nobody moves. SUZIE turns to MOON MOTHER, makes a gesture
imploring her to break the trance.)

MOON MOTHER   Oh!

(She cackles, claps her hands in the air. The trance is broken.
SOL and CINDY separate.)

SOL   Funny, I seem to have blacked out. Cindy, will you see that
Moon Mother gets home?

CINDY   Yes, you stay and talk to Suzie.

(She takes MOON MOTHER by the hand, leads her off to the cage. CINDY
leaves.)

SUZIE   Why did you take her, Sol?

SOL   I took her because I loved her. I never loved you. I never
even felt affectionate about you. (Pause.) Would you like to know
why?

SUZIE   No.

SOL   I never loved you ... because you never loved yourself. (Matter-of-factly.) How could you--you're a cripple.

(For a moment SUZIE is stunned, motionless. Then slowly she picks
up the painting--holds it out to SOL. He takes it from her, stares
at it, horrified.)

SOL   If it only weren't so good. (He leaves.)

SUZIE   It was the last one. It had to be good!

(She takes the red brush, walks down center, slashes her wrist, then
sinks to the floor again, crying. This time she really is going to
get enough tears to wash the floor.)

MOON MOTHER (coming out of the cage with bucket) The last? Sheer
bombast. You think you won't paint again, but you will. (She positions the bucket.) Cry a little to the left!

SUZIE (leaning to the left)   No! Not ever again.

(DR. SHADE enters his office with his back to them.)

DR. SHADE   So! You painted the love you never had, and you hung
it on the wall. Art wasn't art ... art was sex! The stand-in stunt
man.

SUZIE (furious, firing this at his back)   For him, too, art was the
stand-in stunt man! He made love to my art 'cause he was scared to
make love to me!

(Silence on DR. SHADE's part. SUZIE turns back to MOON MOTHER.)

I painted him like that--crippled like that--because all his feelings
are crippled. He can't love anyone but her. Oh, if only she'd
grouch at him--just once. Or burn something on the bottom. (Sadly.)
But that will never happen.

MOON MOTHER   No. Because my Cindy is perfect!

SUZIE   Yeah, perfect. That's how come she can love herself so damn
much. "Bitch ... I don't love you because you don't love yourself.
Bitch!" Well, how am I gonna love myself when I'm not perfect?
Unlike Little Miss Sing-Along in the Sun-Along, I rain!

MOON MOTHER (looks at SUZIE, then smiles and winks at the audience)
"Only wait for the sun and Saturday!"

SUZIE   Oh, my God! It is Saturday!

MOON MOTHER (gleefully singing)   She's coming! She's coming! My
Cindy! She's coming!

SUZIE   I know, I know!

MOON MOTHER   What will you do, take some yowling, howling revenge
on her?

SUZIE   Like ... I could put her in the cage, maybe. And keep her
there! Till all her straight little pearly-white little teeth started
falling out. Then I could let her out and laugh!

MOON MOTHER   My song of the sun! You wouldn't!

SUZIE   No. 'Cause from now on I'm gonna be perfect ... and good
and kind, too! I'm gonna learn to love myself, Mother. I'm gonna
go running around with a basket of ooey little gooey things--giving
to people.

MOON MOTHER (singing) "The Song of the Salvation Army!"

SUZIE   Hey, yeah! I can give to you. Wouldn't you like me to
brighten up your wretched life with a song? Huh? (She runs to get
the ukelele from the cage.)

MOON MOTHER (sigh)   If you must.

(SUZIE returns with the out-of-tune ukelele. "Plink plunk plink
plunk." She sings--with great fervor, but through her nose.)

SUZIE
Only wait for the sun and Saturday!
It's a "tell-me-what's the matter?" day.
How can you be lonely
When I'm just a thought away?

(After the first line, MOON MOTHER puts her hands over her ears and
howls like a dog. Offstage, all the dogs we heard previously join
in the clamor. Above the clamor we hear DR. SHADE intoning.)

DR. SHADE'S VOICE   Fraud--Freud--Fraud--Freud--Fraud--Freud....

SUZIE (stopping)   Gee ... I think I woke up the violent ward.

MOON MOTHER   If you would give to me, give to me what you are--
not what you wish you were.

SUZIE   I wish I were a singing Cindy.

MOON MOTHER   But you are a painting Suzie. So, Suzie--teach me
to paint!

SUZIE   No. I said I'd never paint again.

MOON MOTHER (grabs a brush, paints wildly in the air)
One crooked mind,
Painting straight line

After straight line
After straight line.
Of course, it would be "Art." But we'd call it "Occupational Therapy."
(She leans over to SUZIE, chuckles, says secretively, behind her
hand.) No one would ever know.

SUZIE (sadly)   You mean no one would ever know it was Art.

(MOON MOTHER chuckles again, nods enthusiastically.)

Well ... maybe I could ... if I was sure--really sure--that I wasn't
doing it for him.

MOON MOTHER   For me! We're off on a painting spree--whee!

SUZIE (sadly)   Painting what no one will ever see. (Doubtful pause.)
OK. For you.

(She holds out her hands. MOON MOTHER takes them, smiling. Another
pause--this one full of warmth. Then a fast break. SUZIE begins
to get very excited. Her life, in fact, has just acquired new meaning.)

We're going to make People Art, Mother! And it won't have anything
to do with sex! And it won't have anything to do with ... "genius"!
We don't give a damn if it comes out looking like the floor of the
henhouse, do we?

TOGETHER   No!

SUZIE   It will only have to do with ... with ... feeling. (Slow,
warm.) Our feeling.

(They embrace. SUZIE is excited again.)

Well, where are we gonna get the colors and brushes and stuff?

MOON MOTHER (again whispering conspiratorially)   We're going to
steal them--from the Doctor! Tee hee! I understand he keeps a
goodly supply in his office.

SUZIE   Oh. For that ... that "thing" he keeps working on? Yeah!
We're gonna steal the "things" he does his "thing" with. Come on.

(They creep toward the darkened office. When they reach the throne
and easel, they grab two big brushes that are resting there and run
like hell. DR. SHADE never turns around.)

SUZIE (panting, laughing)   Whee! We made it!

MOON MOTHER (panting, wheezing, cackling with glee)   Let's put them
back so we can do it again!

SUZIE (laughing)   Oh, no!

MOON MOTHER (dancing)
Oh, Dipsy Doodle,
I'm off my noodle,
I've thrown my truss away!
Brrrrrooooops!
She's gone!
Brrrrrooooops!
She's gone!

(She flops to the floor, begins slapping "paint" around from the
bucket of tears.)

SUZIE (standing over her)   You gotta do something about that little
patch of sunlight in the foreground.

(Then she too gets down, takes MOON MOTHER's wrist and guides the
movement of her hand.)

Here ... steady as she goes....   Oh, ooh, oooooh, Hell! Paint!
Paint!

(With wild, joyous abandon, SUZIE begins painting a second row of her
own. DR. SHADE appears out of the darkness--towering over them.)

DR. SHADE   My God, my floor!

(SUZIE, frightened, backs off, but MOON MOTHER proudly displays
her work.)

MOON MOTHER   I call it: "What Do You See That Isn't There? A
Complete Rout in Red and Gold."

DR. SHADE   Who is responsible for this ... drivel! (He stalks
SUZIE.) You? (Suddenly he stops short, covers his eyes and looks
at SUZIE's part of the floor.) Over there it's drivel. But over
here! I'm blinded--blinded as if by the sun! Who is responsible
for this ... Genius? (He stalks MOON MOTHER.) You?

(MOON MOTHER only grins and points to SUZIE. DR. SHADE turns to
SUZIE.)

You. (He stares at her in awe. Finally, in tones of deep and abiding
reverence:) This floor shall never be washed again in our time.

(SUZIE grabs the bucket of tears and defiantly dumps them on her
"picture" on the floor. Sudden change-up from farce to something
very sad and very real.)

DR. SHADE   The sun! You put it out. "Last night I dreamed somebody poured water on the sun and -"

SUZIE   I had to put it out. He loved it.

DR. SHADE (still hushed, incredulous)   Your talent? The golden thing he loved in you? You put it **out**?

SUZIE (passionate)   I wanted him to love me--not the "thing" in me.

DR. SHADE   Can you separate the people you love from the things they are? Him. Can you separate him from his talent? Or even from the color of his eyes? Can you? Can you?

(Pause. SUZIE doesn't answer, turns away. He is right and she knows it. DR. SHADE is quiet, intense. He takes her by the shoulders and turns her around.)

Suzie,... you are the thing.

SUZIE (bitter)   Not anymore I'm not. 'Cause that golden thing ... I put it out.

DR. SHADE   You put yourself out--to get even with him.

SUZIE   Oh,... Oh, no!

DR. SHADE   Oh, yes! "I'll never paint again," you said. "I'll deprive him of the thing he loves in me. I'll never paint again." Bitches- all of you! There's only one who isn't. She comes to sing on Saturday. Thank God, it's Saturday.

(He fades back into his darkened office--then throws his head back into the light and says to MOON MOTHER:)

And you! Get back in the cage!

(She does so.)

SUZIE   He called me a bitch. (Pause.) OK. So, OK. If he's gonna call me that, I might as well -

MOON MOTHER   You might as well--what?

SUZIE   Well ... well, I tried to love, and I landed in the loony bin. So now I'm gonna try -

MOON MOTHER   Hate? You don't know what hate is.

SUZIE (getting upset)   Oh, yes I do! I do on Saturday!

MOON MOTHER (very slowly, deliberately)   You wouldn't.

SUZIE   Put her in a cage, until she got old? I would! Old like you--with all the gold gone out of her! Then she'd know ...

MOON MOTHER   That it's easy to be perfect when you're perfectly beautiful?

SUZIE   Then he'd know.

(Offstage, CINDY is playing and singing. She enters and crosses
center during her song. While CINDY is crossing, SUZIE, as in a
trance, picks up the net and circles around behind CINDY.)

CINDY
So sing a song of the sun with me,
And if he captures you,
It's only 'cause he wants to set you free.
You can't lock light in captivity....

(SUZIE holds the net suspended above CINDY for a moment--then lets
it fall limply to the ground.)

SUZIE   I can't do it.... Cindy...?

(CINDY turns and takes her hands.)

MOON MOTHER (to SUZIE)   Were I an intellectual, I'd say your love
and hate -

SOL (entering)   Are equally ineffectual.

SUZIE   Sol,... you came too!

SOL (smiling at her)   I came too.

CINDY (beaming at her friend and offering the basket)   Suzie, love--
have one. But I'm afraid they're a little burned on the bottom.

SOL, SUZIE, MOON MOTHER   What?

(SOL, outraged, goes stomping over to CINDY, reaches into the basket,
grabs one, bites into it, goes "Ugh!", and spits it out all over the
floor.)

CINDY (furious. CINDY?)   Oh! How can you be so rude! The one time
I leave them out too long, and they get a little ... burned on the
bottom. The one time! Why can't you just smile and swallow? Why
do you have to spit! I hate you! (She throws a sunflower cake at
him.)

SOL, SUZIE, MOON MOTHER   Cindy!

CINDY (pouting)   I'm having a rainy day.

SUZIE   Oh!

SOL (to CINDY)   I'll leave you to rain on Moon Mother, you bad-tempered little bitch!

(MOON MOTHER puts up the umbrella. CINDY, sulking, goes and sits
down under it with MOON MOTHER.)

SOL (to SUZIE)   Come with me. I have something to show you.

(He takes her hand and leads her to the office. Lights go down on
the cage, up on the office. SOL gestures toward his easel.)

Is it finished?

(SUZIE steps back, gazing at it in awe.)

"What Do You See?"

(She looks deep into the large empty frame, is a long time answering.)

SUZIE (ruefully)   I see ... me ... feeling affectionate ... about
you.

(Pause.)

SOL   Do you see anything else?

SUZIE   That's the red part. There is something else--in the gold.
But ... (She stares at it.)   I don't know what it is. You never would
let me see it before.

SOL   No.

SUZIE   'Cause you knew I'd say that. That ... about me feeling
affectionate. You didn't want to hear me say it.

SOL   I didn't want to hear you say what I couldn't say to anyone.

SUZIE   Sol,... why couldn't you?

SOL   Because once you've said it--"I do," or "I don't"--you're
caught. Caught in someone else's idea of what you meant when you
said it.

SUZIE   Oh. You were afraid I'd think you meant ... "Let's go to
bed." (She blushes, looks at the floor.)

SOL   Yes.

SUZIE   Sol,... what did you mean when you said, "I don't even feel
affectionate about you"? I mean ... a little affection, hey...?
(She gestures as if to say, "You'd give that much to any cute little
dog on the street.")

SOL   I meant that I did.

(Stop. She looks at him, incredulous.)

SUZIE (beginning to understand) Then ... then you did give me your
love? Like a closed umbrella in a downpour. "Suzie ... when you
learn to love yourself ... even in a downpour, I'll let you open
the umbrella." Hey, Sol.... A minute ago ... didn't you say it?
Sort of? I love you? Sort of? (She is joyous, triumphant.) Oh,
you did! You did! And you said you couldn't say it to anyone.

SOL   I can ... now.

SUZIE   I ... I made you so you could say it?

SOL (gestures to the painting as they walk toward it)   Now--"What
Do You See?"

SUZIE (another long look into the empty frame)   I see you ... feeling
affectionate ... about me.

SOL   Then ... it's finished. Suzie ... thank you.

(She is a little sad to hear him say it, somehow. At this point
MOON MOTHER comes sweeping into the office, wearing "The Ultimate
Hat!"--profusion of pink, of course. She gets a load of "What Do
You See?", steps back with a gasp, turns to SOL, and says, in the
grand manner:)

MOON MOTHER   But Darling, it's so Now! (She holds out her arms,
puckers up her lips.)

SOL   It's come to this!

(Moment of truth! He hesitates, then throws up his hands in a gesture
of "What the hell!" He crosses to MOON MOTHER, throws his arms around
her, and gives her a mad passionate sexy kiss on the mouth. SUZIE
cheers, jumps up and down.)

CINDY (running from the cage)   Oh, I'm missing it!

SUZIE   He can kiss her now, hat and all! I made him so he can kiss
her!

SOL (to MOON MOTHER--indicating painting)   Now--what do you see?

MOON MOTHER (staring at the painting)   I see the lamp of night becoming
the lamp of day!

SOL   Oh, God, it is finished! Back to the Metropolitan!

MOON MOTHER (clutching her hunch)   He's waking up ... I can feel
him! ... stirring in there. Lunus, did you just yawn? I felt the
rush of air. He's going out of me ... down, down, through the hollow
of my body ... I can feel him!--going out of me. Shall I give him

back to the sky? Oh, yes! The sky so sad and empty. Down and still down.... Oh! Oh! Oh! Am I going into labor so soon? Look out! Here they come again! Five, four, three, two, one! Blast off! (She swats her hunch, sinks to the floor.) "You'll be landing on a crescent." That's what the computer said.... But he was born on the wane, older even than his mother.

SOL   The operation ... is successful!

(SUZIE crosses to MOON MOTHER, takes her hand.)

MOON MOTHER (grinning toothlessly)   He kissed me! A man is better than the moon!

SOL (crossing to MOON MOTHER, taking her hand)   The problem is, there are three of you and only one of me.... Mother, will you marry me?

MOON MOTHER   'Twould serve you right if I said Yes!

SOL   No!

MOON MOTHER   No.
Eternity
With the likes of me
Would prove too long a sentence
For your insincerity.

SOL   Wheww!

MOON MOTHER   "The most beautiful woman in the world." Fie! You lie. For I am old. You find my hunch horrible to behold--for all that little kiss you managed. Oh, for you it was a big kiss, I know ... but you'll never get beyond it.... Nor will any man.

SOL   It was a big enough kiss to get the moon out of you.

MOON MOTHER   So it was. But as for marriage! Try one of these young things, dearie.
As for me,
Tra la la lee,
I'll polish the past
Where he used to be.

(She crosses to the cage, rummages through the rags in her little red cart, chooses one, sits down, and begins to polish her hunch.)

SOL (to SUZIE)   I'd choose you, if you could learn to love yourself. (To CINDY.) And I'd choose you, if you weren't having a rainy day.

SUZIE   Cindy, you don't love yourself in the rain, do you?

CINDY (enthusiastically)   Oh, yes! The lovely pitter-patter of my little bitchinesses.

SOL (to CINDY)   I wouldn't love you if you weren't real enough to rain.

SUZIE (to CINDY)   But in the pitter-patter you're not perfect! (Realization.) Oh! You don't have to be perfect to love yourself.... Then that's it! All I have to do is accept the fact that I make with the pitter-patter a little more often! Wheee, I accept it!

SOL (out of character, joyfully)   Whee! Whee!

(He whirls her around. They stop, look at each other. Big bright glow in the sky--figuratively speaking, please.)

But ... I choose Cindy.

(The glow goes out. He crosses to CINDY. They kiss. The umbrella folds up--sad, funny--over their heads.)

CINDY (crossing to SUZIE and taking her hands)   Suzie,... Suzie, love -

SUZIE (stopping her, sarcastic)   And then there was this slightly sticky rainbow above the room above, on the corner of Cherry and Elsewhere.

CINDY   I know. Suzie,... will you ... (Embarrassed by the cliche.) Oh, dear ... will you ... come see us? That's where we'll be. In the room above the room above.

SUZIE (sadly, squeezing her friend's hand)   No, Cindy. No, I don't guess I will.

CINDY   Suzie,... (CINDY fades off.)

SOL   Suzie, when you come to see us, I want you to bring your work-- what you haven't finished.

SUZIE   Sol,... I said I wouldn't ever paint again.

SOL   Suzie,... (He goes to her, puts his hands on her shoulders. Then, to hide his feelings, he regresses to giving her hell.) And the next time you try sticking yourself in Saint Eugenia's--or suicide-- so I'll feel sorry for you ... remember, I won't.

(He leaves. For a while she just looks after him. Then she crosses slowly in the semi-darkness to the cage. Lights come up dimly on the cage. MOON MOTHER is still sitting in front of it, polishing her hump. Her cart is beside her--all her rags strewn around her in little piles.)

SUZIE (oh-so quiet)   Hey, Mother, it's just you and me.

MOON MOTHER (also very quiet)   Oh, have they gone?

SUZIE   Mother, I think maybe ... maybe ... I want to paint you.

MOON MOTHER   Me? A "monstrosity?"

SUZIE (still quiet--quiet until the end)   Oh, that awful night. Oh, Mother ... I ... I didn't know you then, and -

MOON MOTHER (loud, funny)   Quite all right, child. I once called a Wart Hog, a Wart Hog! (Sadly.) Of course, I apologized later.

SUZIE   I want to laugh, Mother, but....

(The most silence of all. SUZIE positions MOON MOTHER for a portrait.)

There. Just like that ... with all your rags around you.

(SUZIE goes to the empty frame and begins to paint, while MOON MOTHER sings. MOON MOTHER may fade off, pulling her wagon. Lights dim out during the street call at the end.)

MOON MOTHER
I walk alone
      through the wreckage of my friends.
They say I am to blame
      for the way it always ends.
Their hearts go to rags,
      one after the other,
And the cloth of good-bye
      is the saddest color.
Rags! Rags! Old rags to buy and sell! Old rags to buy and sell....

SANDCASTLE

A Play in One Act

By Barbara Allan Hite

CHARACTERS

Jerry
A Girl
Sam
Harry
First Woman
Second Woman
Cynthia

SCENE

A beach.

(Down center a large pile of sand; more sand by the boys' beach
blanket right; more up right of lifeguard stand. JERRY, sitting on
blanket right, is playing his guitar. The tune is played very well,
but is a simple one, even an improvisation, short, which he plays
twice. Near the end of the second playing, the GIRL and a boy run
in, teasing one another and laughing. JERRY puts down his guitar
on their entrance. Transistor radio sound. The GIRL is being chased
by her boyfriend SAM, and she is making a half-hearted effort to
push him back and get away.)

GIRL   Sammy, stop it!... Oh, Lord!...

(She falls against the lifeguard stand now, turns and gives him a
push away with both hands, almost overcome with laughter and exer-
tion.)

Help!

(She turns and runs off left. SAM recovers and follows, dropping
some stuff left. JERRY had put down his guitar on their entrance.
He has a wad of sand and after they leave, he bombs the remains of
yesterday's sandcastle, center, once, from his seat. He gets another
wad of sand, stands up and bombs it again. He goes to the castle,
picks up another sand ball and drops it like a real bomb, making
the bombing noise as it goes down. He picks up another handful
but walks with it left and stands for a count of five or so, staring
out, dripping sand through his fingers. He turns and does some fancy
stuff on the lifeguard stand, climbing up, sitting like the lifeguard

searching the water for drowning people, then finally leans back,
face up to the sun as the GIRL and SAM come back, hand in hand,
out of breath. They spread out their blanket, and she puts on a
bathing cap with flowers while he fixes the umbrella in place. Then
he gives her fanny a whack. JERRY looks for a moment, caught by
the sound.)

GIRL   Quit it, Sam. That hurt.

(They grab surfboards and leave. All is quiet for a moment. HARRY
comes in and sees JERRY in his position. He crosses up to the sand
pile up right and fixes a ball of sand with which he bombs JERRY's
stomach. JERRY after the first instant is not very surprised.)

JERRY   Harold, did I give you permission to use my sand? Did I
give you permission to use my stomach?

HARRY   Your mother said I could, Jer.

JERRY   You're a naughty boy, Hair. Suppose you got higher? (Indicating his mouth.)

HARRY   Would old friend and buddy, sharp-shootin' Hair, make such
a mistake--except on purpose, old friend and buddy?

(As HARRY bends to get some more sand, JERRY jumps him and they
wrestle a bit. They finish and lie there out of breath.)

JERRY   And it used to be so peaceful here.

HARRY   Peace is for the protest marchers.

JERRY   What time is it?

HARRY   Exactly 10:15 by my very own Jack-the-Ripper spy watch.
I was the first kid on my block. Honest, Jer. Scout's honor.

JERRY   You're late.

HARRY (gets up, restless, as he is, brushing sand off)   My aunt
and uncle ... (Depressed about this.) come last night. And my little
cousin Cynthia. (British accent.) Dear little Cousin Cynthia. You
know, old man, the dreamy type. (Fed up.) Emily Dickinson in person.

JERRY   By Jove, I say, we're in for a jolly week.

HARRY   This place gets duller every year. Maybe it's me, old buddy,
lagging behind the times. My mother says she's at the end of her
rope. I should get a job, or something to do. (He sits on blanket,
plunks guitar.)

JERRY (starting to get up, brushing off sand)   You want to build
up the fort again? I started on it earlier, but it wasn't going
very well. It needs you, Hair.

HARRY   Come off it, Jer. I mean something real to do. You know?

JERRY   That was OK yesterday.

HARRY   Yesterday was a real jewel of dullness, Jer. I'm putting
my past behind me. Starting fresh. The life of excitement and adventure. How about that, Jer? After all, I've already got my very
own spy watch?

JERRY   OK, everybody, let's get this sand out of here. Brother
Hair has had enough. In one day he's exhausted the possibilities
of the entire bathing area. The sand holds no charm for Brother
Hair today. He wants to go back to ... to dirt ... or gravel.
Right, Hair? Big Man Stuff?

HARRY   Cut it off, Jer. You know what I mean.

JERRY   Hey, Big Man, I know what. We could take that pile of sand
and reconstruct Las Vegas. How about that, and build poker tables ...
and roulette wheels...?

HARRY   I'm leaving in three minutes. Getting up and walking out.

(A bit of silence. They stretch out, facing the ocean--audience.)

JERRY   Why don't you go for a swim, Hair? Build up the old manly
muscles?

HARRY   I did that earlier.

(Another brief pause.)

JERRY   Tickle ticks. Toothless Tom's tender and tasty tickle ticks
take time to toast tender.

HARRY   Good. That's very good. Did it just come to you just like
that?

JERRY   Actually I've been thinking about that one for hours. But
waiting for the right psychological moment, which is so important,
as well you know.

HARRY   It lifts my spirits, Jer. Truly. Dapper Dan. Dainty Dapper
Dan's dilly doodle dots do double duty daily.

JERRY   Good!

HARRY   Not so good. I had a better one in bed last night, but I forgot it.

JERRY   There. Did you see that? A porpoise. (On knees, looking.)
Where're the damn binoculars? There must be a school. It's really
calm today ... out ... way out. Free.... You know when you're in
bed Sunday morning with nothing really planned for the day but church ...
with pancakes and the funny papers. Do you get that feeling of la-
ziness?

HARRY   Cripes, Jer, cut it off. I want to do something.

JERRY   Can't you feel like you're doing something just being here?
(Feeling sand.)

HARRY   Jer, are you getting duller every year too?

JERRY   You know, I read that dolphins are probably as smart or
smarter than people like you, Hair.

HARRY   No kidding? A truly valuable bit of information. I should
take up reading myself and learn many new and belittling topics of
conversation. Better still I'd like to meet one of those fish in
the scales.

JERRY   No scales, Hair.

HARRY   Ah ha, no scales.

JERRY   What they lack in scales, they make up for in grey matter,
Hair. Don't judge a book -

HARRY   Hey there, you out there, what's your I.Q., old buddy?

JERRY   Ask him how he is at writing a term paper ...

HARRY   Or doing a science project.

JERRY   A Study of Underwater Living, based on personal observations.

HARRY   Did you ever get to see Little Janie Simpleton Morris' project for Science 1A? The most darling little kittens doing all
sorts of tricks. She trained them all by herself. Probably even
had 'em all by herself.

JERRY   Hair. You never took Biology 4 yet.

HARRY   Sex Stimulation? Me? You're kidding. That'd be like sending
that dolphin to swimming classes. (They are both giggling.) You
see, what happened was the guidance counselor suggested it, but I
convinced her it'd be a waste of time, and I haven't heard another
word from her since.

JERRY (following his lead)   Nope, but you ended up in King's office and tried the same thing on him ...

HARRY   And ended up at the school board where they asked me to
teach the class next year after observing a skillful demonstration
of my techniques.

JERRY   But you told them you'd already signed up to give Liz Taylor
a cram course next year. (They laugh.)

HARRY   Did you take that class? (JERRY nods.) You're kidding!
After dating Little Annie Hoffman?

JERRY   Listen, Little Annie Hoffman's a cheap date. She's a little
nothing.

HARRY   Well, no dried-up egghead is going to teach you sex. Typical.
Typical of a man who's all theory and no practice. Jer, you've got
to let yourself go. You've got to use the words and they'll loosen
you up for life.

JERRY   My, my, did you think that up all by yourself, Hair? "Loosen
up for life." Sounds like an ad for mineral oil or something.

(Silence. JERRY fiddles with the guitar. HARRY gets up and finishes
knocking down the fort with his foot.)

HARRY   Well, tell me about it.

JERRY   What?

HARRY   The course--Biology 4--for God's sake.

JERRY   Don't say "for God's sake," Hair.

HARRY   Sheeze. You have to play that thing so slow? What the
heck ... Why not? Everybody likes a funeral now and then. (He
opens up his shirt, sticks out his chest.) Come on, sun--ultraviolet
rays, blast this pearly white chest here. I could at least get a tan,
if I don't do anything else. (He sits, puts his hands back in a pile
of shells.) What in God's name are these? (He has sort of jumped
up on his knees to examine them, fanny to audience.)

JERRY   Shells.

HARRY   Jerry (Turns back around.), there're millions of these kind
of shells on the beach. Why didn't you pick up some unusual ones,
for God's sake? If you're going to go around gathering sea shells,
you might get some good ones.

JERRY   I liked these. I liked the colors. Besides, what difference does it make?

HARRY   You act like some little kid when you come to the beach.

"See the funny fishes, see the pretty shells." A bunch of crummy
shells. How long did it take you to find them? Two minutes? What
are you going to do with them? Make valuable jewelry, make millions
of dollars? (Holding them and letting them drop.)

JERRY (throws the shells away during the following lines) You're
really getting to hack me off, Hair. You sit there waiting for the
world to move in and surprise you, and it's all got to be very large.
Look. (Handful of sand.) Feel that. The feel of that. It's just
something to feel it. But what're you going to do with it? You
can't do anything with it, really. Well, you could, I guess....

HARRY   Sure. Truck it out. Sell it to sandbox owners.

JERRY   But that's not what I mean. I mean ... like ... that it
doesn't matter whether you can do anything with it or not if you
just like to feel it in your hand, when you have time to, like now
when you don't want to do anything else with it. (Giving up.)
Crap, I don't know what I mean.

HARRY (dripping sand on JERRY's head)   You're a nut, you know it?

JERRY (shaking head)   Cut it out, Hair. I'm not in the mood.

HARRY   Don't you like the feel of that, Plato? Doesn't that sand
feel good when you don't have anything else to do? (He stops, then
shoves his heels up and back in the sand like one of those sports
cars.) Baroom, vrum, vrum.

JERRY (gets up)   That's it. What you need is a motorcycle and you
can get on it and ride away to nowhere. With the rest of them.
That's what those guys do. You know, they just ride away ... anywhere ... for the heck of it. They could just go around and around
the same block, and it wouldn't bother them a bit.

HARRY   That's it. Because it's the feeling they get from it. Pure
feeling. What's wrong with that? It's just like your sand deal.
That's true, isn't it?

JERRY   Yeah, I guess it is. (Thinks.) No, I don't think it is,
because in that situation, with the motorcycle, you have the idea
of the noise of the motor, and this is so loud that the person riding
couldn't possibly hear anything else. Maybe he wouldn't even be
able to think of anything else, so that he'd sort of be like in a
trance effect or under a spell. And that, you see, would be cutting
the world out, which wouldn't be th same thing as the sand. The
sand itself is really there in the world. That's the very part of
it that makes it important.

HARRY   You're right. The cycle has a power more like a spell.
At least that's the way I feel it. But still, I wouldn't mind
having one. (Joking again.) And leave this world behind. (Starting
up a pretend motor and going off.) It's better than dope.

JERRY   Remember that time with the jeep? And we'd ride right at
the water edge?

HARRY   I like a jeep. I wouldn't call it a car though.

JERRY   It's too cute.

HARRY   Yeah, it's in another class entirely.

JERRY   People would really panic when they'd look up and see that
thing coming through.

HARRY   It could really take the sand, I'll say that for it.

(Pause.)

JERRY   Maybe we could get the boat today.

HARRY   Yeah. Good thought.

JERRY   Now or when?

HARRY   Not this A.M. This A.M. is for being nice to Cousin Cynthia.
In case she can't find the ocean, I'm supposed to show her up and
down like a good boy.

JERRY   Great. If she's here all week, that'll sure give you something to do, Hair. Something wonderful to do. Something you can
find really rewarding, if you know what I mean.

HARRY (he doesn't know yet)   Yeah, I always wanted to be a tour
guide.

JERRY   Hair, that's not what I mean. Listen, I'll just fade away
into the sunset, leaving you and Cousin Cynthia to explore the wonders of nature here in these ideal natural surroundings. (Gestures
toward SAM and GIRL's stuff.) Everybody's doing it, Hair.

HARRY   Very funny, Gerald.

JERRY   Oh, I won't resent being cast aside, Hair. (Dramatic and
very noble.) I've always known that someday the inevitable would
come to pass, the end of a beautiful friendship.... It couldn't
go on as it was forever, Harold. All good things must end in time.
My dear friend. My dear, dear friend. Adios, but not good-bye.

HARRY   Don't be such as ass, Jerry. (He gets up and goes to the
sand pile up right where his hat had fallen during the wrestling.
He has been made nervous.) Boy, you do, you really do take the
cake.

JERRY (over his shoulder)   The opportunity you always spoke of,
Hair. Now isn't that right?

HARRY   Cousin Cynthia, Jerry? Listen, I'm not in the mood to have
this girl or any girl come down here and ruin this vacation. (While
brushing the sand from his hat, he knocks the feather out and has
to replace it.)

JERRY   Well, don't get all riled up about it. (Turns to HARRY.)

HARRY   Who's getting riled up? I'm just being emphatic about it,
that's all. (He goes to the lifeguard stand and hangs his hat up.)
I just mean what I say. No girls.

JERRY   Well, but last summer you were always saying -

HARRY   That was different. This whole thing I had nothing to with,
and I do not care for these forced kinds of arrangements. (Pause.)
Besides, Cousin Cynthia is a deadpan. Absolutely. She's not my
type.

JERRY   You mean she's not flashy enough.

HARRY (really getting angry)   What do you mean by that little sarcastic remark? Boy, you're so smart. It must be hard to live in
the world with all the dumbbells. How do you do it? You must be
wonderful, huh? Wonderful. I'm going back up.

JERRY   Wait, Hair. I was just kidding.

HARRY   Yeah.

JERRY   No kidding. I didn't mean it. (Change-up.) But I had an
idea.

HARRY   Wonderful.

JERRY   I had the idea that maybe it wouldn't be very pleasant for
her down here on the beach.

HARRY   For her? I'm not thinking about her.

JERRY   I mean it really might be very unpleasant for her....

HARRY (catching on)   Oh, like the nix treatment?

JERRY   Like the nix treatment. But very subtle. You don't want
to cause a family feud.

HARRY   Boy, will we ever be subtle. You know what I think of ...
you know that fat kid last year with the red bathing suit?

JERRY   "You guys want to take a turn on my big red surfboard?"
Poor Norman Goose. "You guys want to borrow my neatsie new swim
flippers?" But that wasn't too subtle.

HARRY   Well, he was like oysters to get out. Besides we're older.
We'll be ultra-subtle now. (He's getting all excited with the pros-
pects.) Snap this picture: Cousin Cynthia will be brushing her
long golden hair, on the beach, where it's very sandy.

JERRY   Aww, that's too bad, but, say, we'll help you wash it out....

HARRY   Hold still, Cousin Cynthia, salt water is very good for the
hair. Like egg and beer.... Do you happen to have some egg and
beer, Jer?

JERRY   Sure thing. I just happen to, all right.

HARRY   Aww, Jer, you're supposed to break the egg before....

JERRY   Shucks. Us boys mean well. (They are laughing now.)

HARRY   Lord, that's too much!

JERRY   Maybe Cousin Cynthia will be drinking a coke on the beach,
where it's very sandy.... (HARRY is laughing so hard he can't speak.)
What? In your coke? Gee, I wish you didn't feel that way. Some
people think it improves the flavor.

HARRY   Improves the flavor!...

JERRY   'Course, you're entitled to your own opinion. Well, try
to think of it like this: Cokes are pretty fattening anyway....
Oh, of course, I don't mean you are -

HARRY   You are! Fat! Fat! Oh, that's too much!

JERRY   Sensational sand!

HARRY   You said you couldn't use it!

JERRY   Wow!

HARRY   Down the bathing suit pants ...

JERRY   Down the bathing suit top....

HARRY   And so Cousin Cynthia will say to her Daddy, "I'd like to
go home now, sir. Those boys are just too mean." "What boys, little
Cynthia, dear?" "Those mean old boys on the beach with the sand,
Daddy." "Oh, my poor little girl. Let Daddy kiss away that hurt
place."

JERRY   Tender family scene.

HARRY   Wait till the next scene. My mother comes in. "Now, Harold,
about that sand you and Gerald are playing with...." "Aw, Mommsie,
you know how carefully Gerald and I play with our sand." "I know

you wouldn't do anything dangerous on purpose, Son, but you know
how scary little girls are, so couldn't you find some other way to
amuse yourselves?" "Well, of course, there's always our swords."
"I knew I could count on you, Son. Have fun now and be <u>careful</u>."

(A mock swordfight, and they lie back laughing as TWO WOMEN come
walking by, left to right.)

<u>FIRST WOMAN</u>   So, as it was, I said to myself: you're enjoying
none of the advantages of a double bed and all of the disadvantages
you could possibly dream of. And, Harriet, I made up my mind then
and there.

<u>SECOND WOMAN</u>   Well, but I think it's so unsettling to make such
a major household change.

<u>FIRST WOMAN</u>   Not so unsettling as a divorce, Harriet. And a lot
less wearing on the nerves. I've been through both, as well you
know, Harriet, and I speak from that experience. You'll find it's
the best solution by far.

<u>SECOND WOMAN</u>   Well, I guess you're right. But I know I'll feel
sooo ... funny ... I mean, how do you ... bring it up? I mean, what
do you <u>say</u>?

<u>FIRST WOMAN</u>   Oh, there are all sorts of reasons you can give.
Illness is only the most common. Personally, I think, and I've tried
several, Harriet, but I think your best approach is to approach it
from his standpoint. You know what I mean? You might begin by
saying, you know, how hard he works and you've noticed he's seemed
a bit tired recently and it occurred to you that he might not be
sleeping well.... Make it seem like a sacrifice that you're making
for him. That way he can hardly help agreeing to <u>try</u> it, and, in
my experience, once the switch is made, it's made for good.

<u>SECOND WOMAN</u> (as they leave on the right)   Well, I guess you're
right.

(HARRY has started rolling back and forth just as they leave.)

<u>JERRY</u>   What in the world are you doing?

<u>HARRY</u> (giggling)   I'm trying to get an even tan....

<u>JERRY</u>   You know, seriously, down where the samd is packed would
be a darn good place to throw knives.

<u>HARRY</u>   Yeah. I guess so.

(CYNTHIA's voice calling from offstage left: "Harold.")

<u>HARRY</u>   Here we go. (He turns over, face away from the sound.)

JERRY Don't go and get depressed now, Hair. You've got to keep your wits up and we'll play it by ear. OK?

(Neither really looks up or at CYNTHIA as she comes in. Is it taking the easy way out to rely on the actress for basic appeal? It's probably a necessity, for speech does not make a young girl lovely. What she says can help or detract, but we all know it's herself that's desirable or not. So let her smile be fantastic and, otherwise, let her not be so physically abundant as to call attention there; let her not be too blonde or, let's say, too anything. And the over-all effect must give at least a hint of innocence and purity.)

CYNTHIA Harold?

(She comes over to the blanket and then circles it to the far side where HARRY is. He turns slightly, but still doesn't really look at her. She is used to this kind of treatment, avoiding eye contact, though in front of the family he would at least hold his head in her general direction. So she is not at first hurt by his lack of greeting. But as minutes go by, and with the other boy there, it becomes painful to her.)

Hi.

(They both mumble something.)

Your mother said she thought you were down here.

(There is no real response. She waits a moment, then turns and moves up to the lifeguard stand to look out to see better.)

You can see a long way out.

(She comes back to the blanket.)

You can see such a long way out from up there.

(JERRY is the first to look at her and he does so during HARRY's line.)

HARRY Oh, yeah, a really long way out. (This is as close as he can openly come to playing his game.)

CYNTHIA I haven't seen the ocean for a long time. There's really something about it.... It's so ... big.

HARRY (under his breath) It's so big. Sheeze.

(CYNTHIA moves over to what was the sandcastle and absently pushes sand up with her foot, patting and fixing it, looking out at the ocean some.)

CYNTHIA I'd forgotten what a feeling it gives you.

HARRY   Oh, man. "What a feeling...."   (He slurs "feeling" in an
ugly way. Silence. CYNTHIA kneels by the castle, her back to them.)

JERRY (finally)   That was yesterday's project.

(She looks at him. She was about to cry. They look for a count of
three, that must seem like years to HARRY. She looks away.)

CYNTHIA   What was it?

JERRY (getting up)   Just a castle.

CYNTHIA   One of the drip kind with the water?

JERRY (moving to the castle)   No, just a regular kind. Squared
off sides and towers.

HARRY (breaking in)   Hey, Jer, Nipper Nix never knots necessary
needle nits ... knowing none need ... knotting.

JERRY (trying a reply)   Petie Pepper puts pretty ... piping pots ...

HARRY   Upon passionate piles ... pouring plenty purple ... pee.

(CYNTHIA rises and turns away upstage to the lifeguard stand again.)

Jer, lets go check on the boat now.

JERRY   You said this afternoon.   (He starts working on the castle.)

HARRY   We don't know if we can get it. (No reply. HARRY rises
and comes over, whispering.) Come on, Jer. Let's get out of here.
Come on.

JERRY   Hair.   (Looks toward CYNTHIA and indicates.)   It's not right.

HARRY   Who said anything about right. I think we should go.

JERRY   I don't want to go yet. I just got here.   (Working again
on castle.)

HARRY   You make me sick.   (He is angry. Goes back to the blanket
to sulk.)

CYNTHIA (coming back down)   Maybe I'll go back up and change. It's
awfully hot ... maybe I should ... go back up....

JERRY   You want to work on this some?

CYNTHIA   Well, I.... You probably know how you want it ... better.

JERRY   If you don't want to....

CYNTHIA   It must have been huge.

JERRY   It was pretty big, I guess. At least it took a lot of destruction.

CYNTHIA   It's funny. We always used to build them up again every day, too. Even if you know they won't last high tide and the night.

JERRY   Or some six-year-old.

CYNTHIA (starts working)   It'd be a boy, though. You'd never see a girl jump on a castle. You know how they do it ... with both feet.

JERRY   Hair and I used to throw sand bombs at ours. A slow and painful death we made.

CYNTHIA   How can you want to work so hard at it, scraping each side and being so careful and then only to ruin it? I never could understand it.

(HARRY throws a sand bomb at this point. She looks at him. JERRY keeps working.)

JERRY   Not yet, Hair, not yet.

CYNTHIA   I always want to keep things.

(Pause.)

Is this right? (Indicating what she has made.) What did you have it be?

JERRY   Yesterday it was the Alhambra and some days it's the Alamo. We really don't know too many castles and things.

CYNTHIA   Well, why would it have to be any real place?

(He looks at her, a look of pure wonderment, not disgust. The woman has moved in.)

JERRY   I don't know; I like to have something in mind. It gives more of a purpose to it.

CYNTHIA   I've never seen it.

JERRY   The Alhambra? You must have seen a picture of it in your Lit book.

CYNTHIA   Washington Irving.

JERRY   Anyway, the object is not to try to copy a place exactly. The place is just supposed to give you a sort of general idea. I never saw it either.

CYNTHIA   I think there is a very elaborate inner part like a garden, but it has a special name.

JERRY   Patio.

CYNTHIA   It has fountains.

JERRY   I don't know, but that can be your project, right off the south end there, and I'm going to do this larger main structure, here.

CYNTHIA   I might put flowers and shrubs and trees in there.

JERRY   Good. Listen, money is no object. We've got to have the best there is. We've got to spare no expense and cut no corners. And that's an order. Hey, you know, that's an idea I never thought of ... rounding the corners. It'd be a great effect, really different. Hey, Hair, let's try that ... listen, what about rounding off all the corners and have no square or rectangular shapes in the whole thing? Hair? What d'you think? Come here a minute.

(HARRY moves over slowly.)

Look, this is really new. You can form it like this easily enough. Now, snap the mental picture. What d'you think?

HARRY   It needs trimming.

JERRY   Yeah, right--a spoon might work. We're going to need some more equipment. A spoon and a knife. Maybe a cup. Be right back. (He exits left.)

(A pause. She works; HARRY watches.)

CYNTHIA   Don't you want to do something to help?

(No answer.)

What was that he called you, Harry?

HARRY (mumbling)   Never mind.

CYNTHIA   It sounded like just "Hair."

HARRY   What's wrong with that?

CYNTHIA   Nothing. It's fine. (No more response.) You didn't tell me his name and I was wondering what it is.

HARRY (still unwilling)   Jerry.

12

CYNTHIA   Jerry? Jerry what?

HARRY   Jerry Compson.

CYNTHIA   Oh. He's the one. You told me about him. I remember now.

HARRY   Yeah, he's the one, but, you know, he goes with this girl down the beach now. I mean there're quite a few he goes with, but this one ... down the beach ... he likes the best. She's something else. You'll probably like her. Maybe you'll meet her ... some time....

CYNTHIA   Is she my age? I really would like to meet another girl my age while we're here. I know your mother keeps telling you that I'm your guest and everything and how you should make sure I'm not, I suppose you would say, bored, but you know, you don't have to think of me that way, as a guest, and you don't have to entertain me. Of course, if there were another girl it would be easier. On you, I mean.

HARRY   Now that I think of it, ah, I think she said she was going to be out of town for awhile, for a couple of weeks ... actually....

CYNTHIA   Oh.

HARRY   Yeah. That's too bad.

CYNTHIA   Harry? That doesn't sound like ... it sounds like you're making that up.

HARRY   All right, if that's what you think, just go ahead and think it. It won't hurt me. You're the one. Just go ahead and think it.

CYNTHIA   I don't know why you're being so ... so....

HARRY   Now what have I done? I'm going back up.

(JERRY enters.)

JERRY   Look at this. I got some knives and a spatula to trim with and some jars and cans. I don't know how they'll work. (He dumps it all out.)

HARRY   I'm going back up.

JERRY   Come on, Hair, you have to do the bridges. He's our expert on bridges and all such joiners ... expansions ... suspensions. Come on, Hair. We'll need something at least, here and there. You can decide. Come on. Let's try a jar tower and see what it does. (HARRY joins in halfheartedly.) You have to pack it pretty tight.

CYNTHIA (indicating her jar tower)   That's a rough effect.

JERRY   You didn't pack it tight enough.

CYNTHIA   I like that rough effect.

JERRY   Well, it could look like stones on the top. Maybe that's better.

HARRY   Oh, hell, Jer. Crap. (He gets up and goes back to the blanket. In a moment he picks up the guitar and messes around with it.)

CYNTHIA (after a pause)   I suppose it is childish.

JERRY   What?

CYNTHIA   Childish. Playing in the sand.

JERRY   It can be (Indicating HARRY.) if you let it be. Your walls should be rounded, too.

CYNTHIA   Oh. Yes.

JERRY   This way. See. That way. That's a good double tier you did.

CYNTHIA   Oh.

JERRY   Hair, don't fool with the guitar.

CYNTHIA   Is it yours? Have you had lessons?

JERRY   Yes and no. It is mine, though you'd never realize it, but I haven't had any lessons yet. I just play naturally, is what you'd say. Naturally bad is what Hair says. For a nonconformist, Hair is not very original. He's getting to be pretty obnoxious though. (Getting up.) Leave the guitar alone, Hair. (Crossing to him.) What's the matter with you? You know I don't like that.

HARRY (hissing)   What is the matter with you?

JERRY   What?

HARRY (indicating CYNTHIA)   What d'you think you're doing?

JERRY (squatting down)   Look, Hair. I felt stupid not talking to her when she came. Don't you think she felt anything? Don't you think she's ... she's trying not to be in the way?

HARRY   So? Big deal. In the way is in the way.

JERRY   But it's not like the fat guy because he was trying to be an intruder and that's the difference.

HARRY   Oh, sure, that's the elephantine difference all right.

JERRY   I mean, what's wrong with her? She's your cousin.

HARRY   If you don't know, I can't tell you.

(Pause. CYNTHIA is uncomfortable.)

CYNTHIA   I'm going to get some flowers for the garden. (She leaves.)

HARRY   Yeah, look at that. A harmless little creature, all right. Little feathery bird with her ways. Flutter, flutter. Picking your eyes out when you're not looking.

JERRY   You'd probably never even notice that beak.

HARRY   I'm not about to be taken in by her.

JERRY   It's not being taken in, Hair. It's just that you reach a certain point where you start to feel odd when you treat someone like that. I mean, ignore them just for no reason.

HARRY   So.... You reach a certain point. And exactly when do you reach this certain point, Jer? Listen, I'm sick of being ... of you implying things, such as maybe poor old Hair hasn't reached the same glorious and high-level point as the chosen ones. I mean it. I'm fed up. All morning you've been talking like that, and if you'd only let me give my side of it, you'd hear my side.

JERRY   OK, OK.

HARRY   I do not want to become involved, and I've given a lot of thought to this. This is what will happen if we try to include her. Pretty soon she'll be giving suggestions and the next thing will be an argument, then with both of us turning against her, she'll feel worse than if we just let her alone in the beginning. You see? Girls can't stand to be beaten. She'd probably even cry, and you know that would not be a good thing.

JERRY   Well, maybe we could make an agreement not to pay any attention to her ideas. I mean, include her up to a point.

HARRY   But that's not the only thing. Suppose we ourselves have an argument and she decides to join up with one or the other, like that time with that kid, Bunky Simpson. Remember what a neat guy he was? And then by the end of the week you and I weren't speaking to each other.

JERRY   That was three years ago, and besides there was this sort of competition going.

HARRY   Not only that, but girls as opposed to boys cause other problems,
too. Because they just don't know how to join in with certain activities. Take the boat, for instance. Look at my mother in the boat.
There she is, squealing and jumping around and not knowing even
where to put her big toe down.

JERRY   I know, Hair, but it all comes down to ... frankly, I don't
see how we have any choice though. We're either going to act like
morons or try to work something out in a mature fashion.

HARRY   Ye gods, cripes in Heaven.   There you go again--Victor
Mature.   (Rises.)

JERRY (rising also)   Well, hell, it's true. Didn't you feel stupid
when we weren't talking to her at first? You must have felt stupid.
What did you feel?

HARRY   How should I know?

JERRY   Did it seem natural to you?

HARRY   Listen, she'd have gotten the idea in a short time, and it
would have been all over.

JERRY   Hair, how are you going to eat breakfast every morning?
She's here for the week. She's staying in your place. You can't
ignore her and you know it. So what I don't see is, why fight it?

HARRY   Thanks old buddy, friend. Do you charge by the hour?

JERRY   Boy, you're an impossible case.

(They turn away from each other, in a mood. The TWO WOMEN walk by
again, right to left.)

FIRST WOMAN   Poor Harriet, I told you it wouldn't take long to
reach that stage. Where's the suntan oil, dear? I definitely feel
a burn coming and that stuff of yours--how much did you say you paid
for it, two-fifty? It was a gyp, Harriet. For two-fifty you got
what appears to be caramel-colored water. Your oil is your best
burn preventative and has been since I was a girl. I hope it's
not too late.

(During the next sequence they stop by the lifeguard stand and
apply suntan oil.)

SECOND WOMAN   I think now that "make love" isn't even the right
term. Love has nothing to do with what he does ... to me ... with
me. But we're both awfully busy ... and tired, you know, tired at
night. When it's ... late....

FIRST WOMAN   How often have I heard that sad song. Do my back, will you please, dear?

SECOND WOMAN   But what ... I mean, what ... can you do?

FIRST WOMAN   Well, of course, in your case, Harriet, you have all those children, and my experience fails me in that area. But from what I've heard said, once you have children, you have limited your possibilities to a very great extent.

SECOND WOMAN   And last night, after the party, it was the first time ... I turned away from him....

FIRST WOMAN   Harriet, you're a martyr. (She finishes herself.)

SECOND WOMAN   You see I do have to get up early with the baby.

FIRST WOMAN   Of course you do. Do my back, will you please, dear?

(They remain up by lifeguard stand, putting on oil.)

HARRY   I'm not ignoring her anyway. I told her right off, cut the scene, Baby, go home and become a blonde. Use Listerine. You know, she wanted to know your name. What's in a name, I said, a man's a man. Anything with pants, I'd say, or maybe better without pants. She wouldn't care what name it was.

JERRY   I can hear you now, Sophisticated Sam.

HARRY   OK, buddy, you be nice. You be really nice. Is that it, Jer? Then she'll be really nice and, crap, I can see you two holding hands down the sand, strolling lovers of the beach. Is that it, Jerry? Crap, you creep, is that it? (Grabs JERRY.) You never laid hands on a girl, so here's one you can't get off your hands. Jerry? Is that it?

JERRY   I'm sick of listening to you, Hair.

HARRY   A bird in the hand. Aw, Jerry, crap.

JERRY   Cut it off, Hair. Now. I mean it.

HARRY   You're going to do that, you're going to do it, Jerry. We were planning, and all the time you were thinking....

JERRY   It's not true, Hair. I was planning too; I wasn't thinking.

HARRY   You make me sick, do you know it?

(He leaves. The GIRL and SAM come back, GIRL first. She is removing her bathing cap; he is sort of trying to goose her with the surfboard. They fall on the blanket and he begins to towel her dry. She, in mock protest, attempts to pour suntan lotion on his head.

They fall back in an embrace. JERRY doesn't notice; he stares off
where HARRY has gone.)

SECOND WOMAN   There. (Finishes back.)

FIRST WOMAN   Whew, it's hot. (She closes her eyes and smooths some
oil on her face. A slight pause.)

SECOND WOMAN   It was late, two o'clock. You know. I just couldn't....

FIRST WOMAN   Of course you couldn't. He shouldn't expect it.

SECOND WOMAN (slight pause as she recaps the bottle to move on)   We've
both forgiven each other so much.

(FIRST WOMAN has moved on ahead. Now SECOND WOMAN catches up with
her.)

FIRST WOMAN   I want to get as black as an ape.

SECOND WOMAN   I'm afraid I'm going to freckle again.

(CYNTHIA enters with flowers, bits of greenery.)

CYNTHIA   What happened to Harry? I saw him leave, but that's not
too unusual, I guess.

JERRY (looking off after HARRY; he answers slowly because it has
shaken him up)   He was really upset.

CYNTHIA   You two did have something planned, didn't you?

JERRY   Not really. It was nothing important. (He **sits** again.)

CYNTHIA   I'm sorry ... if it was because of me.

JERRY   I think it was because of Hair.

(Pause.)

I don't like to plan things on a vacation anyway.

CYNTHIA (she is slightly nervous)   Sometimes I hate vacations. I
mean when you get all those **travel** folders and then someone says if
we have lunch by 12 we can do the Mariner's Museum at 1 and be finished
in time to see them feeding the fish at 4 and on and on. Like a school
bus tour. That's the way my mother does it, and you'd think she
was starved for activity.

JERRY   She ought to get together with Hair. Do you want to sit
down?

CYNTHIA   I know he doesn't care to have me here. (Another brief

pause; then she sits down, carefully. She looks out to sea.) Do
the gulls catch fish or some other sea animals when they dive?

JERRY   I don't know. Fish, I think.

CYNTHIA   They make an ugly sound.... We have a mocking bird at
home who sits on the highest place he can find, either the TV an-
tenna or this tree next door, and there's such a great spirit about
him. He sort of reminds me of a cheerleader. I think he really
likes to entertain people and have someone watching him. And the
funniest thing is that one of the songs he does is a whistle my
mother uses to call us home by.

JERRY   He sings the same thing?

CYNTHIA   It's just three notes. (She whistles.)

JERRY   I never heard of something like that.

CYNTHIA (talking partly to herself) He's really so proud. He sits
there and sometimes he opens his wings a little or flies up in the
air a little way so you can be sure and notice the white on his
wings and not mistake which bird he is. You know, he makes me feel
so glad sometimes. I'll hear him start off while I'm doing the
dishes or something in the kitchen, and I just have to go out to
meet him. Sometimes I just feel like everything inside of me would
like to touch him and hold him. But sometimes he gives me a feeling ...
like a huge tear was swallowing me up, and so that there wouldn't
even be any point in crying.

(Pause.)

You're probably thinking, "Ugh, girls," but you know, it's a very
strange feeling. Look, he does have a fish!

JERRY   Sometimes I feel that way when I'm playing the guitar.

CYNTHIA   Oh.

JERRY   I don't play well or anything. It's just ... something ...
that happens.

CYNTHIA   Do you ever play for people?

JERRY   Oh, sure, I'm really a big recording star. (His tone changes,
the act he thinks she'd expect...?) Well, now, say, what do you do
for a living?

CYNTHIA (caught off-guard)   What?

JERRY   Well, for excitement this summer. I mean, a cute girl like
you doesn't spend all her time listening to mockingbirds, I hope.

CYNTHIA   Oh, that.

JERRY   Don't you go out a lot at home? Dance, take in a movie now and then. There's not much in the way of commercial entertainment down here, I know, and to Hair this is a terrible drawback, but I keep telling him he should learn to make his own entertainment. You know? We could get up something to do.

CYNTHIA   I think it's fun for a change ... not to have a lot to do. I mean, for a change it's nice.

JERRY   Well, you don't want to stagnate. We could probably get up a beach party one night while you're here. (He has never been to one so far.) Maybe even a couple. That'd be different.

CYNTHIA   Aren't they a lot of trouble?

JERRY   Not as far as I'm concerned.

CYNTHIA   Well, if you think ... but I don't know anybody down here. I mean, those parties are ... you have to have a group of friends for it to be ... for it to be fun, don't you think?

JERRY   Come on, girl, loosen up for life, and meet new people. Don't worry, we'll fix it up; we'll have a fire. We could cook hot dogs and even dance. Wouldn't you like that?

CYNTHIA   Well, I guess it is the thing to do at the beach. (She moves to lifeguard stand, takes a mock pose.) Where are all the nightclubs to entertain me?

JERRY (bowing)   We're having them built as quickly as possible, your majesty.

CYNTHIA   Not quick enough! Off with your head!

JERRY (grabbing his neck)   Augh! (After recovery.) Have you ever been to a beach party?

CYNTHIA   I guess everyone has at one time or another.

JERRY   I'll have to think who we could have. It's true you have to have the right group.

CYNTHIA   You must know a lot of people by now.

JERRY   Actually, Hair and I have kept pretty much to ourselves most of the time. Say, but we do know a guy with a motorcycle. Have you ever ridden one?

CYNTHIA   No.

JERRY   Man, that's adventure for anyone.

CYNTHIA   I imagine it's pretty dangerous in the sand.

JERRY   Yeah. Skids. Actually it probably wouldn't be safe for you.

CYNTHIA   I could just watch.

JERRY   Sure. You could do that. I hope he's here now. His family usually comes in August.

CYNTHIA   Oh.

JERRY   We do have a boat here. Hair's father is letting us use it for the summer. That's what we're going to do this afternoon. I bet you'd like that, skimming over the water. It's fast, twelve horsepower.

CYNTHIA   I don't know if Hair.... Well, if you had planned, the two of you, to go....

JERRY   Don't worry so much about Hair. He'll be all right.

CYNTHIA   I don't know him that well, you see. But when I have been with him, in the past, that is, at our house or his, he's always seemed ... like a nice person. (Pause.) Of course, my mother warned me that boys do at times hate girls. At stages, you know. And try to tease them. (Pause. JERRY fingers sand.) I really don't need a lot of things to do all the time. (Pause. She looks out to sea.) Just blue, on and on. It's like the future. I mean, you know fish and things are in there, in the water, and solid land on the other side. But from here you can't see anything. So you forget to look for it.

JERRY   There is a strange experience about it even when the water is calm, and when there's a storm ... it's so ... wild ... that sometimes I want to join in with it. I mean, it's like I feel pulled into it. It's beautiful, too, and you feel like you can't stop it.

CYNTHIA (excited)   That's true. I think it's frightening because it's such a mixture of feelings, and you can't get them all sorted out. But if you jumped into it, maybe you would know what it is ... maybe that's why you feel like that.

(Pause.)

(With binoculars.) If I get these adjusted right, we can see the gulls and how they fish. But I can't get a clear picture. Doesn't each person have to find his own setting?

JERRY   I had them pretty well adjusted this morning. (He takes them.) There were some dolphins out there. (Fixes them, gives them back.) You shouldn't have to change them too much now.

CYNTHIA   Yes. Oh.

(They are embarrassed as he has had to put his arms around her neck
to put the binoculars back. There is a slight pause.)

JERRY   Say, do you want to walk down the beach?

CYNTHIA (looks at him, thinking of his girl)   No, I don't think
so.

JERRY   There's a stand down a way we could get a coke. (Rises.)
Let's do. We'll take the transistor. Come on. (He very awkwardly
tries to help her up, hands under her arms perhaps, but it ends in
an awkward half-fall for her on her hind end.)

CYNTHIA   Oh. Uff.... I'm sorry, I ... I ... didn't know what you
wanted to do.

(She gets up quickly by herself. He lets her apologize as if it were
indeed her fault. Then she notices her flowers, trees, shrubs.)

Oh! They're all dying and squished. (She kneels and gets them up.)

JERRY   Oh, gee. Wait, there's (Looking.) some ... water here ...
somewhere. (He finds the thermos under the junk.) Look. Ice water.
That ought to fix them up.

CYNTHIA   Oh, but don't you think it'd be too much of a shock for
them now?

JERRY (pauses in pouring water into the cap)   Well ... (Tests it.)
No, I don't think so.... Well, but if you want, we could wait for
it to warm up in the sun.

CYNTHIA   Let's put some of them in, half, and see what happens.
I could just get some more, I suppose.

JERRY (in his concern, in his effort to make it up to her, watches
the greenery carefully)   I think they're going to be all right.
(Remembering.) Did you want to finish your patio?

CYNTHIA   Well, if you don't want to....

JERRY   No, it's OK. What I had in mind is a great rounded corner
tower. (She is up as quickly as he.) With some shells maybe. (He
goes to the sand, kneels. She stands looking at the patio.) Look,
there're some shells on the blanket if you could get them. (She
stands.) Oh, I forgot. They're not there. (She begins looking
here and there for shells.)

CYNTHIA   I'd love to find a sand dollar ... with the little angels
inside? We had a camp councilor once who said they were doves ...
doves of peace ... growing inside the root of evil and war.

JERRY   She sounds like a YMCA councilor.

CYNTHIA   She was. If you don't care how exotic the shells are, I can get a lot of these little mussel ones.

JERRY   The color is the main thing. Just bring all the same kind then ... the mussel kind are good.

(He looks at her stooping for shells, as innocently as he can, now, watches until she turns. She is embarrassed. For a moment she stands, just a moment. He turns quickly away.)

I'm going to have trouble getting this top part to stay.

(She kneels this time and collects more. He places the top part on, and it crumbles the layer below.)

Shoot.

CYNTHIA   Here. (She stands watching his work.) I bet you don't play in the sand with your girl down the beach.

JERRY   What girl?

CYNTHIA   The one you go with ... down the beach. Hair was telling me. (She becomes very busy with the patio, working fast to cover up.)

JERRY   Oh. (He stops work, looks at tower. Then finally:) I don't go with a girl down the beach. (He works again. Neither looks at the other yet.)

CYNTHIA   Oh. (She looks up during his next line.)

JERRY   I don't know any girls on the beach. Neither does Hair.

(He stops work and looks at her. They hold this until he begins to work again.)

I think if I put the shells in as braces they might strengthen these sides some.

CYNTHIA (still looking at him)   Well, actually, I'm glad you don't, really.

JERRY   I think these shells ought to brace it.

CYNTHIA   I'll do this side.

JERRY   Not too hard. Don't push them in too hard.

CYNTHIA   They're really pretty, aren't they?

JERRY   You could use a couple more at the bottom there.

CYNTHIA   What made you think of using shells?

JERRY   I don't know. I probably saw one once.

CYNTHIA   That's all I have. And I wanted to put some more on my walls.

JERRY   **Good.** Now, I think we're ready for the top. I tell you what, you hold your hands around that layer as an extra measure. OK? We've got to be careful now. OK. Press together. Ready? OK. (He lowers the top tower.)

CYNTHIA   It stayed!

JERRY   Well, it's not that tricky, really. (He stands, moves front, looks, and makes a few corrections.) Just smooth this off ... the front yard.

CYNTHIA (stands off to look also)   Oh, it's good. I really like it!

JERRY (moving back some)   It's different. It's pretty good.

CYNTHIA   I know! (She goes to him.) Let's put up a sign: "Any- one who knocks this down is a ... is a crab!" (She lets go of his arms and runs to get her flowers.) Oh, my flowers!

JERRY   "Anyone who knocks this down will be sanded to death. And let he who throws the first **grain** be me!"

CYNTHIA (coming back with the flowers)   "And may he get sand in his shoes forever!" (Putting flowers, trees, shrubs in sand.)

JERRY   Or, if he's barefooted, "May he get sand in his toenails ... forever!"

CYNTHIA (finishing the landscape)   There. Oh, you poor things, you came to life and you look beautiful, you really do.

JERRY   They really do. They add a lot of reality. (They look.) Well?

CYNTHIA   You know, I think I'd like to walk down the beach now. But I want to change into my bathing suit first. We could cool off in the water when we go. Do you want me to bring our raft down? (Going.)

JERRY   OK.

CYNTHIA   Will you wait here? (Turning.)

JERRY (fast)   OK.

(Pause.)

CYNTHIA   You will, won't you?

JERRY   Sure.

CYNTHIA   OK. I'll hurry. (Stops. Turns again.) I'll just be
a minute. (Goes again.)

JERRY   Listen, Cynthia. (She turns.) Listen, wouldn't you rather
I knocked it down now ... rather than some stranger?

(She pauses.)

CYNTHIA   No. No, I don't think so.

JERRY   OK.

CYNTHIA   I'll be right back. (She leaves.)

(JERRY looks at the castle. He picks up some wet sand and forms
a bomb, backing up as if he were going to throw it, winding up in
front of the lifeguard stand. Now! But there are noises from
the GIRL and SAM, in a passionate embrace.)

JERRY (low, almost to himself) Stop it. (Then louder, to them.)
Stop it. (He turns away, the sand bomb in his hands and his head
down.) Please ... stop!

3 FILOSOFERS IN A FIRETOWER

By Margaret Collins

CHARACTERS

One (Tom)
Two (Dick)
Three (Jerry)
Sandy
The Man
The Boy
First Trooper
Second Trooper
Myra Hayes
The Doctor
Shenandoah
Eureka
The Fugitive

SCENE

In the mountains. October.

ACT ONE

(Parkway with nature, spoiled or unspoiled, suggested by signs, "Photogenic Scenery 1,000 feet."

Montebello, with marble bench and statuary.

The Firetower with 3 Filosofers.

The philosophers are not sufficiently sure of their identity at
first to have names. ONE and THREE are philosophical enough to
know that one can't take things for granted. Their conversation
is fashionable, but, fashion being what it is, may now be unfashion-
able. TWO is looking through a telescope. He is possibly not a
philosopher at all.)

THREE   That's the trouble.

ONE   What?

THREE   With the new.

ONE   What about it?

13

THREE   It's old.

ONE   I know.

THREE   So there's nothing to do.

ONE   No?

THREE   So there you are.

ONE   Where?

THREE   Is this a tower?

ONE   Perhaps.

THREE   Or a steeple?

ONE   Perhaps.

THREE   Or a nest?

ONE   It might be a womb.

THREE   Do you really think so?

ONE   I suppose not.

TWO (with the telescope)   I see people.

ONE   Where?

TWO   There.

ONE (taking the scope)   What's this? A mirror?

THREE   Perhaps it's a window.

ONE (looking)   I wonder.

THREE   Don't.

ONE   What?

THREE   Wonder.

ONE (still looking)   Is this a microscope?

THREE   That's the trouble.

ONE   What?

THREE (taking the telescope)   With number.

ONE   What about number?

THREE (looking through the telescope the other way)   It may be a telescope. (Returning it to TWO.)

ONE   Then this is a room?

THREE   A shelter?

ONE   A cave?

THREE   I can't agree.

ONE   I'd say we're surrounded by space!

THREE   Pure?

ONE   Empty.

TWO   I see people.

ONE   You already said that.

THREE   Don't be fatuous.

ONE   Perhaps they're angels?

THREE   That was Pope Gregory.

ONE   Then this must be A.D.?

THREE   Anyhow they weren't angels.

ONE   No?

THREE   They were Angles.

ONE   Non-Euclidean?

THREE   My premise is that we're angels, and this is the point of the pin.

ONE   Then it's a steeple?

THREE   Perhaps it's a crow's nest.

ONE   Then this is a ship?

THREE   That's space then?

ONE   It is water.

TWO   They're kissing.

ONE   I doubt that.

THREE   Don't.

ONE   What?

THREE   Doubt.

ONE   Who is?

THREE   Doubting?

ONE   Kissing.

THREE   Well, we may as well look.

ONE   No harm in looking.

THREE   No.

ONE   It doesn't prove that we see anything.

THREE   No.

ONE   So why not?

THREE   Why not?

TWO (with the telescope)   She hasn't any clothes on.

THREE   Do you see an apple anywhere?

TWO   She's beautiful.

ONE   You're only looking.

THREE   You're not seeing anything.

ONE   This is A.D.

THREE   She can't be.

TWO   She is.

ONE   Is what?

TWO   Beautiful.

THREE   You're only looking.

ONE   You're not seeing anything.

TWO (with telescope)   She has long hair. It's red.

THREE   What makes you think so?

ONE   It's probably short.

THREE   I imagine it's blue.

TWO   She's combing it.

THREE   Why?

ONE   Why not?

THREE   I can't imagine why she'd be combing her hair.

ONE   At least not now.

THREE   Particularly not now.

ONE   Perhaps it's later than we think?

THREE   Perhaps it's after when we think it's before.

ONE   Or maybe it's often when we thought it was seldom?

THREE   That's it.

ONE   What?

THREE   Frequency.

ONE   What about frequency?

THREE   Is it usual or unusual?

ONE   Statistics are unsatisfactory.

THREE   That's quantum for you.

ONE   What?

THREE   Unsatisfactory.

TWO (with telescope)   She's stopped combing her hair. I think
she....

THREE   Don't.

TWO   Perhaps she....

THREE   Don't!

(The Parkway, a ledge. "Photogenic Scenery 1,000 feet." Tossed
over a bush or picnic bench are SANDY's clothes. She stands at a
short distance from the MAN, and clutches her coat about her. The
MAN is just a man. SANDY is beautiful. Her hair is red. She is
also a natural, warmly affectionate human being who is not sure
what she wants.)

SANDY   Call it premonition.

MAN   What does it matter?

SANDY   As if someone is watching us.

MAN   Who could be watching us? We're miles from nowhere.

SANDY   I know.

MAN   Who could see us except the trees in the wood, the birds and
the bees -

SANDY   I know. It's silly. I suppose you think I'm acting like
Miss Priss on her wedding night.

MAN   No one has wedding nights anymore. Just nights. And mornings
like this ... and days like today.... (Trying to be persuasive
about the coat.)

SANDY   Perhaps ... later.

MAN   Later? Do you think we drove all the way out here to admire
nature? (Urgent.) Look here. A minute ago -

SANDY (evading)   A minute ago it didn't matter that you have a wife
and a little girl. But now it does. Suddenly. Why? Because it's
October.

MAN (following)   It's been October all week.

SANDY   But I didn't see it. I scarcely looked out the window.
Perhaps it's the flaming dogwood with berries red as blood against
the blue sky.... (Emotional, an echo of some film she has seen.)
Perhaps I love you too much ... or too little ... I'm not making
sense.

MAN   No. That's the trouble with thinking. It doesn't make sense!
Don't do it. Just this -

(He is rough. She is frightened. She tries to run. The MAN ex-
plodes.)

You damned bitch!

(She struggles, cries out.)

(The Firetower.)

TWO   I'd call it rape!

THREE   She asked for it.

ONE   Did she?

THREE   Didn't she?

TWO   We've got to do something!

ONE   What?

TWO   He may kill her!

ONE   Where is she?

THREE   Here or there?

ONE   Who is she?

THREE   Subject?

ONE   Object?

TWO   I can't see a damn thing!

ONE   You're only looking.

THREE   You don't need to see anything.

TWO   The lights went out.

THREE   They always go out.

ONE   We could ask someone.

THREE   Who?

ONE   Would he tell us?

THREE   So there you are.

ONE   Where?

THREE   That's it.

TWO (with the telescope)   Who do you suppose he is?

ONE   Who?

TWO   The boy,

ONE   What boy?

TWO   The one with binoculars.   In a tree.

ONE   He is?

TWO   He was.

ONE   And now?

THREE   That's it.

ONE   That's what?

THREE   Where is he?

TWO   There.

ONE   Where?

TWO   There.

ONE   Where?

TWO   There.

(The Ledge. The BOY is fifteen. He is wearing a pair of binoculars.
The MAN is gone. Behind her coat, SANDY is putting on her clothes.)

BOY (excited and embarrassed)   I thought I saw a pileated woodpecker,
and I only have 187 birds on my life list, so I.... Of course I
knew you weren't a pileated woodpecker, but I climbed out of the
tree anyhow. Not because you were a girl. At least I don't think
so. I was just interested, I guess, because you were people and
I haven't seen any for a week.

(Breathless he looks toward her, looks away, talks some more.)

Before that I saw too many. The wrong kind, maybe. Anyhow, I took
off. I think I'll walk all the way to L.A. Never been south of
Oakland. That's where I live. If you can call it living when you
go to school. I go to school. Or I did.

SANDY (over her shoulder)   So do I. Or I did.

BOY   You look too old.

SANDY   I am. (Reaching for her skirt.) I'm much too old to be
doing what I'm doing. (Climbing into the skirt.)

BOY (embarrassed)   Did they make you repeat a lot? That's what

happened to me. I'm a repeater. That's what they call me. They
don't say I failed. They say I'm a repeater. The poor dopes think
what they say or don't say will make me inferior. As if I don't
know the difference. As if I can't tell what's failing and not
failing. Some boys are fifteen and they can't climb a tree. Do
you see that mountain? There's an oak tree up there I bet no one
can climb. But I climbed it. That's when I saw your hair. These
binoculars of mine--well, I sold enough papers so that when I wanted
to identify a bird I could see every - What I mean is I could have
stayed in the tree and watched you ... combing your hair, but I
figured I might as well come on down and talk to you. When I got
here there was this man -

SANDY (emerging from the coat, dressed)   Yes. There was that man.
Do you mind if I say you're a brave boy and a dear boy? And that
you have four times as much sense as I have, though you failed in
school and I'm a teacher?

BOY   A teacher?... You're a teacher?

SANDY   Teachers are only girls. And I know you don't think much
of girls. You must go back to your tree and your 188th bird, but
like any foolish lady-in-distress who's been rescued by a brave
man, I want to give you a keepsake. (A light kiss. He draws back.)

(The Firetower.)

TWO   Is she serious?

THREE   Not yet.

ONE   She will be.

THREE   The lights will go out.

ONE   Perhaps the girl is disturbed?

THREE   I think it's the boy.

TWO   She's a teacher.

THREE   Teachers are whorish.

ONE   I know.

THREE   Always wanting to give.

ONE   It's absurd.

THREE   Particularly now.

(**The** lights go out.)

Do you see?

ONE (out of the dark)   What?

THREE   Nothing. What did I tell you?

(The lights come up.)

Who wants to see anything anyhow? People are always kissing and
having babies and dying. It's tiresome.

ONE   You've said that before.

THREE   I know.

ONE   Why don't you stop talking about it?

THREE   Why don't you stop talking?

ONE   Why don't you stop?

THREE   Why don't you?

ONE   Why?

(The Parkway. SANDY and the BOY have begun walking. She enters
ahead of him.)

SANDY   That's why I'm ashamed. I was playing a role. **Myra** Hayes
in her last film.... "Maybe I love you too much or too little," I
said. I thought I'd got over her. I guess I regressed. Like when
my little sister is sick, she regresses to being a baby. (Disgusted.)
I was sick with love that wasn't love ... and so I regressed to
Myra Hayes!

BOY   She's not as pretty as you.

SANDY   They used to say she was the most beautiful woman in the
world!

BOY   Maybe they used to.

SANDY (rueful)   She's had five husbands. I haven't had one. (Laughing at herself.) I thought it couldn't happen to me. But it has.
(The laugh doesn't quite come off.) I'm twenty-three ... I thought
by now I'd be married.

BOY   You mean to someone in particular...?

SANDY   He ran away. (That's all she has meant to say but suddenly
she is talking.) Two years ago. Without a word. Or a letter....
One day he walked out of the University. No one heard from him.
No one knew what had happened.... His parents went to the police.

BOY   Why do parents always go to the police?

SANDY   They thought he was dead.

BOY   Parents have crazy ideas!

SANDY   The police checked the Services. Sure enough he was in the
Navy.... Wanted to be let alone. No one knew what his trouble
was. Whatever it was, he didn't tell me. Or write....

(Silence. The BOY waits.)

I thought I could never love anyone else, but after awhile I didn't
know any more. I didn't even know if I remembered.... People change.
But if love changes it isn't real. And if it isn't real it doesn't
matter. So I thought, why kid myself? And so I.... And so this
was the day, and suddenly there I was, and I felt like crying my
eyes out at a patch of sun and a flaming branch of dogwood.

(Silence. The BOY waits.)

If there's such a thing as true love ... maybe there isn't, but
if there is....

(Silence.)

BOY   He'll come back.

SANDY   Do you think so? You sound so positive.

BOY   Sure.

SANDY   Oh, if....

BOY   He will.

SANDY   Why?

BOY   I don't know. But he will.

SANDY   It's got to be soon because.... (Intensely.) It's got to
be soon.

(The Firetower.)

ONE   That was quick.

THREE   How do you know?

ONE   What?

THREE   Whether it was.

ONE   Quick?

THREE   Whether it was.

ONE   What are they doing?

THREE   How do I know?

ONE   You could look. (Taking the telescope from TWO.)

THREE   I could look, but I might not see anything.

ONE (looking)   Is that the same boy? (Giving the telescope to THREE.)

THREE (looking)   He looks taller. (Giving telescope to TWO.)

ONE   Not taller. Just older.

THREE   You always want to count things.

ONE   You want to measure them.

THREE   You have a closed mind.

TWO (with the telescope)   That isn't a boy. It's a statue! (Raising the telescope higher and higher.) Six-hundred feet high!

THREE   Cleopatra's needle.

ONE   Or a winged horse.

TWO   It's a statue of Freud!

THREE   It can't be.

ONE   This is A.D.

THREE   It wouldn't be appropriate.

TWO (looking)   With a beacon on top!

ONE   It must be the Mediterranean.

THREE   And B.C. at that.

(Montebello. The gardens. MYRA HAYES, who only yesterday was the
most beautiful woman in the world, is talking to the DOCTOR. The
DOCTOR wears sunglasses, a smoking jacket. He claims to be seventy,
but he should be played by a man in his thirties.)

MYRA   The last film I made was in Rome. Not that I'm old, of course.
Just a bit old for those roles.... So I've come home. People tell
me you have the answers, Doctor.

DOCTOR   I'm not really a doctor. You know that. And whether I
have any answers, as you call them, depends on you.

MYRA   I know. You haven't a couch or a pulpit. Only a garden with
marble benches, a few pieces of statuary ...

DOCTOR   ... pungent shadows. A chill in the air. And the mountains
drawing color from the sky until they grow purple. Shall I tell
you like Blake of the wrath of tigers? At seventy I am drunk on
the elixir we brew here. Elixir of Life!

MYRA   Seventy?... I'm not sure I can accept that. You don't look
a day over thirty-five.

DOCTOR   Seventy.

MYRA   I want to believe it! I want to believe you're an alchemist,
Doctor! I want to believe that here at Montebello the world is still
whole, science a handmaiden, art a glory, and the prostitutes all
Madonnas leaning from the gold bar of heaven with seven lilies in
their hands.

(SHENANDOAH enters carrying seven lilies, jumps on the bench.)

DOCTOR   Have you met my wife?

(SHENANDOAH jumps down, twirls, throws a lily in the air and leaps
after it.)

Shenandoah is telling you that although she has seven children she
is a person in her own right.

SHENANDOAH (in mid-air)   How do you do. (Another leap and she is
gone.)

DOCTOR   My wife is part Indian and a daughter of the stars. She
thinks she's Head, but of course she's all Heart. It's always been
true that men are the brains and women, God bless them, are women.

MYRA   Speaking of men, Doctor--and women, of course--I feel I should
tell you that men distract me. I want to be alone with myself here.
I want to find out who's been living with me all these years while
the men have come and gone--if you know what I mean. The one who's

been my oldest friend and most trusted companion--ME. There's something in me no man can satisfy. No role I can play is big enough.
I want to give, Doctor! Give! The world is too small. But here
the horizon expands. That's it, isn't it? The Expanding Universe!
I used to think it was love. But love never quite does it. Why
don't we **begin**, Doctor? I'm here. All of me. Waiting.

DOCTOR   We've already begun.

MYRA   You're so calm, Doctor. Like a temple. I wish I were a
temple. Quiet. Serene. Lighted with votive lights. (She is quiet
and serene.) A thousand candles.... Can you see them?... I can't
make you see them. I'm not an actress. I'm a star. But I'd rather
be a great dramatic actress in a small theater ... (She is a great
dramatic actress.) than a star on a million screens. That's why
I'm here. I can't wait to begin.

DOCTOR   You have. Your posture has improved.

MYRA   Yes. I feel it.

DOCTOR   Your eyes are brighter.

MYRA   I'm sure I see you more clearly.

DOCTOR   Of course you do. (Poking her diaphragm.) This is nothing
personal, but if I touch you here.... I can tell.... Yes! Your
metabolism has quickened.

MYRA   Is that bad?

DOCTOR   Nothing is bad. All is good. Everything is Yes!

MYRA   Yes!

DOCTOR   Yes!... Now where was I?... The senses are alerted when
you respond to life--to love--to beauty--because you have faith.

MYRA   In what, Doctor?

DOCTOR   Faith that you exist. That's our triumph. All else shall
be added unto you. To him that hath. But from him that hath not
shall all be taken away. In Shakespeare's immortal phrase, "Sans
eyes, sans teeth, sans taste, sans everything." That's your philosopher. That's your Jacques. Our philosophy is the reverse. Each
day we grow younger. Our talents increase. I have just taken up
the viol da gamba, and my wife -

(SHENANDOAH appears dancing.)

She is on the faculty here.

MYRA   The faculty?

DOCTOR   The universities are a prey to jackals and materialists.
We had to do something. We feel in a modest way that the preser-
vation of civilization depends on us.

SHENANDOAH (to MYRA, dancing)   Of course to men the world is reversed.
You know that, don't you? (Dancing.) Something about the image.
Or the lens. I forget which. But they see everything backwards.

MYRA   What do you mean?

SHENANDOAH (an arabesque)   Take a simple example like my husband.
Bless his dear heart, he thinks he's the brains of this institution,
but I don't need to tell you -

MYRA   I thought so.

SHENANDOAH   You thought what? (She has stopped dancing.)

MYRA   Men are completely emotional.

SHENANDOAH   Aren't they? Their vision's reversed.

MYRA   I've never met the woman who's not jealous of me. I'm sure
you're above it if anyone can be.

DOCTOR   Dance!

(MYRA gives a startled cry and rises straight in the air.)

SHENANDOAH   I can't resist joining you! (Dancing.)

MYRA (upraised hand)   Yes!

DOCTOR (upraised hand)   Yes!

SHENANDOAH (upraised hand)   Yes!

(EUREKA, the maid, enters.)

EUREKA   Yes! (Picking up the lilies scattered about.)   There was
a man at the door. With a knife in his backside.

DOCTOR   What did you do?

EUREKA (a lily)   I took it out.

DOCTOR   Good.

EUREKA   And packed him in ice.

DOCTOR   Excellent.

EUREKA   And gave him a drink.

DOCTOR   He's probably a candidate for the doctorate.   I'll talk
to him.

EUREKA   He's over there.   (Pointing with lily.)   In a tub.

DOCTOR   Send him in.

EUREKA   Yes!

(EUREKA goes. Sound of a lot of ice cubes on the floor. The MAN
appears, brushing himself off.)

MAN (tossing a cube of ice in the air)   I feel better. (Stops.)
Myra Hayes!... What are you doing here?

MYRA   Call him a fan, Doctor. I never saw him before, but he's
still my past--if you know what I mean.

SHENANDOAH (dancing, using the DOCTOR's arm as a bar)
Dance is fundamental.
It's equally good for retarded children, or geniuses.
It does wonders for those who over-verbalize, as well as the inar-
ticulate.
Some need control. (A position.)
Some need release. (A leap.)
Some need bar work. Alone. (She is alone.)
But never for long. (Dancing.)
From the love of beautiful objects ... to the love of beautiful
people.... From the love of beautiful people ... to the love of
beautiful ideas....
And so we ascend!

(She is spinning around in the DOCTOR's outstretched arms, achieving
their most splendid effect, but MYRA is looking at the MAN.)

MYRA (sultry)   How did you get a knife in your butt?

MAN   People exaggerate.

MYRA   What have you been up to?

MAN   It was nothing really. Just a little skin off.

MYRA   Was it fun?

MAN   Fun?

MYRA   I can think of only one really honorable way to get a knife
in the backside.

MAN   There wasn't any knife, I tell you.

MYRA   Don't disappoint me.

MAN   I was climbing a ledge.

MYRA   And...?

MAN   I fell.

MYRA   And...?

SHENANDOAH   The word is Love!   (Drawing them into the dance.)
The word is Now!   (Taking the MAN's hand.)

DOCTOR (taking MYRA's hand)   The word is Yes!

(All dance, carrying the MAN along with them. He looks out-of-it.)

(The Parkway, a roadblock. A vaguely nonfunctional signpost pointing four directions, "101 North--101 South--101 East--101 West."
Two TROOPERS; the SECOND TROOPER speaks first.)

SECOND TROOPER   What's with the firetower? They won't answer.

FIRST TROOPER   Something wrong with their radio.

SECOND TROOPER   That's bad.   (Silence.)   Look at that glow in the
sky.

FIRST TROOPER   It's a long ways off.... You can see a hell of a
ways from up here.

(Silence.)

SECOND TROOPER   Quiet here in these mountains.

(Silence.)

FIRST TROOPER   Tourists are fools. They ride around on a parkway
straight through the woods for a hundred miles. What do they know
about woods? Nothing. Or mountains? Not a thing. If the motor
stops, there they are. Few chocolate bars or a bottle of whiskey.
They haven't even got the right shoes to walk in. Probably a baby
to carry. They can see the lights down there, but how're they goin'
to reach them? So we don't let them in here tonight. Do they thank
us? They curse us. That's what they do. Why do they think I work
at such a lousy job when I could have nice steady machines and fringe
benefits over at Douglas? I love people, that's why. Here I am
in a uniform, packing a gun, and feeling like a woman looking after
a bunch of kids. Maternal, that's all. Maternal. Any man in his
right mind would stick to machines.

SECOND TROOPER   Those lights down there must be Bueno Vallejo.

FIRST TROOPER   No one 'round here calls it that. That's Bueny Valley.

SECOND TROOPER   Looks like jewelry. I'd like to see some dame
come walkin' along this road right now, dressed up like a Christmas
tree, sparklin' from her head to her pretty little feet. And I'd
like to douse out her twinkles one by one, and light up that gal
all by myself.

FIRST TROOPER   Some woman from Minnesota tried to tell me the other
day that oats was wheat. From Minnesota, and she don't know the
difference. That's a tourist for you. Never seen nothin' at home
so they hit the road. (Silence.) Here comes a car.

SECOND TROOPER   It's your turn.

FIRST TROOPER   Go ahead. You like to talk to them.

SECOND TROOPER   Sure. I'm a city boy. (He starts off. Comes back.)
What's the matter with him?

FIRST TROOPER   Maybe he don't like cops.

SECOND TROOPER   Drinkin' maybe.

FIRST TROOPER   Lost his license.

SECOND TROOPER   Stole the car.

FIRST TROOPER   Could 'a killed somebody.

(The Firetower.)

TWO (with telescope)   Do you know him?

ONE   Who?

TWO   The man in the car.

THREE   Was there?

ONE   A man?

THREE   A car.

ONE   I saw headlights.

THREE   I heard a motor.

ONE   Still you can't be sure.

TWO   He looked like a Fugitive.

THREE   A criminal?

ONE   I don't think so.

THREE   Then he wasn't.

TWO   He was a Fugitive.

ONE   You can't label people.

THREE   You're being dogmatic.

ONE   Is he a killer?

TWO   Perhaps he's the hero.

THREE   There aren't any.

TWO (with telescope)   Who is he?

ONE   Who?

TWO   There.

THREE   Who?

TWO   Why don't you stop talking and listen?

(Montebello. EUREKA is setting up an easel. The FUGITIVE enters, watches her.)

FUGITIVE   Two years ago this place was empty.

EUREKA (dancing)   It's not empty now.

FUGITIVE   Who are these people?

EUREKA   It's a school.

FUGITIVE   You mean they teach dancing?

EUREKA   They dance a lot, but they don't teach dancing.

FUGITIVE   What do you do?

EUREKA   I mix the drinks. Make the tea. Look after the children.
Whatever comes handy.

FUGITIVE   I suppose lots of things do.

EUREKA   Oh, yes.

FUGITIVE   Like...?

EUREKA   Well, I mix the drinks. Make the tea. Look after the kids.

FUGITIVE   I see.

EUREKA   Whatever comes handy.

FUGITIVE   Sure.

EUREKA   Some millionaire built this place.

FUGITIVE   I used to live around here.

EUREKA   Here?

FUGITIVE   Around.... I wanted to come back and take a look without being noticed. But there was a roadblock.

EUREKA   A roadblock?

FUGITIVE   Two cops sitting there. I didn't want to talk to them. I want to make up my mind about something. Incognito, you might say. I'm a Fugitive.

SHENANDOAH (entering enthusiastically)   You're a writer! (Shooing EUREKA out.) Mimeograph or paperback?

FUGITIVE   I haven't written a thing for two years. Not even a letter.

SHENANDOAH   You've been soaking up experience, haven't you? Now you're ready to give it form.

FUGITIVE   Form is an empty word. I read that somewhere. Only yesterday.

SHENANDOAH   But wo don't believe it.

FUGITIVE   We?

SHENANDOAH   My husband and I. We have founded a School of Aristotelian Science and Christian Philosophy. We include everything.

(The DOCTOR, wearing a beret and carrying palette and brush, enters with MYRA. MYRA wears gold tights with a medieval-looking red and gold sheath, open down the front. She carries seven lilies.)

MYRA   The word is Yes!

FUGITIVE (to SHENANDOAH)   I'm shopping around. You see my education was interrupted.

MYRA   The'word is Now!

FUGITIVE (to SHENANDOAH)   I went to U.C.L.A.

MYRA   The word is Here!

DOCTOR   U.C.L.A. is a shambles.

FUGITIVE (to SHENANDOAH)   I left rather suddenly. I wasn't sure
whether it was the University or me.

DOCTOR   We include everything.

MYRA   The word is Yes!

DOCTOR   This is Myra Hayes.

FUGITIVE   I thought so.

MYRA   What made you think so? I've changed. And if I like you,
who knows? The word could be -

FUGITIVE   Censored.

MYRA   Well, you don't have to come right out and say so. Maybe
it's censored, but I like to think it's beautiful. At least here.

FUGITIVE   How about now?

DOCTOR (firmly drawing MYRA and her lilies toward the easel)   Stand
over here, please. Art is never humble. Art presumes. It is proud.

MYRA (posing)   Then Beauty is Courage! Is that it, Doctor? I've
never dared to be beautiful. I've merely been sexy.

FUGITIVE   Don't sell yourself short.

DOCTOR (studying his model)   You speak from experience, but what
experience? That's the tough question. You take it on faith.
(Waving his paint brush.) In the eyes of the law a man may be a
killer. Art dares to look with the eyes of God. (Beginning to
paint.)

SHENANDOAH   Nothing is ugly.

FUGITIVE   Murder is ugly.

SHENANDOAH (interested)   Did you kill someone?

FUGITIVE   We're all murderers, aren't we? Some of us know our
victims. Some of us don't. That's the only difference.

SHENANDOAH   When did you leave New York?

14

FUGITIVE   You can't brush it off as New York. It's here.

SHENANDOAH   Of course, it's always been here, and the latest crop
of intellectuals is always discovering it! They're always shook
up. Is death sensational? Is it a cause of grief and making high
moan? That's why the Doctor and I founded our School of Aristotelian
Science and Christian Philosophy. So people would stop being shook
up! Death's been around awhile. The world hasn't always been scared
blue with it. (A movement toward him.)

FUGITIVE (disengaging)   I don't want to dance. I just want to get
married and go back to school.

SHENANDOAH   What school? There aren't any schools. Get married
if you like. But don't go to school.

FUGITIVE   I've got to learn a few things.

SHENANDOAH   Who's the girl?

FUGITIVE   Her name is Sandy. At least it used to be. I've been
away awhile. Things change.

SHENANDOAH   Things change, Q.E.D. (Warmly.) Do you love her or
don't you?

FUGITIVE   I love her.

SHENANDOAH   Then the more they change, the more etcetera!... I'm
sure you'll be happy.

FUGITIVE   I wish I could be sure of anything.

SHENANDOAH   What's love without faith?... You probably know.

FUGITIVE   Yes ... I think I know that much.

SHENANDOAH   You think you know, but at least you said Yes. They
all do. Sooner or later.

FUGITIVE   How do you say Yes to murder?

SHENANDOAH   I'm sure it was an accident.

FUGITIVE   He's dead.

SHENANDOAH   Does it matter?

FUGITIVE   I killed him.

SHENANDOAH   Does it matter?

FUGITIVE   Yes!

SHENANDOAH   You see?

FUGITIVE   Sure. I can put a bullet in my head.

SHENANDOAH   Or else.

FUGITIVE   Or else?

SHENANDOAH   Say yes and be a perfect fool like the Doctor and me!

FUGITIVE (angry)   What do you do about anger?... Sure it was an accident. (Pulling a gun.) He pulled a gun in a brawl. But you can't say I didn't hate him. It was an old feud. The law calls it an accident. The law decides I'm free. Free, Hell! If he wasn't a stranger, it wasn't an accident!... How can I ask Sandy to marry me?

(SHENANDOAH has been startled by the gun but not at all unnerved.)

SHENANDOAH (warmly)   You mean you're ashamed?

FUGITIVE (turning the gun over in his hand)   No, I'm not ashamed. I have regrets. There's a difference. (Putting the gun away.) How can I ask a girl like Sandy -

SHENANDOAH (following)   How can you ask any girl but Sandy?

FUGITIVE (turning)   Do you know her?

SHENANDOAH   Should I?

(The FUGITIVE looks at her, knowing he's been had.)

FUGITIVE (laughing)   Yes!

SHENANDOAH (modestly victorious)   We're coeducational, of course. And we have apartments for married couples. With maid service! (Calling.) Eureka!... What's the matter with that girl? What can she be doing? Eureka!

EUREKA (appearing)   Ma'am?

SHENANDOAH   Is that apartment on the third floor available?

EUREKA (playing for the FUGITIVE)   The one with the view?

SHENANDOAH   The other one.

FUGITIVE   But I'd like -

SHENANDOAH   The one with the view has a window.

FUGITIVE   But I'd like -

SHENANDOAH   Don't be conventional. You want to write, don't you?

FUGITIVE   But -

SHENANDOAH   Then you don't want a view.

(Dismissing EUREKA, who dawdles.)

I'm sure you'll be happy. Sooner or later they all say -

MYRA (elsewhere, waving the lilies, upstaging everyone)   Yes!
Yes! Yes! Sex is Art! And Art is Substance!

(EUREKA gives the FUGITIVE a flirtatious look and swishes out.)

SHENANDOAH (crossing to rearrange MYRA's lilies)   May I...?

(The MAN enters. It is his first view of MYRA in lilies, red-and-
gold sheath. He does a long take.)

MAN (to the FUGITIVE)   I don't get it.

FUGITIVE   What?

MAN   Myra Hayes. All those sophisticated roles she plays. She must
really be off her rocker.

FUGITIVE (bored)   Who cares if she's off her rocker? Get going,
bud. That's what you want, isn't it?

MAN   I almost flipped when I walked in here and found Myra Hayes.
I spent my life at the flicks. How lucky can a man be? It makes
you wonder. Fate and all that. If it hadn't been for that damn
little Sandy I wouldn't -

FUGITIVE (tensing)   Sandy?

MAN   Damn little bitch.

FUGITIVE   Did you say Sandy?

MAN   I said she's a damn little bitch.

FUGITIVE   Take it easy.

MAN   Why?

FUGITIVE   Because I say so.

MAN (laughing)   You got something going for that little whore?

(The FUGITIVE pulls the gun. The MAN stops laughing.)

Maybe she isn't the one. (Backing toward wall.) Red hair...?
Teaches school...?

FUGITIVE   I can't see Sandy teaching. She's not the type.

MAN   Neither's Sandy.

FUGITIVE   She's only a kid.

MAN   This one's no kid. (Gaining confidence.) She'd better keep
out of my way. Because if she doesn't -

FUGITIVE (bored)   Forget it. Her hair's not red. Anyhow you wouldn't
know her. She's from Bueno Vallejo.

(He has turned away. The MAN stares at him with fresh apprehension.)

I shouldn't have made such a thing of it. I'm ... well, accident
prone. Rebellion breaks out.

(He still has the gun. The MAN watches him warily. EUREKA hurries
in.)

EUREKA   Ma'am!

SHENANDOAH (to EUREKA)   Where are the children?

EUREKA   At loose ends, ma'am.

SHENANDOAH   Take them into the gymnasium and turn on some Bartok!

EUREKA   Yes, ma'am.

SHENANDOAH   And don't forget the marjoram.

(EUREKA is still there.)

Well, what is it?

EUREKA   Your class, ma'am. They're still waiting.

SHENANDOAH   How long have they been there?

EUREKA   About ten hours.

SHENANDOAH   They might try a sarabande!

EUREKA (on her way)   Yes, ma'am.

SHENANDOAH   It's all in the book.

(EUREKA pauses again.)

Awfully good diagrams. Tell them not be fainthearted and I'll come along later and give them the coup de grace!

(EUREKA goes out.)

MYRA (crossing to the FUGITIVE)   The coup de grace.... (Looking at the pistol.) Tell me about it.

FUGITIVE (stowing the gun)   I'm sure I can't tell you a thing.

MYRA   Really?

FUGITIVE   Not one thing.

(The Roadblock.)

SECOND TROOPER   What about those crackpots at Montebello? Aren't they in the way of the fire?

FIRST TROOPER   They're all right.

SECOND TROOPER   But look at the red glow.

FIRST TROOPER   I told you it's a long ways off.

(Silence.)

SECOND TROOPER   They say Shenandoah's an easy make.

FIRST TROOPER   I doubt that. I think she's sincere.

SECOND TROOPER   About what?

FIRST TROOPER   I don't know. It's kind of a religion. Save-the-world type of thing. They convert people.

SECOND TROOPER   For a few thousand bucks.

FIRST TROOPER   So what? You can't separate money and religion. You go to church, don't you?

SECOND TROOPER   I read in the paper that Myra Hayes is there. Looking for some of the Doctor's philosophy.

FIRST TROOPER   Shucks. Do you believe that?

SECOND TROOPER   The Doctor's seventy, isn't he? What else has he got but philosophy? (A scream. He whirls, listening.) What was that?

FIRST TROOPER   Bobcat.

SECOND TROOPER   But it sounds like a woman screaming.

FIRST TROOPER   It's a bobcat.

SECOND TROOPER   How do you know?

FIRST TROOPER   Because I was raised in these mountains. That's
how. First time I heard one, I like to tore down the front door
trying to get in the house to my daddy.

SECOND TROOPER   What if somebody gets murdered? They blame the
police.

FIRST TROOPER   And if we catch anybody, they blame us for catching
him. Poor boy, they say. And they write a bloody ballad. We could
lay down our lives and they'd still sing about Jesse James. You
think you can be a hero? Well, you can't.

SECOND TROOPER   Damn good song ... (The scream.)

(The Firetower.)

TWO   He says it's a bobcat.

THREE   Do you believe him.

ONE   I think it's a woman.

THREE   Which woman?

TWO   There have been several.

ONE   One was dancing.

TWO   I don't think it's the dancer.

ONE   One was called Myra.

TWO   I don't think it's Myra.

ONE   One had red hair.

TWO   It doesn't sound like a woman with red hair.

ONE   Is it music?

THREE   It's sound.

ONE   Noise?

THREE   Jargon.

ONE   In the beginning?

THREE   In the beginning was jargon.

TWO   He says it's a bobcat. (The scream.)

(The Parkway. SANDY enters ahead of the BOY.)

SANDY (frightened)   Do you hear that?

BOY   Of course I hear it. It sounds like a girl.... What can
we do?

(They listen.)

SANDY   It's stopped. Do you suppose ... someone's...? (She clings
to him.)

BOY (arms around her)   Whatever it is, it's moving. Probably some
kind of animal.

SANDY (shuddering)   Oh....

BOY   It's moving away.

(Silence.)

SANDY (moving away a little)   I can't understand why there aren't
any cars.

(The BOY is shaken by his encounter with her fear and her warmth.
He is trying to be practical. He looks at his watch.)

BOY   It's only eight-thirty.

SANDY   Where's the moon?

BOY   It won't be up for a couple of hours.

SANDY   How do you know?

BOY   It's past the full.

SANDY (lightly)   You know so many things I've never thought about!...
Like the habits of the moon and the names of the stars. I've spent
half my life in the moonlight and all I know is that sometimes it's
big and bright and sometimes a sliver. To me trees are just trees,
leafy and green. Birds sing. Flowers bloom. I don't know the
names of anything!

(Silence.)

BOY   What's your name?

SANDY   My name?

BOY   I've been with you all this time and I don't even know.

SANDY   You've been more than just with me. You've protected me.
My name is Sandy.

BOY   I like that. It sounds like--well, like you. Like someone
to have adventures with. Why don't you come on and go to L.A. with
me?

SANDY   L.A.?

BOY   You can have the sleeping bag, I don't care. I've got a
couple of pans and--you know--powdered milk and dehydrated soup.
And before we run out of grub we can stop off at some town and work
for a couple of weeks in a store or something.

SANDY   I'd love to. I'd really love to. But I never walked anywhere.

BOY   You'll get used to it.

SANDY   And I have a job.

BOY   Take off!

SANDY   I wish I could! But if I just ... took off, some people
would worry.

BOY   Who?

SANDY   Oh, my mother, I suppose.

BOY   If you worry about your mother worrying you'll never do anything.

SANDY   I suppose not. But sometimes I wish....

BOY   What do you wish?

SANDY   I don't know!... I just don't know. (She walks away.)

BOY   You think your mother's disappointed in you, don't you? That's
a trick they play. You can't be like they want you to be because
you aren't what they think you are. Some of them cry. Some of them
laugh. And some of them--like mine--slap you in jail and don't give
a damn what happens to you! You've got to fight them, that's all.
But you don't have to hate them. That's what I keep telling myself.
I climb up to the top on one of those trees and I say, so here you
are, so you don't have to hate her.

SANDY   Why would your mother put you in jail?

BOY   For running away. She said it would teach me.

SANDY   Teach you!

BOY   Like jail was a school. School was a jail. I don't get all this about teaching. I only get about learning. Learning's OK. But teaching -

SANDY   You taught me.

BOY   I did?

SANDY   That makes you a teacher.

BOY   I'll be damned if it does!

(The Firetower.)

THREE   The world is a jail.

ONE   Perhaps it's a school.

THREE   Or a hospital.

ONE   Without doctors?

THREE   Or teachers.

ONE   All men are sick.

TWO (gently)   There are guardians.

ONE   And policemen?

THREE   The world is a desert.

ONE   A wasteland.

THREE   You said that before.

TWO   Perhaps it's a garden?

ONE   Of vipers.

THREE   Cannibals.

ONE   A jungle.

THREE   Blackboard, that is. With terrible equations.

TWO   They say the desert is beautiful. They say it blooms.

THREE   It's a wasteland.

TWO   Perhaps there is music?

THREE   There are vibrations.

ONE   Waves.

THREE   The shoreline's receding.

ONE   The ocean floor can be measured.

TWO   Perhaps there are patterns.

ONE   Anyone can make patterns.

THREE   It's a need of the pattern-maker.

ONE   Are you a mathematician?

THREE   Do you dance?

TWO   She has red hair.

THREE   Does it matter?

ONE   No.

THREE   That's just as bad.

ONE   As bad as what?

THREE   As saying "Yes!"

TWO   But her hair is red!

(The Parkway. Moonlight. SANDY enters with the BOY.)

SANDY   Look at that glow in the sky!

BOY   It's a long ways off.

SANDY   But it looks like ... a fire.

BOY   Yeah.

SANDY   I'm terrified of forest fires. I live in Bueno Vallejo and
when I was little, the town was almost burned out.

BOY (reassuring)   That one's a long ways.... You can see a hell
of a long ways from here.

(Silence.)

SANDY (uneasy)   Maybe that's why there aren't any cars?... Maybe
we're walking the wrong way.... Maybe....

BOY   There's nothing the other way either. Except woods.

SANDY   Nothing but woods? And this empty road?... If I had to run
for my life, I couldn't.

(An anxious silence. The BOY tries to break out of it.)

BOY   I don't see why you're called Sandy. Your hair is red.

SANDY   I couldn't stand my real name. It's so funny it's really
out of it.

BOY   What is it?

SANDY   You'll laugh.

BOY   No I won't.

SANDY   Cassandra.

BOY   I never heard that name before. (He tries it.) Cassandra.
I like it.

SANDY   Do you?

BOY   Almost better than Sandy. I don't know. I like them both.

SANDY   And I like you.

BOY (overwhelmed and fighting it)   My name's Pampanelli. Isn't
that something? If he was my father I'd be proud. But he isn't.
I mean he doesn't care. Why should I have his name? Someday I'm
going to get a new one. I don't know where exactly. But it's going
to be there. And it's going to mean something. And I'm going to
be--like they say--a new man.

(Silence. SANDY changes pace.)

SANDY   I can't believe the police are looking for you.

BOY   I guess so. I guess they're looking for me. It seems a big
waste of their time because I'm not against the law. I don't want
to do anything.

SANDY   You want to climb trees. And I want to climb ledges and lie

in the sun. But that's not what we're supposed to do. I'm supposed
to be at a blackboard and you at your desk.

BOY   I bet you teach English.

SANDY   Do I look like an English teacher? (Sitting on parkway
bench and struggling with a stone in her shoe.)

BOY (kneeling to help)   Don't you?

SANDY (laughing)   Yes.

BOY (removes the shoe, shakes out the gravel)   What grade?

SANDY   Mostly ninth. I have four sections.

BOY (putting her shoe on)   That's what I thought. I thought it
was ninth. Like I said, I'm a repeater. So you see I'm only in
ninth.

SANDY   You and I are delinquents.

BOY   Maybe in L.A. no one would care.

SANDY (laughing)   They always care. Sooner or later.

BOY   But L.A. -

SANDY   Sooner or later they care. (She gets up.) I thought by
now I'd be married. I thought by now....

BOY   Why don't you wait a couple of years?

SANDY (turning)   You're a dear.

BOY   You think I'm a kid. You've forgotten what can happen in a
couple of years.

SANDY (away from him)   In a couple of years nothing's the same....

BOY   That's right. You'll see! It won't take me long. I'm not
going to college. People say you grow up in college but it takes
four years. I haven't got time. I'm starting now. Give me a year
and I'll ... I'll call you Cassandra!

(Suddenly SANDY is on the verge of tears.)

What did I say?... I didn't mean to.... You're tired, aren't you?...
Why don't you lie down?

SANDY   Lie down...?

BOY   Here on this bench. I won't go to sleep. I'll watch. And if a car.... (He is **wrapping** her coat, which he had been **carrying,** around her.) Why don't you lean against me?

SANDY   Can I?... That's wonderful.... Are you really comfortable?

BOY   I'm not just comfortable. I'm happy.

SANDY   So am I.... That feels good. Could you...?

BOY   Could I ... what?

SANDY   Move. Just a little ... there....

(She is asleep. The BOY watches her in silence.)

BOY   I wonder if I could.

(The Firetower.)

TWO   Is he a killer?

ONE   Death again.

THREE   They make songs of it.

ONE   They down their liquor.

THREE   They raise their mugs.

ONE (singing)   "Come away, come away, death ..."

THREE (singing)   "And in sad cypress let me be laid."

ONE   They don't know what they're saying.

THREE   Or feeling.

ONE   Or doing.

THREE   Why not forget them?

ONE   And do what?

TWO   Is he a killer?

THREE   Everything is dead.

ONE   And dying.

THREE   Everyone talks about love.

ONE   Everyone is dying.

THREE   What is music?

ONE   What is melody?

THREE   Everything is dead.

ONE   And dying.

THREE   Some kill with knives.

ONE   Some with a song.

THREE   Everything is dead.

ONE   Everyone is dying.

TWO   But she has red hair.

THREE   Who cares?

TWO   Her hair is red.

ONE   Does it matter?

TWO   Yes.

ONE   That makes you four-thirds of a ghost.

THREE   Much less than a whole.

ONE   So what?

THREE   So who cares?

TWO   But her hair is red.

(The Parkway. First pale daylight.)

SANDY   Of course I dreamed lovely dreams. You were in some of
them.

BOY   You mean I was on the ledge?

SANDY   Oh, no, I was on the ledge with the man I was engaged to,
and you were writing things on the blackboard.

BOY   Four-letter words? Is that all I could do! Write four-letter
words on the blackboard?

SANDY   I think they were poems.

BOY   Poems? That's worse.

SANDY   They were beautiful.

BOY   Did you like them?

SANDY   You are my favorite poet. I'm your first Influence. And the sun's coming up! Look!

BOY   Sure. It also rises.

SANDY (laughing)   You're funny. What do you know about Hemingway?

BOY   I read lots of his stories.

SANDY   They say repeaters can't read.

BOY   That depends.

SANDY   On what?

BOY   On a lot of things. Such as if it's got enough sex anyone can read it.

SANDY   Look over there!

BOY   The firetower!

(They are running toward it.)

SANDY   People!

BOY   Radio!

SANDY   Food!

BOY   News!

SANDY (to the FILOSOFERS)   Where are the cars?

BOY   What's happened?

SANDY   Where is everyone?

BOY   What are you doing?

THREE   Doing?

ONE   Nothing.

BOY   Don't be silly. Nothing is something.

SANDY   We waited all night for a car.

BOY   So we walked.

SANDY   And slept.

BOY   And the sun came up. This is a firetower. (To ONE.) You must be Tom.

ONE   Sure. (Coming down.)

BOY   You're the radio man.

(TOM takes a radio out of his pocket and listens. The BOY looks at TWO.)

And you're Dick.

(TWO comes down. The BOY looks at THREE.)

I don't know about you.

SANDY   Tom ... Dick.... He must be Harry!

BOY (looking at THREE)   He's Jerry.

(THREE comes down.)

JERRY (taking an object from his pocket and holding it up)   What's that?

BOY   It's an egg.

JERRY   I find it extraordinary.

BOY (to TOM with radio)   What does it say?

TOM   It says there's a fire.

DICK   Where?

TOM   In the mountains.

(DICK begins to gather equipment. Stows things in pockets, hangs them around his neck.)

BOY   What's that, Dick? It looks like a mask.

DICK   It is.

BOY   For smoke?

DICK   Yes.

BOY   Do you have a walkie-talkie? Will there be firejumpers? Will you jump? Can I come along? Why not?

TOM (at radio)   The fire's a long way off. Bueno Vallejo.

SANDY   But I live there! I ought to go back!

JERRY   How?

TOM   You can't walk.

JERRY   No one can take you.

DICK (staring at the BOY)   You had a knife.

BOY   I always carry a couple of knives. And these binoculars.

DICK (to SANDY)   You have red hair.

SANDY   Not really. It was a mousy brown and -

DICK   You were combing your hair. Was it a garden?

SANDY   It was a ledge.

DICK   I'd like to go there with you. You're beautiful.

SANDY   Not really.

DICK   I knew you were. But the others -

SANDY   Were there others?

DICK   Just Tom and Jerry.

SANDY   That's funny.

DICK   What's funny?

SANDY   You mean why is it funny?

DICK   I mean what is funny.

SANDY   Tom and Jerry's a drink.

DICK   Do they?

SANDY   What?

DICK   Drink?

SANDY   Look. This could go on all day!

DICK   It does.

SANDY   But you've got to fight that fire.

DICK   Why?

SANDY   It's my home town.

DICK   How do you know?

SANDY   I live there!

DICK   Then I want to help.

SANDY (warmly)   You're a dear.

BOY (to JERRY)   What do you do?

JERRY   I'm an observer.

BOY   What do you observe?

JERRY   Everything.

BOY   You mean like in a science laboratory you measure and record things?

JERRY   I suppose you might say I measure things. If you don't care about being too accurate.

BOY   I bet you're a teacher.

JERRY   Perhaps I was a teacher, and so I learned that teaching is fatuous. I'm an observer. I know a great deal about you.

BOY   That's nothing. So do I. I suppose you know I'm wanted by the police.

JERRY   That makes you a good subject.

BOY   Kings have subjects. I'm a citizen. I learned that much in school.

JERRY   I mean a good subject for an experiment. You've been in some rough places.

BOY   Yes, I've been in some rough places with a lot of tough boys.

JERRY   I like boys.

BOY   You know something? Since yesterday I like girls.

JERRY   She doesn't seem very willing.

BOY   Look here, you! I ought to slug you!

JERRY   Well, you needn't. I assure you she doesn't appeal to me.
Not in the slightest.

BOY   Then shut up about her. (He goes to TOM.)

JERRY (to DICK, who is trying the smoke mask)   Where do you think
you're going? Outer space?

DICK   We can't just stand here.

JERRY   Why not?

DICK   Bueno Vallejo is threatened.

JERRY   Then what's keeping you?

DICK   I'm an objector.

JERRY   Then stay here.

DICK   I can't. I've got to fight it. Someone has to. Something
has to be done. (He sits down.)

BOY   Can I come along?

DICK   Why?

BOY   It's an adventure.

DICK   What makes you think so?

BOY   I've been in a lot of tough places.

DICK   This is no spot for a kid.

BOY   I'm not a kid! How many times do I have to tell you? I read
that in some places fifteen is a man. Or like if you were a knight,
I could be your squire and carry things. You sure got a lot to carry.
Or if you was in bad trouble, maybe I could get help. Or give first
aid. And I can climb. Like I could be your patrol. These binoculars
are the best.

SANDY   He's very strong. And he just passed his test in lifesaving.
Yesterday.

DICK   Do you think he's old enough?

SANDY   He's old enough for anything. All he needs is leadership.

DICK (to the BOY)   OK, pal. (He gets up.) Let's go. (The BOY starts off after him.)

BOY (turning)   Goodbye, Cassandra.... Wait for me!

ACT TWO

(Montebello. The DOCTOR has traded his beret for a white turban
and is talking to the FUGITIVE. MYRA is dancing a pavane with the
MAN, ridiculous now in a tunic. On the marble bench, alone, SHEN-
ANDOAH watches and listens.)

MAN (to MYRA)   All this dancing seems a bit forced.

MYRA   It's supposed to be a symbol of something.

MAN   Symbol of what?

MYRA   Of spontaneity.

MAN   That's what I mean. It's not spontaneous.

MYRA   Symbols never are.

MAN   It's unnatural.

MYRA   What's more unnatural than love? I ought to know.

MAN   Let's not kid about it. (Leering.) Love is sacred, isn't it?

MYRA   I don't know whether love is sacred--but sex is divine.

(They dance up right and pose.)

FUGITIVE (to the DOCTOR)   Hell, I've accepted Law and Order. I'm
ready to be sandbagged and otherwise clobbered by a family. I'll
even get a job! What else can a man do?

DOCTOR   You've tried hell, I suppose.

FUGITIVE (off-balance)   Hell?

DOCTOR   You know. You're a Fact. I'm a Fact. That sort of thing?...
But of course when Qualities go, Facts begin to slip!... Have you
noticed? And so there you are.

FUGITIVE (cautiously)   Where?

DOCTOR   Limbo.

FUGITIVE   Limbo?

DOCTOR   You know. I'm not a Fact. You're not a Fact. So there

16

you are.

FUGITIVE (cautiously)   Where?

DOCTOR   You'd make a fine teacher.

FUGITIVE   I don't want to teach.

DOCTOR   That's what I mean. You'd make a fine student.

FUGITIVE   I'm not sure I can learn.

DOCTOR   That's what I mean. You'd make a fine student of philosophy.

FUGITIVE   I want to get married.

DOCTOR   That's what I mean. Sandy's your Unmoved Mover.

FUGITIVE   Right. She doesn't think about things. She does them.

SHENANDOAH (breaking in)   So does Myra.

DOCTOR   That's what I mean.

FUGITIVE   You can't compare Myra and Sandy.

SHENANDOAH   Can't I?

FUGITIVE   Myra's a wreck. She's down under. She's got fish in her cabin.

SHENANDOAH   She may be a wreck, but you men are all skin-divers. Taking soundings. Tapping her hull. You can't quite relinquish her legendary treasure.

MYRA (to the MAN, dancing)   Some people need to dance because it's so physical. But you're physical enough. You need to dance because dancing is measured. That's why I chose a pavane.

MAN   It's like making love.

MYRA   All art is like making love.

MAN   Then why make art? Why not -

MYRA   Art is substance.

MAN (crowding her)   I assure you you'll find me very substantial.

MYRA   Art is eternal. If you were to make me, you'd make nothing.

MAN (crowding her)   Who do you think you're kidding?

MYRA   Don't be so restless.

MAN   What else do you have in mind?

MYRA   Your immortal soul. (Reinstating the pattern of the dance.)
That's why I chose a pavane.

(They dance up right and pose.)

FUGITIVE (to the DOCTOR)   Why don't you throw him out?

DOCTOR   He's a guest. He came here with a knife in his back.

FUGITIVE   Don't look at me! I never saw him before.

DOCTOR   That's what they all say. But it wasn't your knife. It
must have been Sandy's.

FUGITIVE (belligerent)   Sandy's?

SHENANDOAH (crossing to them, indicating the MAN)   His Sandy's.
What's in a name? The world's full of Sandys. But suppose it was
your Sandy. Could you be sure it was the same girl?

FUGITIVE (belligerent)   Let's leave philosophy out of this.

DOCTOR   Can you?

FUGITIVE (turning)   It's academic to ask!

SHENANDOAH   Is it?

FUGITIVE (turning)   Maybe not, but I say the hell with it. (Turning back to the DOCTOR.)

SHENANDOAH   Do you?

FUGITIVE   Look here! You can't do that! It's too easy.

DOCTOR   Isn't anger?

FUGITIVE (exploding)   Isn't anger what?

SHENANDOAH (smiling)   Easy.

FUGITIVE (laughing)   You people play dirty!

DOCTOR   Sooner or later, but it costs less when it's sooner.

SHENANDOAH   I suppose Sandy loves you?

FUGITIVE   I don't mean to brag, but she's not the sort who has
doubts.

DOCTOR   How do you know?

FUGITIVE   You talk like a materialist. I know Sandy. That's how.

SHENANDOAH   Two years. You think you'll surprise her, but who'll be surprised?

FUGITIVE   She loves me. She's waiting.

DOCTOR   She may love you, but she may not be waiting.

SHENANDOAH   Had you thought of that? Suppose you find her in the kitchen frying eggs for some man.

FUGITIVE   There won't be any eggs. And there won't be any man.

SHENANDOAH (lightly)   There's an old proverb about don't count your chickens if they're all in one basket.

DOCTOR   Women are kin.

SHENANDOAH (finishing the parody)   We all have one touch of Myra.

FUGITIVE   Not Sandy.

SHENANDOAH (amused)   Then you'd better....

FUGITIVE   What?

SHENANDOAH (an elegant gesture)   Go. If Sandy's a paragon and Myra's a wreck--why are you here?

(But the FUGITIVE is looking at MYRA who has become bored with the MAN.)

MYRA   Eureka!

EUREKA (appearing)   Ma'am?

MYRA (with a gesture toward the MAN)   Art makes him restless. Why don't you give him a rubdown?

EUREKA   Ma'am...?

MYRA   What are you being paid for?

EUREKA (pleased)   Yes, ma'am.   (Taking the MAN in tow.)

MYRA   And don't take too long! These things can go on for hours.

EUREKA (on her way)   Yes, ma'am.

SHENANDOAH (to EUREKA)   Tell the sarabande group to sleep on the

floor! They've got to be fresh for the Sunrise Service!

EUREKA   Yes, ma'am. (On her way again.)

SHENANDOAH   And check the three youngest!   (To the FUGITIVE.)
I don't know why, but my children are always uncovered. From birth.

EUREKA   Yes, ma'am. (On her way again.)

SHENANDOAH   And bring me my dulcimer!

(EUREKA and the MAN go out. MYRA is looking at the FUGITIVE.)

(The Firetower. An indefinable air of domesticity. SANDY is frying
eggs.)

TOM   Yes and no.

SANDY   Don't be silly. It's one or the other.

JERRY   You can't do that.

SANDY   Do what?

JERRY   Put us on the spot.

TOM   Not both of us.

SANDY   Oh, can't I?... Do you want your eggs sunnyside up or not?

TOM   You decide.

JERRY   I don't care.

SANDY (to TOM)   You can't make a girl decide everything. (To JERRY.)
And you do care. About a lot of things. Some bright day -

TOM   There aren't any bright days.

SANDY   Don't kid me.

JERRY   Not around here.

SANDY   You love it. Sitting up here like two owls with your books.

TOM   I could read anywhere.

JERRY (to SANDY)   Why don't you give up?

TOM   People are fools.

SANDY (turning back to the eggs)   One or two?

TOM   "Do Not Disturb" it says here on the door. We're already
disturbed.

JERRY   Disturbed as hell.

SANDY (waving the spatula)   That's the trouble with men. You'd
sit up here talking until Judgment Day and not even fry an egg!
(Back to the frying pan and radio.)

TOM   It might be hot enough if we wait for the fire.

JERRY   What fire?

TOM   On the radio.

JERRY   What does it say?

TOM   It says it's a long way off.

JERRY   I suppose people may be killed.

TOM   People are always dead.

JERRY   And dying. (Eager.)   What's the word?

TOM   Word?

JERRY   On the radio.

TOM   There isn't any.

JERRY   The word is nothing.

TOM   In the beginning.

SANDY (turning from the radio, distressed)   But that's horrible!
He's dead!

TOM   Who's he?

JERRY   Who can say?

SANDY   He was killed in the fire!

TOM   Who?

SANDY   Dick.... (She stands a moment in a daze. Then with a gasp
turns back to the frying pan.) Oh! I burned them!... But never
mind. I'll do you some more in a jiffy.

(Turning back to them. JERRY offers an oversized agate egg from
his pocket. She ignores him.)

He's dead.... I can't believe it.

TOM (mechanical) People are always dying.

JERRY   Or already dead.

SANDY (ignoring them)   And the most horrible thing of all is....
I can't believe that either. That someone would do such a thing.
That anyone could.... (To TOM.) They think someone set fire to
the woods on purpose. Some sort of ... maniac. (To JERRY.) A ...
what do you call them? A ... firebug. And now.... He's dead.
Fighting it.... It's horrible. (Turning back to her cooking.)

TOM (mechanical) People are always dying.

JERRY   Or dead.

SANDY   Oh, shut up. (Serving the eggs, blinking back tears.)
There you are. (Slapping down a couple of plates.) Sunnyside up.

TOM (protesting)   But I don't -

JERRY (protesting)   No, I -

SANDY (in tears)   Shut up and eat!

(They stare at her. Stare at the eggs. Pick up their forks.)

(Montebello. The DOCTOR, with academic hood and extravagant hat,
stands with the MAN at the easel. The MAN wears a beret and clutches
a paint brush, but is watching MYRA do arabesques. SHENANDOAH is
playing the dulcimer and singing to the FUGITIVE who is also watching
MYRA.)

SHENANDOAH (singing)
O holy day, high holy day,
The best day of the year,
Little Matty Groves to church did go
Some holy words to hear,
Some holy words to hear.

DOCTOR (to the MAN)   The word is Yes.

MAN   Yes, hell! I've been here twenty-four hours! And I don't
get to first base!

DOCTOR   Myra's a philosopher.

17

(MYRA does a figure. The MAN mutters.)

She came here as open-handed as a little child.

(MYRA does a figure. The MAN mutters.)

And as trusting.

(MYRA does a figure. The MAN makes a vicious gesture as if stabbing something.)

And don't make obscene gestures. They will do you no good. You have nothing to give such a woman. What do you know of Art?

MAN   I -

DOCTOR   Nothing. Women adore Art. They adore Artists.

(MYRA does another figure.)

SHENANDOAH (to the FUGITIVE , who is watching MYRA)   Perhaps you could talk to her.

FUGITIVE   Does she talk?

(MYRA takes another pose.)

SHENANDOAH   That's what I mean. I'm not sure Art can do it. Perhaps you could help her see what she has in a new light.

(MYRA does another figure.)

FUGITIVE   No one can say "Yes" to Myra.

(MYRA does another figure.)

SHENANDOAH   You could try.

FUGITIVE   I could cut my throat.

(MYRA does a figure.)

SHENANDOAH   There's no harm in trying.

FUGITIVE   You and the Doctor are sentimentalists.

(MYRA poses.)

SHENANDOAH   Nonsense. We're fools! It's not the same thing.

FUGITIVE (watching MYRA)   When I find Sandy I'll marry her, and that'll be that.

(MYRA poses.)

SHENANDOAH   Why aren't you on your way?

(He stares at MYRA.)

DOCTOR (to the MAN at easel)   Brace up, man, you can at least be
a connoisseur!

(The MAN looks at MYRA and mutters.)

If Myra wanted to endow an art gallery, where would you be? The
divorce courts are littered with husbands who can't keep up.

MAN   Who said anything about divorce?

DOCTOR   Myra's had five husbands.

MAN   Who said anything about husbands?

(He watches MYRA who is undulating toward the FUGITIVE.)

MYRA (to the FUGITIVE)   Dancing is fabulously stimulating. You
should try it.

FUGITIVE   I'd rather get married.

MYRA   Anyone in particular?

FUGITIVE   No comment.

MYRA   You mean she's not anyone? Or she's not particular? (Laugh.)

FUGITIVE (angry)   Look here. Maybe you used to be the most beautiful woman in the world, but you're not any more. You're making
yourself ridiculous!

MYRA   Used to be?... You impossible male! You're too young, too
stupid, too masculine to understand that Art is eternal! Art is
substance! (Desperate.) Beauty is courage! (She sweeps away down
right. Perhaps her despair is genuine.)

FUGITIVE (to SHENANDOAH)   That was a lousy thing to say to her.
But it's true.

SHENANDOAH   Of course it's true. That's why she can't bear it.
Truth is what you can hardly bear to know.

FUGITIVE (angry)   What do you want me to do about it?

SHENANDOAH   I want you to dance with her. Truth can get along without
you. It's there. But there are transitions ... repetitions....
Illusions are lovely garments. They don't fool anyone, but they're

beautiful to wear.... We each know our nakedness. We are sick with it.

(But the FUGITIVE is on his way to MYRA.)

FUGITIVE (to MYRA)   I know you couldn't care less, but you frustrate the hell out of me.

MYRA (expectant)   Do I?... I want you to be honest.

FUGITIVE (snow-job)   That's why I said what I did. Because of all the women you're the most beautiful. (They begin to dance.)   The very nonpareil....

MYRA   Oh...? (She sighs.)   That's lovely!...   What does it mean?

FUGITIVE   Unequalled. Peerless. Incomparable.... (They dance.)

MYRA   You see I'm not analytical. I'm just happy or unhappy without knowing why. And so ... and so I've had five husbands and it never seems to work out. We're made for each other today. Can't stand each other tomorrow. Even the Prince.... I loved being a Princess. But came the day when I just couldn't take it any more-- if you know what I mean.... Keep me dancing! (They dance.)   You see I need help.... It's like driving down one of those long, straight roads at night--not a curve, just a straightaway--road, that is ... and there's something about it that's absolutely hypnotic. Because I don't know myself, that's why. I've been analyzed, of course. Well, at least more or less ... here and there. But that was pretty hypnotic too. There's always a couch in the landscape somewhere. Couches and ... benches ... and floors, of course. You can't go much of anywhere there isn't a floor.... This is bad. Really bad. I feel as if ... I'll have to ... lie down.... (Leaning all over him.)

SHENANDOAH   I suppose you have children?

MYRA   Children?

(SHENANDOAH is drawing her upstage to the bench.)

Oh yes. Yes, I have children. Two of them. Daughters. (She sinks down beside SHENANDOAH.) I love my children. But I never see them. The Prince was the father of one of them--the older, I believe ... or was it the younger? Anyhow he was definitely the father of one of them. I find this sort of thing confusing, don't you?... Always looking for love, and always crying "Eureka!"

EUREKA (appearing)   Ma'am?

MYRA   You're interrupting.

EUREKA   Ma'am...?

MYRA   Are you the Maid of All Work? I suppose that means you're any man's meat.

EUREKA   At least I'm no man's poison. Which is more than some people can say! (She flounces out.)

MYRA   The little tart! (To SHENANDOAH.) Are you sure that True Love exists? Because I've been just about everywhere and met everyone, and if it doesn't I might as well ... (Drifting toward the FUGITIVE.) give up right now and ... enjoy myself ... the way you do when the world is new and you have a new Adam....

(They are drifting together.)

DOCTOR   Dance!

(MYRA turns and gives him a dazed look.)

Dance!

(A few languid steps.)

Dance!

MYRA (air-borne) Yes! Yes! Yes! (She dances out alone.)

DOCTOR (crossing to the FUGITIVE)   Forgive me for interfering, but things were a bit out of hand.

MAN (to the FUGITIVE)   "Yes," hell!

DOCTOR (to the FUGITIVE, indicating the MAN at easel)   I told him to paint a nude descending a staircase as if he had never seen one.

FUGITIVE   A nude?

DOCTOR   A staircase. You can't ask too much. This is his first lesson.

SHENANDOAH   Imaginary play comes later.

DOCTOR   For all of us, my dear. But not yet. (Taking her hand.)

FUGITIVE   Well, I guess I've got to leave all you happy people and be getting along.

SHENANDOAH   You aren't going?

FUGITIVE   I've got to get along. Few people to see. Few things to do.

SHENANDOAH   You'll be back?

FUGITIVE   I'm a criminal. I can't be sure.

DOCTOR   Sure of what?

SHENANDOAH   He wants to get married.

DOCTOR   There really aren't any good schools. You know that.

SHENANDOAH   You'll be back?

DOCTOR   Yes.

MAN (at easel)   "Yes," hell!

DOCTOR (to FUGITIVE)   The world is an ugly place.

FUGITIVE (to the MAN, with a wave of the hand)   The word is Love!
(He laughs and goes out.)

DOCTOR (drawing SHENANDOAH aside)   My dear, everyone's busy. Everyone's happy. Do you think we might...?

(Patter of seven pairs of little feet, laughter of seven little
voices.)

SHENANDOAH (calling)   Eureka! The children! They're up early.

EUREKA (appearing)   Yes, ma'am?

SHENANDOAH (radiant motherhood)   Take them out and throw them in
the pool.

EUREKA (on her way)   Yes, ma'am.

SHENANDOAH   They've got to sink or swim, and it may as well be sooner.

EUREKA   Yes, ma'am. (She goes.)

DOCTOR   Do you think we might...?

(SHENANDOAH gives him a look that says Yes. It also says No.)

(The Firetower. TOM and JERRY have a chessboard on their laps.
There has been a long silence. The pieces seem immovable. They
are stuck.)

SANDY (pointing)   Perhaps....

TOM   No one asked you.

JERRY   Three people can't play.

SANDY   I'm sure you could teach me.

JERRY   Don't talk that way.

SANDY   What did I say?

TOM   He was a teacher.

JERRY   People want to learn the wrong things.

SANDY   Are you sure?

JERRY   Of what?

SANDY   That they're wrong?

TOM   "Do Not Disturb."

JERRY   You have disturbed us.

SANDY   How can you tell?

TOM   Because we're disturbed.

SANDY   You can't expect things to last forever.

TOM   Like what?

SANDY   Like 3 Filosofers in a Firetower. Things change. (Taking
the chessboard, she stands between them.) We have ... well, you
might say we have regrouped.

TOM   We sure have.

(He turns away left. JERRY turns away right.)

SANDY (crossing down)   That's the way it is!... It poses a question.

TOM   What?

SANDY (laughing)   It's my question.

TOM   Your question? (Indignant.) As if questions could belong
to anyone.

SANDY   Well, they do. Because the question is me.

TOM   How can a question be -

SANDY   I'm it! That's how!

TOM   Let me get this straight. You ask -

SANDY   Oh, no. You're going to ask me!

TOM (triumphant)   Then it's my question!

SANDY (sitting on his lap)   OK!

TOM (bewildered)   OK what?

SANDY (arms around him)   Just OK. You asked me and I said -

TOM (baffled)   Asked you?

SANDY   And I said OK.

TOM   But you don't even know me.

SANDY   So?

TOM   You never saw me before!

SANDY   So?

TOM   But I didn't suppose....

SANDY (light and affectionate)   You didn't suppose it could be so
easy, poor boy. So you read about it, didn't you? All those books...!
And never looked out the window or got down on the ground because
you were afraid to ask. Well, now you've asked and I've said OK!...
You've had your first one. The rest will be easy.

TOM   But I haven't had anything!

SANDY (arm still around him)   How do you know?... Perhaps you have.

TOM   But -

SANDY   We've been here for hours, haven't we?... And Jerry's asleep.

JERRY (sternly)   I'm not asleep.

SANDY   How do you know? (To TOM.) You see? You can't be sure....
You'll never be the same! Of course, Jerry's the one....

JERRY   The one what?

SANDY (rising)   The one I'm interested in. (Crossing.) There's
something about him....

JERRY   About me?

SANDY   ... that's mysterious.

JERRY   Mysterious?

SANDY   I thought so!

JERRY   You thought what?

SANDY   That you like to think of yourself as mysterious.

JERRY   I'm an observer.

SANDY   Did you look at me through the telescope while -

JERRY   No.

SANDY   Why not? Why didn't you?... You knew I was there on the
rock in the sun combing my long red hair. You knew I -

JERRY   Don't.

SANDY   Don't what?

JERRY   Don't say it.

SANDY   I thought so. I'm an observer too. I saw you talking to
him. He's a good kid. He knew the answers, didn't he?

JERRY   He knew some of them.

SANDY   He'll make it. (Crossing away from him.) I only met him--
yesterday, wasn't it?... It was yesterday. That's how it is. You
meet someone and you don't know why but you love him.

(Her head is turned away from them both. TOM is staring at her.)

TOM   That's how it is.

JERRY   Is what?

TOM (looking at SANDY)   You don't know why.

JERRY   Why not?

TOM (not listening, looking at SANDY)   She's beautiful. I see that
now.

JERRY   Don't.

TOM   But she is.

JERRY   You're only looking.

TOM   Her hair is red.

JERRY   You're not seeing anything.

TOM   But she is.

(SANDY turns to him. No one is aware the FUGITIVE has walked in.)

FUGITIVE   The little hut, as I live and breathe. (He takes in the plates, the frying pan, the left-over eggs.) Enough for chamber music of all kinds--Two Males, One Female. You can play it lavish or plain, but it packs a wallop. Two males?

TOM (the only innocent)   I'm Tom and -

FUGITIVE   Jerry. Don't be funny.

TOM   Oh, do you know him?

FUGITIVE   Don't be funny. The female is always Eve. Hello, Eve. Shall we send the boys away? Out to the streets? Off to sea? The Navy's good for two years.

TOM (crossing to radio)   This is a firetower.

FUGITIVE   Bound to be a fire. Sex will do it every time.

TOM (with radio)   It's threatening the town.

FUGITIVE   Small towns are like that. (Staring at JERRY.) They can't take the Bald Sopranos who wear wigs and dye their hair. (Staring at SANDY.) But in a cozy set-up with Two Males, One Female, and a couple of fried eggs, everyone's happy, so why not?

(He has reached the boiling point long ago, but he doesn't pull his gun. He talks it.)

Cheer up, boys and girls, I won't spoil your fun. I just want to listen to your radio. You know, the kind of radio that has news bulletins about criminals and that sort of thing? Don't be afraid, kids, I'm on my way and I'm not talking. How could I?... Answer me, baby. You stand there staring at me with those big eyes like I'd killed something. Who, baby?... It couldn't have been you because you're standing there with your Two Males and I know you're happy. And it couldn't be you, mister...!

(He whirls around at JERRY, pulling the gun. JERRY stares at him stonily. No one moves. The FUGITIVE suddenly pockets the gun, turns to TOM.)

What's the word, Tom?   What does the man say?

TOM   The fire's out of control!

FUGITIVE   What fire are you talking about?

TOM   Forest fire.

FUGITIVE   Is there a forest fire?

TOM   They're evacuating the town!

FUGITIVE   What town?

TOM   Bueno Vallejo.

FUGITIVE   I knew I was on my way.

SANDY   finding her voice)   Don't!   (Crossing a few steps toward him.)

FUGITIVE (turning)   Why not, baby?   Answer me that.

SANDY   Because Dick....

FUGITIVE (angry)   Is he a "friend" of yours too?

SANDY   He was ... killed!   Fighting the fire!

FUGITIVE   That's how it is, baby.   Some people get killed.

(He goes.   SANDY sinks to the bench, crying.)

TOM   Did you know him?

SANDY   I....   (Tears.)

TOM   Don't you know?

SANDY   I ... can't say.

JERRY   What I want to know is did that guy know her?

TOM   He shouldn't have said those things.

SANDY   He thought they were true.

TOM   Why?

JERRY   Why not?

SANDY (crying)   Why didn't I answer him?   I just stood here....

TOM   Perhaps -

JERRY   Perhaps not.

SANDY   Oh be quiet!   You don't know anything!...   He won't come
back.   He'll do something crazy....   Look, you can see the smoke
off there to the south....   I can't stay here!   I can't stay here
at all!

TOM (going to her)   Come on, Cassandra, we'll take you to Montebello.

SANDY   I can't.

TOM   You'll be safe there.

SANDY   But I don't -

TOM (tender, urging her right)   Come on.

(They take a few steps. He stops.)

JERRY   Go on! What's keeping you?

TOM (crossing to the radio)   You'd better take her to Montebello. I've got to stay.

JERRY   Why?

TOM   Someone has to.

JERRY   Why?

TOM (to SANDY, tender)   Jerry will take you to Montebello.   I'd like to, but I've got to stay here.

JERRY   Your word may be here.   (Rising.)   Perhaps mine is now.

(As he takes SANDY's arm, there is a suggestion of his latent cruelty. They start off right.   TOM is at the radio.)

(The Parkway, roadblock.)

FIRST TROOPER   Who ever caught a firebug with a roadblock?

SECOND TROOPER   They're fiends, that's what they are. Devils.   On that great day when punishment fits the crime, may they burn in the everlasting fire.

FIRST TROOPER   Is that some of your Christian charity?

SECOND TROOPER   "'Vengeance is mine,' saith the Lord." And from what I learned at my mother's knee, he's no chicken.

FIRST TROOPER   Well, all we're supposed to do is catch 'em. Not roast 'em, thank God. I told you I like people.

SECOND TROOPER   Sure you like people. That's why you got to stop some devil from running around loose burning up innocent children and helpless old folk in their beds.

FIRST TROOPER   It's depressing.

SECOND TROOPER   Whoever said that because you got television life's a bed of roses?

FIRST TROOPER   If it weren't for the universities we'd have law and order. It's those crazy students -

SECOND TROOPER   This one's no student. He's a teacher. Name of Jerry Thatcher.

FIRST TROOPER   So he's a teacher.

SECOND TROOPER   Used to come up here weekends. Hike with the boys.

FIRST TROOPER   Where'd you get that info?

SECOND TROOPER   Came in a few minutes ago.

FIRST TROOPER   It's depressing.

SECOND TROOPER   What's depressing? Any fool can see it's not education puts the fear of God in a man. It's the church.

FIRST TROOPER   Sure, sure. You church people are biased. Anyhow I don't get it. If this bug is so educated, why didn't he stay in his bloody classroom!

SECOND TROOPER   Maybe he got fired.

FIRST TROOPER   He's got Academic Freedom, hasn't he? You fire a professor and there's hell to pay.

SECOND TROOPER   Damn right. The whole town's going up in smoke!... And fellows like Dick got to pay for it.

FIRST TROOPER   Dick...?

SECOND TROOPER   That's the word.... He didn't make it.

(Silence.)

FIRST TROOPER (angry)   Always got to catch someone. Stop somebody from some damn thing. Some lousy mother's son of a Home-town Boy who didn't make good. Never can tell how many criminals you're dealing with until you start counting the parents and children.

SECOND TROOPER   What would you say at a rough guess?

FIRST TROOPER   I'd say we're outnumbered.

(The BOY enters in a hurry.)

Well, kid, where do you think you're goin'?

BOY   Dick sent me back. See?

FIRST TROOPER (with a look at the SECOND)   Dick...?

BOY   He's gone with the firejumpers. He sent me to -

FIRST TROOPER   Your name isn't Johnny Pampanelli?

BOY   You got the first part right.

SECOND TROOPER   We're looking for a boy about your age.

BOY   My name's ... Richardson.

FIRST TROOPER   Richardson?... You're sure about that.

BOY   Sure I'm sure. You can ask Dick.

SECOND TROOPER (with a look at the FIRST)   If you say so, kid.

BOY   Ask Dick.

FIRST TROOPER   Sure.

BOY   I was with Dick. See? Like his squire. I carried some of
his stuff.... (Uneasy.) Look here. What's wrong? He went with
the firejumpers, didn't he? After that I didn't see him. He wasn't...?
You mean he...?

(He looks at them. Silence.)

SECOND TROOPER   That's the word.

(The BOY turns away.)

FIRST TROOPER (going to him)   That's how it is, kid.

(Montebello. The DOCTOR is looking critically at the painting which
the MAN holds. The DOCTOR still wears academic hood and hat, but
the MAN has returned to civilian dress.)

DOCTOR   Not bad. Of course the nude's pretty conventional, but
the staircase is superb. Though I wouldn't expect Myra to see this.
It's a funny thing about women. You've probably noticed their vision's
reversed. They get their images backside to or hindside before or
some such thing.

(MYRA enters with SHENANDOAH. MYRA too wears civilian clothes--some-
thing from Rome or Paris--and outsize sunglasses.)

MAN (to DOCTOR)   You aren't complaining?

DOCTOR   Complaining?

MAN (looking at MYRA's rear)   Maybe, as you say, Doctor, she's got her backside to or her hindside before, but it all adds up. I should be so lucky. I should die happy if she never even turns around! So I've been here thirty-six hours and haven't had the grand tour. So why hurry? It's only a matter of time, Doctor. Only a matter of time until....

(MYRA takes off the sunglasses and turns, giving him that certain smile.)

Like Samson said when he pulled down those pillars, man, let the heavens fall!

(He drops the picture, crosses toward MYRA. The DOCTOR stops him, points sternly at the picture. The MAN stoops for it.)

MYRA (to SHENANDOAH)   Some people have such broad backs. It makes you think of a target. I used to be a pretty good shot, but I never knifed anyone. I wonder who did.

SHENANDOAH   I'm sure you will meet her.

MYRA   Is she here?

SHENANDOAH   People turn up. Haven't you noticed? She has red hair.

MYRA   I always wanted red hair but the studio -

(SANDY, reluctant, miserable, enters with JERRY.)

SHENANDOAH   You must be Sandy!

SANDY   How did you know? (She sees the MAN. Freezes.)

MYRA (to the MAN)   Who are those people?

MAN (looking at SANDY)   Does it matter?

MYRA   How could she knife anyone?

MAN   Look here. This is my last offer. Do you think I'm a man or -

MYRA   I think you're a man. Don't tell me I'm wrong.

MAN   I can think of better places. How about you? (Drawing her up left.)

JERRY (crossing) Myra Hayes! (Taking her arm.) It fascinates me to see such elegance as yours in those low-brow films.

MYRA (turning)   Elegance?

JERRY   I've always wanted to know what you think of love.

MYRA   Think?... Of love?... Does one?... I'm rather impulsive.

MAN (aside)   This is my last offer. You have exactly one hour.

(He bolts. SANDY sinks down on the bench. SHENANDOAH fades toward the DOCTOR.)

MYRA (to JERRY)   How could she knife anyone?   Look at her. I have majestic rages. My tempests are famous. Does she hope to compete with her little teapot? (She sweeps over to SANDY.) What are you crying about?

SANDY   I'm not crying. I'm just miserable.

MYRA   Being miserable doesn't become you. You lack the talent for it. You should be sunny. All this red hair and running around with older men. You ought to go home and marry a nice young man and have babies. You foolish child, get a mop, get a sponge, but for heaven's sake stop that crying! What are you crying about anyhow?

SANDY   The world!

MYRA   Don't be grandiose. It's only maternal feeling. You're awash with it. Go home and have babies.

SANDY   I'll never see him again.

MYRA (to JERRY)   What's the girl talking about?

JERRY   Bueno Vallejo.

MYRA   What about it?

JERRY   It's burning.

MYRA   You mean there's a real fire? How horrible! Fires are thrilling! I always follow the fire engines. Don't you?

JERRY   How about the firemen?

MYRA (laughing)   You're wicked. I like you.

JERRY   I know you do, and I can't imagine what has happened to me but I feel unspeakably gay.

MYRA   It's the fire. It's exhilarating! (To the DOCTOR and SHENANDOAH.)   Why don't we all go and fight it?

DOCTOR   Why should we?

MYRA   It would be thrilling.

SHENANDOAH   Is it a real fire?

JERRY   They're evacuating the town.

SHENANDOAH   What a pity!

JERRY   I find it fascinating.

MYRA   It gives me the real frisson!

JERRY   I hadn't expected to feel pleasure. I thought of it as
science, but you're right. It has more the quality of Euripides
and the Women of Troy. Of course! And here's our Cassandra weeping
for her city. (Turning back to MYRA.) Have you ever played Andromache?

MYRA   Andromache...?

JERRY   You'd be splendid. You move beautifully. And with that
thrilling voice.... When they take your infant son and dash him
from the walls....

SHENANDOAH   Of course there's always Helen.

JERRY (to MYRA)   Why don't you play Helen? We'll let Shenandoah
be Andromache.

MYRA   Who are you?

JERRY   Your husband.

MYRA   Not my lover?

JERRY   Good heavens no! I'm Greek to my fingertips. I'm Menelaus.
When the city's reduced, I take you home.

MYRA   Why not? You'd be different.

JERRY   Well, Cassandra, dry your eyes and begin. Or rather, don't
dry your eyes. Wail, girl! Moan!... Don't tell me you haven't the
lines. Good heavens, is no one educated? Doctor! We need six
Trojan Women. Have you got them about?

DOCTOR   In the library, I suppose.

SHENANDOAH   Eureka! Where is that girl?

(EUREKA enters with books, a girdle for SHENANDOAH, and a laurel
wreath for the DOCTOR.)

JERRY (already declaiming as the books and props are passed) "Up from the ground--O weary head, O breaking neck. This is no longer Troy...."

DOCTOR (replacing his academic hat with the laurel wreath)   You'd make a fine teacher.

(EUREKA leaves with the DOCTOR's hat. SHENANDOAH is adjusting her girdle.)

JERRY "See. Only smoke left where was Troy. Let us weep for her."

(The DOCTOR and SHENANDOAH have found their places. They follow JERRY and stand with him, open books in hand.)

MYRA (to SANDY who is still on the bench, oblivious of the others) It was ridiculous of you to put a knife in his backside.

SANDY   I didn't. I can't really talk about it. But I feel I should warn you....

MYRA (eager)   Warn me?

SANDY   He's not a bad sort. Just ... violent.

MYRA (intrigued)   Violent?

SANDY   It was the humiliation.

MYRA (enthralled)   What happened?   What did he do?

SANDY   We were on a ledge -

MYRA   And you knifed him!

SANDY   No, I didn't!

MYRA   I can see it all! You standing there with a mysterious smile. Promising ... or withholding? He is wild! He lunges at you! (Looking around.) Where is he? (Panic.) He asked me to meet him. But where? An hour, he said! But where? Eureka!

EUREKA (entering)   Ma'am?

MYRA   The ledge!

EUREKA   Ledge, ma'am?

MYRA   You must know! A lover's ledge!

EUREKA   Yes, ma'am.

MYRA   Hurry!

EUREKA   I may be the Maid of All Work, but I have my pride!

MYRA   Are you accusing me...?

EUREKA   Yes, ma'am, meaning no offense, ma'am. (Dropping that game.) The gentleman's waiting.

MYRA   Where?

EUREKA   For me, ma'am.

MYRA   You're a tart!

EUREKA   Yes, ma'am. He said if I'd come along first -

MYRA   First!

EUREKA   Yes, ma'am. So I can show you the way.

MYRA   Show me!

EUREKA   Yes, ma'am. He thinks of everything. (She goes out.)

MYRA   He's brutal. He's repulsive. (Suddenly she bolts.) Eureka, wait!

(The Parkway. The sign says "Forest Fires Destroy. Use Your Ashtray." The FUGITIVE, in a hurry, encounters the BOY in a hurry.)

BOY (pushing the FUGITIVE aside)   Dick sent me. See? I've got to find Sandy!

FUGITIVE (in a rage)   Sandy! Does everyone know Sandy?

BOY   Take it easy. You can't say anything about Sandy.

FUGITIVE   Why not?

BOY   Because I won't let you.

FUGITIVE   Has she taken on Junior too? (Laughing.)

BOY   Shut up! (Pulling his knife.) Look, mister, I've got other things on my mind and I don't want to fight you, but you're going to be quiet, see? Because this knife says -

FUGITIVE (jumping him)   Says what, sonny boy?

(He gets the knife. The BOY is down.)

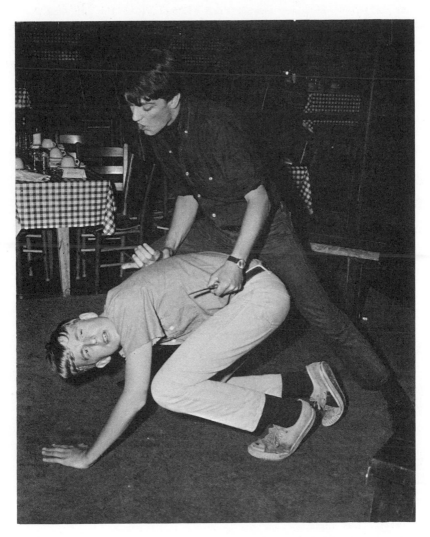

18

You see this? I'll say what I damn please! Like the man said,
Sandy's a whore!

(The BOY struggles to his feet. The FUGITIVE knocks him back.)

And I'm a bastard for saying so ... and taking a knife from a boy.
(Walking away.) I'd give it back to you, son, but I don't trust
you.

BOY (getting up)   What's eating you?... Why do you care so much?...
Who are you?

FUGITIVE   Call me a Fugitive, son. I thought I'd come home. It
took me a couple of years to figure it, but I figured the answer
was here. But this is no answer. (Looking at the knife.) You
know those compasses they give you in school with a sharp point
that's the center? And a little old stubby pencil that rambles until
it makes a circle? It rambles for a couple of years and makes the
prettiest little circle you ever did see.... How crazy can a man
get! Thinking the center's not going anywhere. Not moving. Not
changing into a red-headed slut in a firetower with Two Males, One
Female, and all that rot!

BOY   How dumb can you be! You sure jump your conclusions like you
did me!... Did you learn to fight in the Navy? Sandy said you was
in the Navy.

FUGITIVE   It wasn't the Navy's fight. It was another deal.

(The BOY waits.)

I killed a man.

(The BOY waits.)

The law decided it was an accident. I had just about figured the
law was right but--well, now I don't know. Look at me! I blow!
I'm unstable. Arrogant as hell--like you pulling a knife to defend
a lady's virtue. Like me using a kid as my whipping boy and wanting
to clobber the whole bloody world. At least we're not mean and
cold-blooded, but Great God in Heaven, kid, we've got to learn!...
I thought I had. And then I walked in that four-letter firetower
and found her with Jerry!

BOY   If you ain't too dumb! Do you think Jerry means anything to
Sandy? Anyhow Jerry....

FUGITIVE   You see I used to know Jerry. Two years ago I was at
U.C.L.A. Figured I'd marry Sandy and settle down and that would
be that. But I had a teacher--philosophy it was. That's the hell
of it. It's the philosophy teachers. They'll do it every time.
Anyhow a bunch of us came out here one weekend. You know, "Let's
be rugged, boys. Let's hike." So we hiked and we cooked and sooner

or later there I was with the Professor.... They say it's great.
But I decided to fight it. The next day I left school. I didn't
tell Sandy or write. I just left. That was pretty extreme, but
that's how I am. Maybe I've got Puritan guts, but I figured I'd
better find out, and if I was going to be one of those I'd keep
out of Sandy's way. I figured she'd know it was just one of **those**
things.... Good God, what was she doing in the firetower with Jerry?
I thought she wasn't confused. Doesn't she know anything? The
hell with it.

BOY   Man, you've got trouble unless you wise up. You don't know
Sandy.

FUGITIVE (patronizing him)   Well, now, son ... tell me about Sandy.

BOY   I guess if you're Sandy you like everyone, and you want the
best for them. And because you think they're equal, you treat them
different because they are, and they want different things, and you
want them to be happy.

FUGITIVE   Sounds as if you've got it made, kid. But it's not like
that. You can't play along with everybody. There are some people
you can't play along with at all. Sandy can't say **Yes** to everyone!

BOY (angry)   Do you think she says **Yes** to them all? I ought to
slug you!... Like yesterday. I was up in a tree looking at birds
and the next thing I'm on that ledge and there's this man roughing
up a girl and I jump him.... Well, anyhow, the man is gone and the
girl is Sandy, so I naturally look after her ... and finally she's
asleep with her head in my lap and I'm just ... watching for cars.
That's the way it is, but anyhow I tell her maybe in a few years
I'll be a bit older and more like what she's looking for ... but I
won't be, because she's looking for you.

(The FUGITIVE waits.)

Well, like you say about the center. How's the center supposed to
know she's the center if she doesn't hear a damn word for two years?
Sure she dyed her hair and she came up here with that guy, but in
a mixed-up way she was looking for you.

(The FUGITIVE waits.)

That's why I figured on waiting. I don't want to be no man's stand-
in. I figured on waiting. But ... well, you've come back and that's
how it is. That just about does it.... Just about wraps it up....
If you ain't too dumb.

FUGITIVE   I don't know.... I'm awful dumb. (Giving the BOY his
knife.) Why don't we go find her?

BOY   Come on. Dick says the fire can break out anywhere.

(Montebello. SANDY sits alone on the bench. SHENANDOAH, the DOCTOR, and JERRY are still reading Euripides.)

JERRY   That's your cue, Cassandra! You enter dressed like a priestess, a wreath in your hair, a torch in your hand.

(SANDY doesn't move.)

Well, we'll skip that. Over to where Helen comes in. (He turns, looking for MYRA.) Where is she?... Gone? She can't have. She was to read Helen. (He closes the book, turns away.)

SHENANDOAH   Helen, Helen! "Is this the face that launched" etcetera. Men are fools!

DOCTOR   But, my dear, this is Euripides.

SHENANDOAH   That's what I mean. Men are fools. Andromache's worth six of her. (They resume their reading.)

JERRY (to SANDY)   You look like my sister ... my poor tragic sister.... Some people are made for suffering. We say it ennobles them, don't we? And we admire nobility.... I admire suffering. When you look so tragic, you are beautiful, Cassandra, weeping for your burning city. (Sitting beside her.) The world is unjust. Men are depraved, All we can do is observe. Of course it's all inconclusive. One needs a great deal of data to make one reliable statistic. Euripides had an elegant imagination, hadn't he? But a firetower is a better place than the walls of Troy. Let Andromache weep for her son. Let Helen go. You are my sister. You will suffer because I love you....

(TOM rushes in to the DOCTOR and SHENANDOAH.)

TOM   You people don't answer your phone. You don't listen to the radio. The whole mountain could be afire and you'd sit here on your marble benches and read poetry!

SHENANDOAH   Euripides. Please be quiet.

DOCTOR   You're interrupting us.

TOM   It's arson, I tell you. (To JERRY.) You saw him. You can identify him. He had the brass to come right up to the firetower.

JERRY   The Fugitive?

SANDY   No!

JERRY   I know him better than you do.

SANDY   I don't believe you. Why do you say these things?

TOM   We should have known he was a crackpot--the way he talked to

Sandy. We've got to catch up with him! (He dashes out.)

SHENANDOAH   That man's compulsive. Why does he want to catch
people? The Fugitive is a nice boy who wants to get married and
go back to school.

DOCTOR   I'm sure we can help him.

SHENANDOAH   If we can find him. But we don't want to catch him.
Do we?

DOCTOR   Aristotle will have a lot to say to him.

JERRY   Aristotle was a bit of a firebug himself. You might say the
same of St. Paul. A spiritual firebug. "The Kingdom's within."
That's anarchy, isn't it, Doctor?

SANDY (crossing away from him)   How can you joke at desolation?

JERRY (following)   Wrap yourself in ashes and moan, Cassandra.
You love a villain! What will you do?... Run? Run away!... Lose
yourself in the forest and become consumed! (Holding her, laughing.)

SANDY   Is there nothing you can live on but anguish?

JERRY (following)   Cruelty is a splendid virtue, Cassandra. Art
is shot through with it. The theater's sadistic by definition.

(She turns away.)

Why grieve? All men are cruel.

(SANDY is motionless, whispering some inaudible words.)

What are you murmuring?... A prayer...? Where in the world did
you come up with that? Cherubim and Seraphim left long ago. Do
you think you can resurrect them for a one-night stand of hell?

SANDY   You have resurrected them.

JERRY (laughing)   I?... Dear girl, I am Satan!

SANDY (slowly)   I know who you are.... You can't bear being alive,
can you? And so you kill.... You want people to die! (Silence.)
Tom expects you to go, doesn't he? Before he comes back? (Urgent.)
Why don't you? He gave you the chance.

JERRY   Tom's a Yes-man. I could burn this place to the ground and
he'd deny I had evil intentions. And the No-men will sit at their
roadblock and never catch me. So the small choices will die for love,
and the rotten apples will live for hate, and I shall go on uncon-
strained, free - !

SANDY   Oh, Jerry, why do you talk so fast? You don't have to prove
anything. Not anything at all.

JERRY   You really are splendid, Cassandra!... Come with me.

SANDY   Come with you...? (Retreating.) I couldn't!

JERRY   Come with me.

SANDY   How can you ask?

JERRY   I don't ask. I implore you.

(SANDY looks at him in terror, knowing there is no answer, and that
she must answer him. She turns away.)

SANDY (turning back) OK, Jerry.... OK.

(Silence.)

JERRY (baroque again)   Couldn't you be more eloquent? I submit
you one of the half-dozen crucial propositions and toss in my soul!

(He starts out with SANDY. Their exit is interrupted by EUREKA.)

EUREKA   Ma'am!

SHENANDOAH   You're interrupting.

EUREKA (breathless)   Yes, ma'am, but -

SHENANDOAH   I'll be the judge of when you are needed.

EUREKA   Yes, ma'am, but -

SHENANDOAH   Then don't interrupt us.

(TOM enters on the run.)

TOM (to EUREKA)   Did you tell them?

EUREKA   No, sir.

TOM   Get the children!

EUREKA   Yes, sir! (She goes out.)

TOM (to DOCTOR)   The fire's too close for comfort, sir.

DOCTOR   Whose comfort? I'll be the judge of that.

TOM   No, sir. We have orders to evacuate everyone at Montebello.

SHENANDOAH   Beauty's eternal. Montebello will last forever.

TOM   But you won't, ma'am.

SHENANDOAH   Don't be presumptuous. My beauty is for my husband.
I live in his eyes.

DOCTOR (firmly)   De gustibus non disputandum.

TOM   OK if you say so, Doctor. Just keep moving. I won't argue
with you. Just keep moving.

SHENANDOAH (indignant)   Young man, you are a relativist, and everyone knows where that leads. Straight to the bottom. Not many have
the spirit to live as we do here on the mountain tops and greet each
dawn -

TOM   Just keep moving.

SHENANDOAH   Young man, you have the soul of a plumber!

TOM   Just keep moving, ma'am. Plumbers are necessary.

SHENANDOAH   Not in the mountains. You're a relativist, and we know
where that leads. Straight to the bottom.

TOM   Just keep moving.

SHENANDOAH   You're a clod. Why do we listen to you! We know the
fire will recede! The wind will change! We will hold our Sunrise
Service! We will greet the dawn with splendid affirmation!

DOCTOR   Yes! By all means!

JERRY   Will you really? I ought to be on my way but I can't resist
staying if you're going to perform a miracle. I should hate to miss
it by half an hour. Half a millenium's different. Even the chagrin
of half a century may be borne with fortitude. But half an hour?
I think I must risk it. (Turning.) Look, Cassandra! Is it the
rosy dawn?... How could I have been such a fool as to think of
running away?... And the marvelous thing is that I didn't plan it.
It happened. You are perfect. Even your name. What will you do
in your terror? Will you come to me? (Voluptuously.) Do you
remember Jason's golden princess robed in flame? Your hair will
burn.... I shall cover you -

(TOM rushes JERRY as the FUGITIVE and the BOY enter up left. SANDY
runs to the FUGITIVE. TOM turns, and in that instant JERRY has gone.)

SHENANDOAH (to the BOY)   Who are you?

BOY   Sandy's my friend.

SHENANDOAH (to the FUGITIVE, who is embracing SANDY)   So good to
see you again.

DOCTOR (trying to shake the FUGITIVE's hand)   I knew you'd be back.
We have a little Aristotle waiting for you.

SHENANDOAH   Not yet, dear. (Looking absently at SANDY's arms around
the FUGITIVE.)   Let him take off his things.

BOY   We're after that bug.

SHENANDOAH   Bug?

DOCTOR   Volkswagen, dear.

BOY   I mean that firebug.

DOCTOR   Hot-rod.

BOY   Look, Doctor, don't be so damn smart. I talk English too, and
I mean a firebug that sets fires and burns up innocent babies and old
folks like you.

DOCTOR   You mean you have the presumption to look for criminals
at Montebello? I refuse to allow it.

TOM (to the BOY)   Your name isn't Johnny Pampanelli?

BOY   My name's Richardson.

TOM   They say the Pampanelli boy may have set these fires.

BOY   My name's Richardson. Ask him! (Turning to the FUGITIVE who
is busy with SANDY.)

SANDY (to the FUGITIVE)   ... Anyhow there were three philosophers
in a firetower, and I fried their eggs! (Laughing.)   That's Tom ...
he cares.

FUGITIVE   At a distance. A firetower is just right for him. He
has his radio.

SANDY   And he'll always have me. (The FUGITIVE reacts. She teases.)
Didn't I tell you? It's all in his mind, but he'll love me forever.
Jerry's smarter.

FUGITIVE (angry)   Jerry's smart all right. He'd philosophize us all
right out of existence!

SANDY   I loved Dick. He wasn't really a philosopher at all. He
was the most like you.

FUGITIVE   Dick...?

SANDY   He went to fight the fire.

FUGITIVE   Poor guy.

SANDY   Poor guy? (Crying.) He's wonderful!

FUGITIVE   Yes. (Comforting her.)

SANDY (trying to recover)   Let's invite Tom to dinner some night, shall we? (Eager.) And we'll all buzz up to Montebello and jump in the pool with the maid and the kids and dance the sarabande and -

FUGITIVE   Sure. Just tell me how many there will be on our honeymoon? Not that I mind entertaining, but I think the management should know. Space is limited.

SANDY (kissing him)   Silly, can I help it? Anyhow I asked Johnny to stop off and see us on his way back.

FUGITIVE   Johnny! (Realizing she means the BOY.) Look here. That boy's growing!

SANDY   So are you, I hope!

(EUREKA enters on the run.)

EUREKA   Ma'am, there's a fire!

SHENANDOAH   Don't stand there.

DOCTOR   Do something!

EUREKA   I put it out.

DOCTOR   Good.

EUREKA   And tied the man to a tree. Come and get him!

(The FUGITIVE, BOY, and TOM are on their way. They all follow EUREKA out.)

SHENANDOAH   Who do you suppose it can be?

DOCTOR   Perhaps he wants a degree in philosophy.

SHENANDOAH   Perhaps he's a dancer.

(The FUGITIVE, BOY, and TOM return.)

FUGITIVE   Well, if there's one thing a woman can't do!

SHENANDOAH   Name one!

FUGITIVE   Tie knots!

BOY   He's gone.

SANDY   Jerry...? Let him go!

FUGITIVE (grabbing SANDY) Come on! We've got to get to those cops
at the roadblock!

(They go out with the BOY.)

TOM (melancholy, to the DOCTOR and SHENANDOAH)   Just keep moving.
(He goes out after the others.)

SHENANDOAH (uncertain for the first time)   You don't think we should ..
leave?

DOCTOR   There's no question of leaving.

SHENANDOAH   I thought not.

DOCTOR   If we perish -

SHENANDOAH   We perish.

DOCTOR (smiling)   Of course.

SHENANDOAH   Montebello is safe.

(EUREKA enters on the double.)

EUREKA   Glad tidings, ma'am. Of great joy. The wind has shifted.
Montebello is saved. But the children -

SHENANDOAH (panic)   What about the children?

EUREKA   They're up early again.

SHENANDOAH   Then do something. Don't come to me for everything!
Improvise!

EUREKA   Yes, ma'am.

SHENANDOAH   And tell the sarabande people I will definitely see
them.   After the Sunrise Service!

EUREKA   Yes, ma'am. (She goes.)

DOCTOR   We still have a few minutes.

SHENANDOAH   Yes.

DOCTOR   Do you mean Yes? Just like that?

SHENANDOAH   I mean <u>Yes.</u> Just like that. But first -

<u>DOCTOR</u>   I thought so.

<u>SHENANDOAH</u>   Not many have the spirit to live as we do high in the
hills and greet each dawn with a cry of joy!

(She leaps into the air. When she comes down they are dancing.

Curtain call: Lights pick up TOM, alone, ascending the long flight
of stairs to the tower. He picks up the telescope. MYRA and the
MAN are on the ledge. On the Parkway EUREKA is tying JERRY to the
bench. She tightens the knot. The BOY is with the TROOPERS at
"101 North." SANDY and the FUGITIVE are kissing.)

STYOPIK AND MANYA

A Comedy in One Act

By Nicolai Evreinov

Translated by Christopher Collins

CHARACTERS

Manya
Styopik

SCENE

Their living room.*

MANYA (in a loud voice)   Stepan Ilich! I'm going to pour the tea now--if you want to drink yours cold, that's your business.

STYOPIK (from the room offstage right)   In a minute, in a minute.... Great Lord, I'm coming.

MANYA (spreading butter on some toast)   The teapot's ready. Are you going to fritter around all morning?

STYOPIK (coming in from the door right, in a sweater and some thread-bare trousers, with a towel in his hands)   But tell me, Marya Ivanovna, shall I dry myself off, or not?

MANYA   You should get up sooner. Always misbehaving. Just like a little boy.

STYOPIK   Aah. Married people shouldn't quarrel. No indeed.

MANYA   Are you going to have some tea, or aren't you?

STYOPIK   I just came to find out what the temperature is outside.

MANYA   I'm not saying a word until you get dressed.

---

*The playwright probably expected a realistic domestic setting of about 1900. Theater Wagon's production has utilized some commodious and not-too-modern living room and its furnishings, a space large enough to hold both audience and actors.

STYOPIK (spotting a magazine)   Ah, the <u>Country Journal</u> is here.
(Goes over to the table.)

MANYA (seizes the magazine and holds it under the table)   The <u>Coun-
try Journal</u>, the <u>World</u>, and the <u>Citizen</u>. You shall have all of
them as soon as you drink your tea.

STYOPIK (tries to get the journal anyway)   I just wanted to see
if it **was** true that -

MANYA   Leave it right there, please.

STYOPIK   So. You're the strongest, and you're going to take advantage of it. Very nice. So now we know. Now we know.

(He goes off right, shaking his head. She puts the magazine on the
table, spreads some butter on the toast, and pours some tea in a
cup for herself and for him in a glass.)

MANYA   Just incredible: won't drink his tea unless it's hot, but
as for me.... Always keeping me waiting. Let it get cold then,
it's not my fault. God is my witness, it's not my fault. (Yells.)
I **poured** the tea! (Puts a little cream in her own tea and starts
to drink with great relish.)

STYOPIK (wearing a robe over his trousers and **sweater,** comes in right
and goes, all sweetness, to his wife)   Well now, I'm all ready.
Good morning, dear.

MANYA   Did you say your prayers?

STYOPIK   I did.   (Kisses her **tenderly**.)   See how early I got up
today.

MANYA   For once in your life.

STYOPIK   But allow me to point out what a good boy your husband
is--never causes you the slightest trouble.

MANYA   The slightest trouble! Who was it that coughed all night?

STYOPIK (sits down, pours some cream in his tea glass, and stirs
it with his spoon)   Oh well, I'm going to take a walk this morning
anyway.

MANYA   Don't **even** dare think about it.   (Puts some toast in front
of him.) Sick as a pup three days ago and now off for a walk. The
Good Lord's going to be angry this time for sure.

STYOPIK   In the first place, I'm entirely -

MANYA (interrupting)   Please don't argue, you'd do much better to
drink your tea, and then I have a little surprise for you.

STYOPIK (drinks his tea and eats his toast)   I'm going for a walk just the same.

MANYA   Now you're **trying** to make me cry. I don't cry enough as it is ... yes.... You have no reason to ... and who was going to clean his pipe today?... You can read your magazine in a little while, then clean your pipe. We're going to make a little rice pudding today.... And I'm **going** to mix up a little rheumatism treatment, and you're going to help me.   Look at all the work there is, and you're going off for a walk.

STYOPIK   A man can't live without a little air.

MANYA   Don't be so naughty, it won't get you anywhere. (Takes an unopened letter from her pocket and draws it past his nose.) See that? (Hides the letter behind her back.)

STYOPIK (brightening up)   Who's it from?... Who?

MANYA   You're going to be a good boy now?

STYOPIK   Yes, yes.... Who's it from?

MANYA   Be so kind as to finish your tea. It's a letter from our Lida, that's who.

STYOPIK (examining the letter)   Get me my glasses. Quick.

MANYA (goes to the mantelpiece)   Only kindly don't order me around ... I'm not a child. Thank the Lord I'm over sixty. (She brings his glasses.)

STYOPIK   For some time now. Eight years to be exact.

MANYA   What do you mean, "eight years to be exact"?

STYOPIK   All right, all right, you're not even a year old, you haven't even been born yet. Only get me a knife or something.

MANYA   Give it to me if you can't do anything yourself. (Takes the letter and neatly, slowly opens it.) Drink your tea.

STYOPIK (drinks his tea)   I wonder if she and her husband went to visit the monastery at Zagorsk or not.

MANYA   I'd **much** rather hear whether she's taking sewing lessons or not.

STYOPIK   Well, hurry up.

MANYA   Is there a fire somewhere?

STYOPIK   I finished my tea.

MANYA   But who didn't finish his toast?

STYOPIK   I'll get to it in a minute.

MANYA (hands him the opened letter)   See, Styopik, how nice I am:
while you've been playing with your tea I could have read the letter
twice through, but I know it would make you mad if I found out anything first, and so I -

STYOPIK (interrupting)   Listen. (Makes out the writing with some
difficulty.) "Dear papa and mama."

(MANYA gets out a stocking and knits.)

"... after my last letter, in which I...." Heavens, such Oriental
handwriting.

MANYA   Oriental?

STYOPIK   It's absolutely inscrutable.

MANYA (laughs, with mock pain)   Oh, you're the witty one. It's
your eyes that are Oriental, that's what.

STYOPIK (reading)   "... in which I tried to give you at least some
slight idea of how unbearable married life has become for me...."
(Takes out a cigarette case, and lights a cigarette.)

MANYA   "Unbearable?" Her husband's the sweetest man, worships the
ground she walks on, the children are perfect little darlings. She
plays the piano, sings ... all kinds of magazines.... God in heaven.

STYOPIK   "... married life has become for me, of how unhappy I am,
so you shouldn't be too terribly surprised...." Not be surprised?
(He laughs.) The reports we wrote at the office were pretty bad,
but we never cooked up a sentence like that.

MANYA (smiling)   Oh, you're the witty one.

STYOPIK   "... surprised to learn that I...." The handwriting's
frightful!

MANYA   She's going to take a little vacation?

STYOPIK   "... that I ... that I...."

MANYA   Let me have it. I'll see if I can make it out.

STYOPIK   No, I'm going to.

MANYA   "Me, me, me" all the time. And then you don't do anything.

STYOPIK (lively)   "... that I'm giving up...." So that's it. And

I thought, what letter is that`... "that I'm giving up...."

MANYA   The sewing lessons?

STYOPIK   "... giving up on my mm ... mm...."

MANYA   Giving up on her music lessons. That's all we need. Ten years she's spent on them.

STYOPIK   No, no, wait a minute: "... mm ... mm...." Please get me the magnifying glass.

MANYA (gets up and looks on the mantelpiece)   Lord, lord, where did you put it? (She goes off right.)

STYOPIK   "mm ... mm...." (A look of pained surprise comes over his face; he throws away his cigarette, and yells in a mournful voice.) Manya, Manya!... (Now reads the letter with the greatest concern.)

MANYA (returns with the magnifying glass)   Well, what is it?

STYOPIK   Marriage, marriage.

MANYA   What about marriage?

STYOPIK   Giving up on her marriage, on her husband. Anton Ivanovich.

MANYA (sinks in amazement into her chair)   Lord Almighty, stars in heaven!

(STYOPIK takes the magnifying glass from her and reads.)

You must have made a mistake. Let me see it. You probably made a mistake.

STYOPIK   Oh no. "... that I'm giving up on my marriage" ... and then ... "I'm in love with another man."

MANYA   Another man?

STYOPIK (reading rather swiftly)   "Of course, you're people of another generation and won't understand and will condemn me, but what can a person do when your feelings run away with you? Besides you two, there's no one for me to talk to about what I should do.... Anton Ivanovich doesn't know anything yet. I won't tell him until I decide whether I should get a divorce or just move out. If you have even one drop of pity left for me, don't turn me away ... but help me--I don't know what will become of the children,...."

(MANYA starts to sob.)

"I don't know anything except my love for.... My God, how I am suffering.... I wanted to come see you and ask you personally,

but I didn't have the strength.... Let me know how you feel about
a divorce right away, and don't abandon me. I beg you, don't turn
your backs on your poor sinful daughter." (With a trembling voice.)
"A million kisses to both of you. Loving you with all my heart,
Lida."

(MANYA bawls.)

Manya, please don't cry or I'll cry too. (Barely holding back his
tears.) I'll cry too.... (Blows his nose tearfully.)

MANYA (wiping her eyes)   Just like I said, it was that dream; nothing
good will come of it when you dream about a black stallion, nothing
good at all. You laughed, but now look.

(She bawls louder than ever. STYOPIK gets up and paces around the
room.)

STYOPIK (after a pause)   Manya, I want to ask you something of
extraordinary importance.

MANYA (through her tears)   What now?

STYOPIK (smoothly)   Tell me the God's truth now, Marya Ivanovna.
That is, cross your heart....

(She stops crying.)

Now tell me. Could you take, say, a brick in your hand and hit Lida
with it?

MANYA (frightened half out of her wits, crosses herself)   God save
me, Styopik, what are you talking about?

STYOPIK   You're a strange one, Marya Ivanovna, my heavens. I'm
speaking allegorically and you're taking it all literally. I ask
you, metaphorically as it were, and you should look me straight in
the eye and answer me--could you throw a stone at her or not?

MANYA (defensive)   Meaning?

STYOPIK   Meaning ... meaning, you understand perfectly well. I
ask you now, like Christ asked the Pharisees, is your conscience
so clean that you could throw a stone at your own daughter?

MANYA   And yours, Stepan Ilich?

STYOPIK   You answer me first.

MANYA   Why me?

STYOPIK   Well, you're ... a lady, and ladies go first.

MANYA (narrowing her eyes)   Stepan Ilich, why have you got such a
guilty look on your face?

STYOPIK   It's not me, Marya Ivanovna, you're the one with the guilty
look.

MANYA   Just because you've got a sick mind doesn't mean everybody
else does.

STYOPIK   Marya Ivanovna, your eyes tell me more than your lips.

MANYA   **Styopik, enough** jokes.... Here we are with a disaster on
our hands ... and instead of discussing it -

STYOPIK   I am discussing it. I ask the question: Can we judge
our little Lida, **that** is, can we be so cruel?

MANYA (interrupting)   What do you mean, not judge? Is it a sin
or isn't it?

STYOPIK   So you're going to throw the stone.

MANYA   Oh, forget the stone! You've got a real fixation on stones
today!

STYOPIK   You don't like me to speak allegorically. All right then,
non-allegorically.

MANYA   What are you driving at?

STYOPIK   The truth, Marya Ivanovna, the plain truth. (Loudly,
deliberately.) Were you ever unfaithful to me or not? Answer me.

MANYA (really agitated)   And you?

STYOPIK   I'm asking you.

MANYA   I'm asking you.

STYOPIK (quickly getting impatient)   Give me the key to the chest
of drawers.

MANYA   What on earth for?

STYOPIK (deliberately)   Give me the key.

(She produces the key and hands it to him. He strides off right
with an alacrity unexpected in a man of his years.)

MANYA (barely able to keep up with him)   Goodness.... (She stops
at the door, hardly able to catch her breath.)

Styopik, what are you doing? Why all the big mystery? (Suddenly frightened.) Don't you dare open the bottom drawer. (Backing away from the door in fright.) I can't stand for you to touch the pistol, you hear. I'll run lock myself in the kitchen, I really will.

STYOPIK (comes in with a small box in his hands)   Marya Ivanovna, stop being afraid and get ready for something of extraordinary importance. (Sets the box on the table.) Here's the box with the bullets.

MANYA (shrinking)   Take it away.

STYOPIK   Marya Ivanovna, you've always poked your nose into everything, but you didn't dare look in this terrible box. And so this is where I've kept a great secret from you for the last twenty-five years.

(MANYA timidly approaches the table; he opens the box and takes out the bullets, then from under the bullets, a lovely pink garter and two photographs.)

There!... (Shows her the garter.) That's her garter, and that's her picture (Shows her one picture, then the other.) with her clothes on, and with her clothes off.

MANYA (amazed)   Where did you get them?

STYOPIK   Marya Ivanovna, may people condemn me, may God strike me dead, but twenty-five years ago I was unfaithful to you.

MANYA   Unfaithful? (Seizes one of the photographs.) With who?

STYOPIK   Her name was Matilda. She was a cafe singer.

MANYA   When was that? When you used to go to St. Petersburg on business?

STYOPIK   Yes, but don't get mad, Manya. After all, that was twenty-five years ago.

MANYA (laughing)   Why get mad? Do you really suppose nobody ever cared for me except you? Do you really suppose that during your trips to St. Petersburg your cousin Grigory Dmitrievich was wasting any time?

STYOPIK (amazed)   Grigory Dmitrievich?

MANYA   Do you suppose that that's my mother's hair I've been keeping in my locket all these years? My sweet husband, they were replaced by somebody else's long ago ... and -

STYOPIK (interrupting)   So that's why you cried so much when he died.

MANYA (sadly)   Twenty-five years ago. (She sits down.)

STYOPIK   And, and you weren't unfaithful to me any more **after** that?

MANYA   Well, you retired, you were around all the time.

STYOPIK   I wasn't unfaithful after that either.

MANYA   My sweet husband, I don't doubt you for an instant.   Why, even if you'd wanted to, you....   (Laughs loudly.)

STYOPIK   Now that's mean, that's really mean.

MANYA (looking at one photograph)   Was she a blonde or a brunette?

STYOPIK (sits down and looks carefully at the other photograph)   A redhead.

MANYA   Oh you. But why take her picture all naked?

STYOPIK   Oh, just for ... fun.

MANYA   Goodness, the things people think of.

STYOPIK   You'd do better to explain how you and Grigory Dmitrievich -

MANYA   What is there to explain?   Surely you remember what a hard-driving man he was.

STYOPIK   It's been twenty-five years.

MANYA   Twenty-five years.

STYOPIK   I was only forty-eight then, I was almost a boy, a pup. I still had my whole life ahead of me ... and you were....

MANYA   Skip the **arithmetic,** thank you.   I was simply a fascinating woman, and that's the main thing.

STYOPIK   Lord, how could so many years have passed? There's her garter, as if I'd just taken it off her leg. And such logs. And the songs she used to sing! I even wanted to marry her....   My God, how could so many years have passed? (Sniffs the garter.) You can still smell the perfume.

MANYA   That's your imagination.

STYOPIK   Oh no, indeed. (Sniffs again.) Ah, she was so beautiful, such fun. Where is she now? Still alive? Does she remember her songs? Twenty-five years passed....   I was so young then, there wasn't anything I couldn't do....

MANYA   And all the while Grigory Dmitrievich was telling me nicer things than I ever heard from you.

STYOPIK   And how she used to make me laugh, the rascally girl.

MANYA   There was no comparing Grigory Dmitrievich! His kisses used
to make shivers run all over my body.

STYOPIK (deeply moved)   Oh God, those were the days! Youth! No,
this garter can't fail to move me. (Kisses it tenderly.) Dearest,
glorious, when I took you off her leg, there was no rheumatism, no
trembling hands. I didn't even wear glasses then. I could see like
an eagle. (Takes out a handkerchief, wipes his eyes, and blows his
nose.)

MANYA (looking carefully at the photograph)   Yes, those were the
days all right.... I was built just as good as she was, and Grigory
Dmitrievich used to call me Venus.

STYOPIK (sighing)   Matilda ... Matilda. (In a different tone.)
But tell me, Manya, if you had found out then that I was unfaithful,
what would you have done?

MANYA   What would I have done? I'd have left you.

STYOPIK   Left me? Left your own sweet Styopik? Left him to the
mercy of Fate? I'd have gotten sick, been robbed, and you wouldn't
even have cared!

MANYA   And if you had found out about me?

STYOPIK   If I'd found out.... (A pause.) No, I can't even imagine.
I'd have.... No, I don't even want to think about it.

MANYA   But still, now you....

STYOPIK   Now ... hm.... Manya, twenty-five years is long enough
to.... But would you have really left me?... (Goes over to her.)

MANYA   I don't know.... I would have been sorry to leave you, and
at the same time.... No, I would have stayed, but I would have been
so unhappy, so unhappy....

STYOPIK (kissing her on the head)   Well, there you see, Manya, it
was a good thing we kept quiet.... How could I have lived without
you? I wasn't afraid to confess now, because I knew you'd look at
it with a historical perspective, but before now, who knows what
honesty might have led to? (Sits next to her.) And so I did it
all now on purpose, so as to get you to answer our Lida's letter
properly.

MANYA   What? What?

STYOPIK   Here's what: something like this--"and so, even though
you may think of us as some Philemon and Baucis, and even call us
old fogeys into the bargain, just the same, we, so to say, have

come to the conclusion...."

MANYA   Ah, I get it now. Oh Styopik, Styopik, what a clever old
man you are!

STYOPIK (warmly)   You understand, Manya, she simply needs to break
loose a little. Like everybody else. And then go back to her marriage again. She loves her husband and doesn't want to leave him,
but she just needs to break loose a little. So? So that's what
we'll say--that leaving her husband would be rather stupid and that
actually -

MANYA (interrupting enthusiastically)   Absolutely right, you're
absolutely right. So we ought to explain.... But she wants an
answer as soon as possible.... I think the best thing would be
to send **her** a telegram. She'll come here; then we can talk things
over properly.

STYOPIK   Excellent. (He goes off.)

MANYA   Postponing something like this could be very dangerous.

STYOPIK (returns with ink, pen, and paper)   Take the pen and write.
(Puts the things on the table.) "Get on the train immediately" ...
or better yet, "come right away."

MANYA (pen in hand)   Better, "immediately."

STYOPIK   Fine. "Come immediately. We will solve the problem."

MANYA   I think it'd be better "will solve," leave out the "we."
Five kopecks a word, after all.

STYOPIK   So "we" aren't worth five kopecks?

MANYA (with mock pain)   Ooo. You're the witty one. (She writes.)

STYOPIK (yells in the direction of the door off left)   Dunya! Dunya!

(MANYA gets up and rushes out left, waving the paper in the air to
dry the ink. STYOPIK is left alone, takes one of the photographs,
sits down on the sofa and gazes at it smiling and weeping.)

MANYA (entering)   I sent it. Sixty kopecks, that's all. (Going
over toward STYOPIK.) You just can't get enough of her, can you!

STYOPIK   I'm, so to say, looking at myself through her.

MANYA (sits and looks at one of the photographs)   A quarter of a
century. The hairdoes they had in those days!

STYOPIK (babbling with great happiness)   She used to call me a
rascal. She used to say "You're a little rascal, that's what you

19

are." I'd ask "Why am I a rascal?" and she'd answer "You really
are a rascal, that's all there is to it." (He laughs and weeps.)

MANYA   Ah, you philanderer.... I bet you were really naughty....
(Kisses his head tenderly, smiles, on the verge of bawling.)

CIRCUMSTANCES

CATALOG

CONTRIBUTORS

20   21

20 The Undisciplined Death Of Freddie Hall at
   Skyland Lodge, on the Skyline Drive, Virginia

21 A Blank Page Entitled "Climax" at the Barksdale
   Dinner-Theatre, Hanover Courthouse, Virginia

22

23

22 A Blank Page Entitled "Climax" at the Hotel
   Albemarle, Charlottesville, Virginia

23 Do You Daydream? at the Hotel Albemarle,
   Charlottesville, Virginia

CIRCUMSTANCES

Like many theater people, Theater Wagon's producer wears two other hats: chairman of the department of dramatic arts at Mary Baldwin College and founder/director of the Oak Grove Theater, now in its twentieth season of subscription audiences.

The relationships between Theater Wagon and educational and community theaters have proved extraordinarily productive. Each theater has its own resources, but these resources are shared, not duplicated. Each has its own audience, but these of course overlap and reinforce each other. Actors, acting at different times for each group, have unusual opportunities in plays from Euripides to Ionesco and in musicals from the 12th-century Saint Nicholas Miracles to The Canterbury Tales, by way of The Beggars' Opera, for which one of our actors wrote musical interludes in suite form for recorders and guitar.

Cordial relations between these town-and-gown theaters may be due in this case to a shared preference for the personal quality of small colleges and small theaters: small by choice rather than little when they'd rather be big. There are similarities in values. Everything is close at hand. Much can be done with a minimum. Ingenuity and versatility are requirements, of course, but individuals can be effective. The outdoors is always near the indoors, and there are more trees than houses.

These circumstances, which Theater Wagon shares with its educational and community counterparts, determine our style of production,

which aspires to work at minimal expense in any small theater, good-
sized room, or garden. We use simple, suggestive staging; plenty
of space for actors to move in; color in costumes and props; musical
instruments an actor can carry, hang on a wall, or lean against
a tree. The emphasis is always on the play and the actor.

What Theater-Wagon audiences like about our actors is their
honesty, their freshness, their preference for affection over af-
fectation. The physical circumstances of our performances--audi-
ences never over 300, the back row never more than fifty feet from
the stage--are themselves encouraging to our actors to enjoy the
intimacy, to project a role like a hearty handshake.

Since Theater Wagon is customarily on tour, and thus meets an
unknown audience at each performance, the actor is in a very different position from his opposite number in a community or university theater, where many in the audience are known to be his friends.
In a real sense Theater-Wagon encounters with audiences make professionals of its actors. The amateurish may be excused by friends
in a community theater as a good try; our actors cannot lean on
such a crutch. They do resist, however, the commercial actor's
temptation, faced with unknown audiences, to become cynical, to
take it easy, and to rely on tricks that get a laugh or else, on
what we call the superpunch.

The quality of our plays, which are themselves honestly com-
posed, helps the actors to stay honest and to enjoy their work.
Moreover, the customary presence of the concerned Theater-Wagon
playwright counterbalances any temptation a director may have to
make over the play in his own image and to bend play and players

to his imperious will or at least to his gimmicks. The playwright
and the director may be a well-married couple of some years' standing. Even when they are not a couple, the relationship between
director and playwright is close and trustful, not a bitter rivalry.
Actors are encouraged to try things, to create, to help themselves
to grow in their roles. They know that the director knows that
creation is slow and uncertain, and that the director has to be
the most patient person in the theater. At the same time they rely on him to choose the emphases at each rehearsal and to sense
when the actors are ready for each emphasis.

Some of our actors themselves are husbands and wives, as in
Birdwatchers and Styopik And Manya, and from their considerable
experience in playing together (on and off stage) work up a short
play of this sort without need for a director to be continuously
present. The actors likewise value and reach for ensemble playing.
Our playwrights do not write plays as vehicles for stars; the plays
expose a strong design of human relationships. The actors there-
fore play together and frequently testify that this experience
is ecstatic.

Theater Wagon's choice of place and audience for a performance
being largely influenced by the probable pleasure of playing in
that place for those people, we expose ourselves to a fairly brisk
demand for ingenious staging, since the places chosen are seldom
within the gates of well-equipped theaters. A commentary on the
staging of the plays in this collection describes some of the virtues made out of these rugged necessities.

In <u>Love Is A Daisy</u> the staging challenge on a small open stage, surrounded by an audience banked up on platforms on three sides, is that the brief first scene is in a mountainside clearing, the remainder of the play inside a valley farm kitchen. The solution, discovered by the playwright sometime after she finished the script, is for the farm kitchen to open out of a nest of hinged panels, revealing the occupants, while Hugo is throwing off on them to the girls and is simultaneously introducing the new <u>personae</u> to the audience. The necessities of intimate staging stimulate an original and integrated projection of the play.

Minimum staging seems best for <u>Birdwatchers</u>. No scenery; merely two camp chairs and hand properties. Any effort to go beyond this by showing an actual bird sanctuary on the stage, with sunlight and recorded **birdsong** filtering down through leafy bowers, would be to betray the playwright, who created a play for two actors (herself and her husband) to perform in an open environment.

There are occasionally situations and plays in which nothing will do but a measure of naturalism. In <u>Sandcastle</u> there is probably no substitute for clean, white (not brown) sand, but on a tarpaulin it is controllable, and the set is completed by the ubiquitous scrim. For Evreinov's <u>Styopik And Manya</u> almost any not-too-modern living room and its furnishings will suffice. <u>A Merry Death</u>, on the other hand, is a cabaret play, made complete with an immensely tall clock, a table **with** stools, and an old brass bed, the bars of the headboard at one point making the semblance of a jail for Harlequin.

The fantasy quality of <u>On The Corner Of Cherry And Elsewhere</u> demands either something extremely atmospheric--film does this sort of thing better--or something simple and functional. The pivotal set piece here is the cage, for which we find that a fragile yet practical structure of red lattice-strips creates the properly fantastic tone, as do the easels with empty picture frames, and the Victorian Gothic "throne" for Dr. Shade's office.

When <u>3 Filosofers In A Firetower</u> was considered for production by other groups, and was produced in Alexandria by one of them, the scenic requirements were thought to be extremely expensive: an actual firetower with space for three, a Parkway roadblock at an intersection, and a palatial terrace at Montebello. Ours is a simple and we think a more effective design: three stepladders of varying heights arranged in a pyramid as a firetower, with railings below it; for Montebello a marble bench and a sculptured Greek bust on a pedestal; for the Parkway a rustic bench, with composite road-sign adjacent. These simple elements are backed outdoors by trees, indoors by the usual skydrop scrim.

One of our favorite stagings is that for <u>A Blank Page Entitled</u> "<u>Climax</u>," of which some photographs precede this section. This musical play requires a stretch of the George Washington Bridge and a cross-section of a Hudson-River coal barge, with the murky Hudson between. Our designer, Tom Cabe, has so constructed these set pieces that, knocked down, they fit on the deck of a station wagon, yet, assembled on stage, they create a charming and practical set. Actors leap into and out of the barge; they scale the bridge, fish off it, jump from it.

Implementing these settings on tour are the spotlights and
tall, home-made lightbridges for them, as well as several hundred
yards of electric cable and a sophisticated, home-made dimmer-con-
trol unit. "Home-made" is to say that our ingenious technical director, Richard Johnson, designed and constructed them.

Stage settings being simple by necessity and choice, the visual element is enhanced not only by lighting but also by colorful
costumes and hand props, which are often metaphors of the play.
Because our audience is close enough to be strongly affected by
specific objects, our playwrights, directors, and actors depend
a good deal on appropriate details and metaphoric use of hand props.

The shells and flowers of Sandcastle, for instance, are simple
enough to procure and transport, and are a tender metaphor of ju-
venile love. So for Harlequin is the monstrous thermometer in A
Merry Death, with the surging red-ribbon mercury tube and its exploding top. The outsize telescope in 3 Filosofers, Dr. Shade's stick-
dog leading him around on a dowel-leash, the paint brushes and red
latex-paint of On The Corner Of Cherry And Elsewhere contribute
powerfully to the tone and theme of these plays and are carefully
sifted into the action by playwrights and actors.

Some of these hand props are frankly theatrical; others like
the seashells are "real." Anything natural or handmade creates
a warmth and intimacy of its own. Because we are a small and in-
formal company we sometimes use cherished objects like the silver
teapot, lace cloth, and handmade Russian box which heighten the
immediacy of Styopik And Manya. Handwoven coverlet, earthenware
jugs, antique bowl, pitcher, and washstand of Love Is A Daisy do

much for the tone and sense of the play by contrasting with those
modern contraptions: the downed plane and car, the television and
the telegram. Similarly with costumes, some are created like those
of Harlequin and Pierrot, derived from Cézanne's painting of the
subject, while The Lady And The Unicorn, a play about a historic
house, is enhanced by a genuine heirloom dress of gold silk, circa
1836, worn with its original jewelry. No play in our repertory
has played with more different settings, both indoor and outdoor,
but throughout this variety and enclosing a variety of actresses,
the gold-silk dress moves respendently.

Handwoven coverlets and heirloom dresses give a sense of the
past in the Now, of relating to things that someone has handled or
worn. But whether our props are antiques or from Sears, whether
our setting is a theater or a summer circle of green, Theater-Wagon
forms are more architectural than existential, baroque rather than
electronic--in other words, social. We see even our empty spaces
as intensely human; inviting movement, asking for snatches of
song. In the empty forest the spinster with the Audubon card
confronts the man with his thermos of martinis, or Shenandoah scatters
lilies and reads The Trojan Womon. On the empty beach the young
people decorate a sandcastle with seashells and wildflowers. In
the loony bin, Suzie and Moon Mother gleefully paint the floor.

As a company of players and playwrights, Theater Wagon's top
priority is the freedom to play our own work in places we enjoy
for occasions we believe in. The places may be as elegant as the
boxwood gardens of Gunston Hall or as simple as a clearing in the
woods. The occasion may be a party in the Berkshires or a free

performance for wheelchair students at a rehabilitation center.

Theater Wagon's system of repertory is very probably unique,
involving more than forty actors who live in such disparate places
as Norfolk, Washington, Boston, and half a dozen towns in the Shenandoah Valley, and who are able to converge for hilarious, hard-
working weekends of rehearsing and playing any one of eight plays
in our current repertory. Three of those eight plays have been
alive for years. Others were recently added. One is a revival
from our first tour.

Wagon actors work together, travel together, party together.
Some are in college, some have teen-age children. Some go off
to graduate school or to Europe, but they return. As one of the
company explains, "We all have a tremendous loyalty to Theater
Wagon. We may move almost anywhere, but we come back for a month,
a week, or a weekend. We can be found spending precious vacations
with the Wagon, and dropping precious babies at sitters so we can
rehearse morning and afternoon and perform at night, grabbing meals
from somebody's casseroles, making music and square-dancing to un-
wind when the play is over."

We are often asked who subsidizes us. Our subsidy is the energy of a great many talented people. Some are professionals in
educational theater. Others are professionals in law, medicine,
corporate management, engineering, cable television, real estate,
banking, farming, dog breeding, construction, interior decorating,
architecture. Talented, experienced actors, they have no desire
to go commercial. In commercial theater, actors spend too much
time playing in places they don't enjoy for occasions they don't

believe in. Wagon actors prefer to give rather than be hired, but
their giving is a commitment stronger than a contract. In the "real"
world they have responsible jobs. In theater they treasure a freedom to create their work and believe in their play.

M.J.C.
F.C.,Jr.

24

25

26

27

Two St. Nicholas Miracles at Trinity Church, Staunton, Virginia
24-25 **The Three Clerks**. 26-27 The Image Of St. Nicholas

28

29

30

28-30 The Ship Of The Righteous at The Blue Ridge School,
Dyke, Virginia

31

32

31-32 <u>Yaqui</u> at the 1971 Theater **Wagon** Festival, Verona, Virginia

33

34

35

36

37

33-37 A Chance Of Love at The
Boar's Head Inn,
Charlottesville, Virginia

38

39

38-39 **Bliss Towers** at The Oak Grove Theater, Verona, Virginia

40

41

42

Take Away The Lady
40-41 At Bryce Mountain Resort, Basye, Virginia.
42 At Coolfont, Berkeley Springs, West Virginia

43

44

45

46

The Lady And The Unicorn
43 At Ashlawn, near Charlottesville. 44 At **Gunston Hall**,
Lorton. 45 At Woodrow Wilson Birthplace, Staunton.
46 At the Langhorn House, Lynchburg, Virginia

A BLANK PAGE ENTITLED "CLIMAX," by Jeannie Lee. An intimate music-play about a young wife who rejects civilization and escapes to a coal barge floating around Manhattan. Her husband attempts "dialogue" but finds she is all wrapped up with the mythical Great Silkey of ballad fame. On the barge she faces a choice: demon lover or humdrum husband? Songs with guitar help her to make up her mind. "The script is fresh, witty, and very unusual, and the music, some 30 songs, makes the evening of theater a refreshing experience. It is musical fantasy and delightful.... Amusing study of the imaginative vagaries of womenfolk caught up in the doldrums of life. Escape from the 'drip, drip' of reality conjures up the dashing hero, an oceanic hobo with a fine touch of Gaelic." - Alton Williams in Richmond News-Leader. Illus. 21,22.

BLISS TOWERS, by Margaret Collins. David trusts everyone, even his wife Adele, who trusts no one. In an adjoining apartment lives a bachelor playboy, a high-scoring man of affairs. He campaigns to get Alice, David's sister, who has more money than brains, but he discovers that Adele also is available. All ends well. "Four people have a great time in Bliss Towers, and, watching them, you will too.... Farcical brew, laced with spirits of sharp dialogue and wit.... Joyous." - Barbara Rich in Charlottesville Daily Progress. Illus. 38,39.

A CHANCE OF LOVE, by Pierre de Marivaux, trans. by Fletcher Collins, Jr. A delightfully romantic French comedy of the 18th century. A lady masquerades as her maid to win a gentleman who is democratically posing as his valet. Performed under the title Le jeu de l'amour du hasard more than a thousand times at the Comédie Française. Collins' translation was made for the theater, plays well. Illus. 33-37.

DO YOU DAYDREAM?, by Margaret Collins. Psychologist Dr. Dove, hung up on statistical determinism, is intent on match-making one of his adopted sons into a computerized marriage. Of course the girl finds Dove's choice less attractive than his brother. When she introduces her twin sister to the complex, even the computer begins to splutter. "Rapid-fire dialogue, barbed satire, and a wild series of situations kept the audience chuckling.... The playwright has created a marvelous character in Dr. Dilwyn Dove, who devotes his life to compiling statistics about people and 'eliminating qualitative judgments.' But his own behavior does not corroborate his findings, as we see when he meets the voluptuous redhead." - Richmond Times-Dispatch. Illus. 23.

THE LADY AND THE UNICORN, by Margaret Collins. The setting is Fanshawe, a historic mansion, whose gallant owner has been dabbling in

embezzlement to save her home from foreclosure. She in turn is saved
from prosecution by an internationally known billionaire who appreci-
ates legend and has been tracking down the owner's daughter. One of
our most extensively performed plays. "Witty ... stimulating ...
pithy observations about art, love, history, and money." - Jon Longaker
in <u>The Commonwealth: The Magazine of Virginia</u>. Illus. 43-46.

THE MOTEL AND THE CHICKENHOUSE, by Margaret Collins. The titular
structures are neighbors, off an interstate. To the motel comes
George, a successful young novelist who is trying to re-hitch his
mother to her ex-husband. To the chickenhouse come Ted and Joan,
looking for a feature. Joan sees the chickenhouse as a Pinteresque
stage-set and its owner as a grotesque. The real story turns out
to be Virgil, who owns the motel. "Brilliant and fascinating, lyrical
and human, it is laugh-provoking and thought-provoking." - <u>Winchester
Star</u>.

OUR FEET ARE SO CRUCIAL TO THE WAY WE **FEEL**, by Barbara Allan Hite.
The story of a young woman who is about to turn on the gas for the
unrequited love of her boss, with whom she has had "one lunch, at
Schrafft's." She is interrupted by an encyclopedia salesman. He has
his problems too, but his humor and sympathy give her a new perspective
before the boss and her mother arrive.

SAINT NICHOLAS MIRACLE PLAYS, transcribed from a 12th-century manu-
script and edited by Fletcher Collins, Jr. These four charming,
medieval music-dramas have been transcribed and edited for production by the author of <u>The Production of Medieval Church Music-Drama</u>
(University Press of Virginia, 1972), but have not yet been published
or reproduced in quantity. Theater Wagon has successfully produced
two of the four in three Virginia churches. The editor will entertain requests for a sample copy of scores of the four, from producers
seriously contemplating a performance. Illus. 24-27.

THE SHIP OF THE RIGHTEOUS, by Nicolai Evreinov, translated by Christopher Collins. A tragi-comedy written in the 1920's, and featuring
a play within a **play**, and meanings within meanings. It focuses on
a commune of idealists as they embark to sail "away from the human
herd that tramples on high ideals": peace, love, brotherhood, happiness. Collision between their escapist dreams and their inescapable
psychological drives provides Evreinov with a fast-moving interchange
of tragedy and farce. Successfully produced by Theater Wagon in
two theaters. Illus. 28-30.

TAKE AWAY THE LADY, by Margaret Collins, with music by Fletcher
Collins, Jr., Jeannie Lee, and Francis Collins. A hijacked jet,
making an unscheduled landing, deposits its assortment of passengers
in a Lovers' Paradise, where the clock seems to have stopped during
the Middle Ages. Under the spell of a love potion that misfires,
a pretty young schoolteacher falls for the king instead of the prince.
This causes no end of trouble for the king's sorceress-mistress, who
has political ambitions. The premier tries to unmask the naive,
émigré scientist, whose Russian wife comes to the rescue as a catalyst.
Almost everyone in the cast sings or dances or both. The medieval

flavor of the music is heightened by recorder and guitar accompani-
ments. Scores available. Widely performed by Theater Wagon, a play
which delights all ages. Illus. 40-42.

THE UNDISCIPLINED DEATH OF FREDDIE HALL, by Barbara Allan Hite. A
deadpan comedy about a con man's effort to generate memorial funds
for himself by means of funeral trappings and Freddie, a very live
corpse. Freddie tries to do a good job, but he is a born loser.
Events are complicated by a pair of over-the-hill entertainers, a
batty old lady misquoting Scripture, and a chicken which considers
itself miraculous. Illus. 20.

YAQUI, by Margaret Collins. Yaqui has given up the world to live
in a greenhouse. His creed is to simplify, be natural, do without,
give away. But he is involved with Rose, an older woman on whom
he is passionately dependent. He is outraged by Lisa, a young,
would-be suburbanite who represents every thing he detests, and
who insists on building a house on the estate. There are also the
fay if not actually senile owners of the estate, who bumble **into**
the situation and wind up throwing bricks over the shrubbery for
the sheer delight of it. Illus. 31-32.

    For further information about these plays, including quotation
of royalty for use, address the playwrights' agent, Theater Wagon,
Inc., **437 East Beverley Street, Staunton, Virginia** 24401.

CONTRIBUTORS

BARBARA ALLAN HITE (Birdwatchers and Sandcastle) teaches at Virginia
Wesleyan College, acts with the Norfolk Theatre Center, has three
children, and, in her spare time, writes, directs, and acts for Theater Wagon. An accomplished actress in both comedy and tragedy, she
has played Antigone, Clytemnestra, and Lady Bracknell, as well as
leading roles in Oh Dad, Poor Dad, The Birthday Party, and The Mad-
woman of Chaillot. Barbara and her husband, Rick Hite, professor
of drama at Virginia Wesleyan, created the roles in Birdwatchers
(Illus. 5-6), and translated and played the leads in Casona's Siren
Cast Ashore at Oak Grove and on tour. Barbara, a graduate of Mary
Baldwin, has her M.A.T. from The Johns Hopkins University. Rick,
a Dartmouth graduate, has an M.A. in Romance Languages from Hopkins
and a Ph.D. in dramatic arts from Michigan State.

NICOLAI EVREINOV (A Merry Death and Styopik And Manya) is known in
the books as a wide-ranging producing-director of the early 20th
century. He replaced Meyerhold at Vera Komissarzhevsky's theater,
and was regisseur at the Crooked Mirror Theater in Moscow for seven
years. He wrote aggressively and prolifically on his theories of
theatricality, past and present. His The Chief Thing was performed
in New York by the Theater Guild. The two one-act plays included
in this collection and toured by Theater Wagon demonstrate his crafts-
manship, sympathy, irony, and wild theatrical humor.

CHRISTOPHER COLLINS (Translator) is author of The Plays of Nikolai
Evreinov (Ardis Publisher, Ann Arbor, 1973). For the Oak Grove Thea-
ter he has also translated Chekhov's Uncle Vanya and A Marriage
Proposal. Graduate of Washington and Lee University, with a Ph.D.
in Slavic languages from Indiana University, he has taught at Syracuse
University and the University of Virginia, and was a Fulbright Fellow
in 1971 to work on Evreinov. He is also the author of Zamjatin: An
Interpretive Study (Mouton, The Hague, 1973). He is vice-president
of Theater Wagon, and one of its photographers and guitar-pickers.
As an actor he has possessed such roles as Jess in Love Is A Daisy
(Illus. 3) and the Doctor in 3 Filosofers (Illus. 14, 17).

JEANNIE LEE (On The Corner Of Cherry And Elsewhere) is a composer and
guitarist as well as a playwright. She wrote the music for the songs
in Cherry And Elsewhere, as well as lyrics and music for some thirty
songs in her A Blank Page Entitled "Climax." A native of Philadel-
phia, she moved with her family to the Shenandoah Valley so they
could all participate in the Oak Grove Theater and Theater Wagon.
Her mother, Betty Lee, is one of Oak Grove's most popular comic
actresses, and plays Moon Mother in Cherry And Elsewhere (Illus. 11).
At Oak Grove Jeannie has played in The Glass Menagerie, The Beggar's
Opera, Royal Gambit, and toured with Theater Wagon in The Motel And
The Chickenhouse , Love Is A Daisy, Take Away The Lady, and The Lady
And The Unicorn. Her musical training was at Hartt School of Music
in Hartford. She is a junior at Mary Baldwin College.

MARGARET COLLINS (Love Is A Daisy and 3 Filosofers In A Firetower) is
the co-founder and co-producing director of Theater Wagon. She and
her husband, Fletcher Collins, Jr., with their four sons, have provided

the Wagon with its home-base at Pennyroyal Farm near Verona and at
The Oaks in Staunton, where outdoor and indoor rehearsal stages are
available, and where actors have been fed and lodged for years. She
serves the Wagon as playwright, tour manager, publicity director,
and cook. A graduate of Wells College, she has an M.A. from Yale
and has published articles in This Week and Mademoiselle.

FLETCHER COLLINS, JR. (Editor) is producing-director for Theater
Wagon and Oak Grove Theater, professor of dramatic arts at Mary Baldwin
College, and author of The Production Of Medieval Church Music-Drama
(University Press of Virginia, 1972), which reflects his transcriptions
and productions of eleven medieval dramas, performed in Winston-
Salem, N.C., Folger Shakespeare Library Theatre in Washington, Christ
Church Georgetown, Upperville, Richmond, Alexandria, and Staunton,
Virginia. He is a native of Pittsburgh, with Ph.B. and Ph.D. from
Yale. He has been president of the Southern Folklore Society, as an
eminent collector of folksong in North Carolina and West Virginia.
He has been assistant to the general manager of Fairchild Aircraft,
and manager of the organization division of Republic Aviation. He
has taught theater at Elon College and for many years at Mary Baldwin
College, has served as president of the Carolina Dramatic Association,
and on the festival committee for the Virginia College Drama Festival.

BETTE ALLAN COLLINS (Editorial Assistant) has worked for the Syracuse
University Press, and is an assistant in the Graduate School of Busi-
ness Administration at the University of Virginia. She and her hus-
band Christopher, with small daughter, live in the country near
Charlottesville. One of our most versatile actresses, she has played
at Oak Grove such roles as Audrey in As You Like It, Elyena in Uncle
Vanya, and the girl in The Knack. For the Wagon she has played both
Susan and the mountain woman, Kelly Shepherd, in Love Is A Daisy
(Illus. 2-3), the young artist in Cherry And Elsewhere (Illus. 9),
the fading film-star in 3 Filosofers (Illus. 14-15), and in The Lady
And The Unicorn the young girl (Illus. 44) and the older woman (Illus.
43). She also directed A Chance Of Love, Ship Of The Righteous, Freddie,
and Feet.

TERRY KOOGLER SOUTHERINGTON (Editorial Assistant) typed this book,
"camera-ready." She teaches mathematics at Madison College, and is
the author of Reunion, a one-act play which was successfully produced
at Mary Baldwin and the Virginia College Drama Festival. She has
acted in Ship Of The Righteous (Illus. 29) and The Lady And The Unicorn
(Illus. 46). With her husband, F.R. Southerington, she co-produced
a new version of Strindberg's A Dream Play at Oak Grove in 1973. Terry
is a native of Fairfield, Virginia, and a graduate of Mary Baldwin.

F.R. SOUTHERINGTON (Foreword) is a Hardy and Strindberg scholar, an
Oxford Ph.D., and a professor at Mary Baldwin College. He is the
author of Hardy's Vision of Man (London: Chatto and Windus, 1971;
New York, Barnes and Noble). In preparation is his Strindberg: A
Critical Biography. Three of his Strindberg translations have been
produced by Mary Baldwin, Theater Wagon, and Oak Grove. In addition
he has had major roles in three Theater-Wagon plays (Illus. 33, 35, 41).

TOM CABE (Photographer: Illus. 5-6, 19, 22) is an engineer. He designed the set for A Blank Page, toured with the Wagon to Pennsylvania and Connecticut, and directs at Oak Grove.

RICK CHITTUM (Photographer: Illus. 24-27, 42) is a video program director in Staunton. He has played Garland in Love Is A Daisy and Igor in Take Away The Lady.

WILLIAM FRANCISCO (Photographer: Illus. 33-38) is a farmer, and has operated lights and sound for A Blank Page and Cherry And Elsewhere.

ROSS HERSEY (Photographer: Illus. 23) played Dr. Dilwyn Dove in the premiere of Do You Daydream? at Oak Grove Theater.

CHRISTOPHER COLLINS (Photographer: Illus. 1, 7-11, 13-16, 20, 28-32, 39-41, 45,46).

Commercial Photography is by Milius Associates (Illus. 43); Alwood Studios (Illus. 12); Roland Van Essen (Illus. 2-3, 21); C.S. Henderson (Illus. 4); Charles Battie (Illus. 44).